Mining for Gold on the Internet

NEVER GIVE YOUR NAME OR PERSONAL INFORMATION OVER THE INTERNET!!!

NO SEX; AGE, SS#, NICKNAME, DATE OF BIRTH, TOWN YOU WERE BORN, MOTHER'S MAIDEN NAME, FAVORITE COLOR

ANYTHING!!!

Mining for Gold on the Internet

Mary Ellen Bates

McGraw-Hill

New York San Francisco Washington, D.C. Auckland Bogotá
Caracas Lisbon London Madrid Mexico City Milan
Montreal New Delhi Singapore
Sydney Tokyo Toronto

McGraw-Hill

A Division of The **McGraw-Hill** *Companies*

1 2 3 4 5 6 7 8 9 0 AGM/AGM 0 9 8 7 6 5 4 3 2 1 0

ISBN 0-07-134981-2

Printed and bound by Quebecor/Martinsburg.

McGraw-Hill books are available at special quantity discounts to use as premiums and sales promotions, or for use in corporate training programs. For more information, please write to the Director of Special Sales, Professional Publishing, McGraw-Hill, Two Penn Plaza, New York, NY 10121-2298. Or contact your local bookstore.

This book is printed on recycled, acid-free paper containing a minimum of 50% recycled, de-inked fiber.

To D.D.W. and L.G.D.

Contents

Introduction

Online trading is quick and easy; online investing takes time.
U.S. Securities and Exchange Commission Web site

If all it took to make your fortune by online trading was an Internet connection and some ready cash, we'd all be happily retired by now, sipping drinks by the pool. Unfortunately, the SEC's investor education Web site had it right—it takes time and attention to successfully invest, whether online or through the time-honored tradition of using a full-service broker.

Mining for Gold on the Internet not only introduces you to electronic investing but shows you where to get reliable, high-quality information about investment issues; how to find online help in planning your financial future; and how to research a company that you're considering investing in.

Pleased to Meet You

I made a few assumptions about you as I wrote this book.

First, you are at least modestly familiar with the Internet. You have a browser (Netscape Navigator or Internet Explorer, for example, or one of the proprietary software packages like America Online or CompuServe); you know how to type in an Internet address, or URL, to get to a Web page; and you have access to the Internet. Note that while high-speed access (such as what you may have at work) is nice, it isn't necessary. I researched this book before I had my lightning-fast DSL line installed, and no site mentioned here requires special equipment, high-speed connections, or software add-ons.

Second, you already have an idea of what your investment strategy is, or you are interested in using the resources on the Web to help you determine your strategy. I'm not going to tell you whether one kind of investment is smarter than another—I'm not even going to tell you that investing in one kind of company or another is the best move. (Okay, here's one tip—playing the lottery is *not* your best long-term investment strategy.) You know your objectives, your resources, and your tolerance for risk. Use the resources I've described in this book to decide for yourself how to allocate your investments to best meet your goals.

Third, you want to use the tools, knowledge, and sources available on the Internet to help you make the best investment decisions possible. I'll be giving you tips on how to determine the reliability of a Web site, how to find sites that are more likely to be trustworthy and unbiased, and how to keep up to date on the companies and industries that interest you.

My goal is to not only point you to some of the best resources on the Net for financial and investment information, but also to give you the tools to find your own favorite sites. As I sat down to write this introduction, I saw a cartoon of a couple getting on the Internet for the first time. After powering up the PC, the wife turns to the husband and asks, "Where's the button I push to set up a Web site, go public and make a gazillion dollars?" Unfortunately, this book won't tell you where that button is, but it will help you find a treasure trove of information online to help you invest more intelligently.

A Quick Tour of *Mining for Gold*

While I'd like to think that you will sit down and read through this book in a single, spellbinding sitting, I'll bet that won't happen. Don't worry—it's written to be read a chapter at a time. If one chapter relies on something I've discussed in more detail elsewhere, I'll give you a pointer to that chapter. I include in the text the Internet address of each site I mention, and there's an Appendix at the end with a list of all the resources described in the book. One caveat when you type in the URL to go to the site yourself: be sure to type upper and lower case just as it appears in the text. While most URLs are case-insensitive (www.xerox.com will get you to the same place as www.Xerox.com or even wWw.XeRoX.CoM), those URLs that include subdirectories (www.sec.gov/oieal.htm, for example) need to be typed exactly as you see them in the book.

Chapter 1 is a refresher course and overview of how to find information on the Net. I talk about the difference between search engines (those sites that attempt to capture and index everything on the Web) and catalogs (sites built by humans, often librarian-types, and designed to point you to the best of the Web). I give tips from a professional online researcher (that's me) on how to evaluate the reliability of a site and how to search for information efficiently. I also cover various methods of accessing the Net, including the proprietary online services such as America Online.

Chapter 2 tells you how to review and evaluate sources for basic financial and investment information. You'll find glossaries, tutorials, and how-to's on reading an annual report, evaluating relative risk among investment strategies, and how to think like an investor. I also look at stock-picking games and other no-risk tools for familiarizing beginning investors with the basic concepts of personal investment.

Chapter 3 addresses where to find information on managing credit, planning for retirement, and investing for your specific needs. It includes sites that help you to determine your net worth, establish how much you need to put away to meet your savings goals, and understand your options for pension and individual retirement plans.

Chapter 4 covers how you can use the Net to track your portfolio and obtain online stock quotes. I review sources for stock ratings and "picks and pans" of the stock market. I show you where to find investment analysts' research reports, earnings estimates, and other third-party analyses of companies and industries.

Chapter 5 shows you the tools you can use to screen stocks and reduce the universe of possible companies to invest in, down to a size you can handle. You can compare screening tools to decide which one, if any, works best for you.

Chapter 6 looks at bonds and their place in your portfolio. I review sources of information on both corporate bonds and government bonds, and point you to rating services that help you evaluate the relative risk of various bonds.

Chapter 7 covers mutual funds and how to find information on a fund's investment philosophy, fees and expenses, and management team. I show you mutual fund screening tools to help you select the best fund, as well as tutorials that cover the benefits and downsides of mutual funds. I also have pointers to several sites that let you track news about individual mutual funds.

Chapter 8 gives a quick rundown of some advanced investment options, for those of you who are willing to tolerate additional risk for higher possible returns. I look at how to find information about upcoming initial public offerings (IPOs), where to go to learn about real estate investment trusts (REITs), what to watch out for in microcap stocks, and how to find out about day trading.

Chapter 9 lets you see your tax dollars at work. The federal government maintains sites with a wide variety of information—the full text of companies' financial filings, statistics indicating economic trends and forecasts, and data that lets you compare a company's operating expenses to the industry average. This chapter points you to the government Web sites that have financial and investment-related information.

Chapter 10 looks at how to track companies and industries through news sources online. Not only will you get pointers to real-time news sites, but you'll also see how to get the online versions of newspapers, magazines, business journals, and newsletters. I also include sources for electronic-only publications, or e-journals.

While most of the chapters in this book look at free or low-fee Net services, Chapter 11 introduces you to the high-powered online services that the pros use. When you need in-depth, high-quality information from a wide variety of sources, these professional research services may be your best bet. I review the features, resources, and search tools of some of the big players so that you can decide whether it's worth the expense to use one of these services.

Chapter 12 gets into the nitty-gritty of researching a company on the Net, whether it's for a possible investment or to scope out a competitor or a potential employer. I talk about what information you can glean from careful examination of a company's Web site, how to find out what others are saying about the company, and how to use the Net to monitor its activities.

Chapter 13 shows you how to find electronic discussion forums, message boards, and email lists on financial and investment topics. I review Usenet newsgroups and discuss how to see what's already been said on a topic. I also look at the members-only investment forums of America Online and CompuServe.

Chapter 14 focuses on financing college expenses, one of the largest investments many families make. I look at Net resources for finding college loans, scholarships, and other financial aid, and other alternatives for paying for higher education.

Chapter 15 looks at scams, frauds, and other ways of losing money through the click of a button. I talk about how to run a reality check on what you see online, how to find out if a proposed investment opportunity is legitimate, and where to find resources on the Web to help detect and report investment scams.

Chapter 16 is a guide to some of the major brokerage firms offering online trading and research. I include a checklist of e-brokerage features to look for—both must-have and would-be-nice—and point you to sources for ratings of the various electronic brokerage firms.

Is It All on the Net, for Free?

In case you were wondering, no, not everything you want is on the Net, for free, at the click of a button. But you knew that, right? While most of the resources I have included in this book are available at no charge, I have also described sites that charge for access, usually in the $5- to $20-per-month range. Most of the information in these pay-per-view sites is not available elsewhere; usually it's either produced by the site owner or is copyrighted information licensed by the site owner. I have also included sites that, while free, require that you register in order to gain access to all the information available. If you choose to register, be sure to read through each screen in the registration process. Somewhere along the line, often buried at the bottom of a page in small print, is a box you can check to indicate that you do not want to receive mailings or newsletters from the site. Unless you live a sheltered life and never receive email messages from friends or co-workers, or unless you really do want to hear from this site frequently, make sure this box is checked.

As you read this book, you'll notice that I don't rely much on search engines such as Alta Vista, Hotbot, or Northern Light. It's not that I have no use for them—I've just found that they often return far too many irrelevant sites and not enough of what I'm looking for. I also know that only about 15 percent of the material that is publicly available on the Web is included in any one search engine. (See "Accessibility of information on the web," *Nature,* vol. 400, no. 6740, 8 July 1999, pp. 107–109, available at www.nature.com.) Think about it—even the biggest search sites that claim to cover the entire Web are missing far more than they include. That's a sobering thought. And no search engine can capture the material that is buried in databases within Web sites, such as the archives of magazines and newspapers, or any material that isn't in plain text, such as tables, graphs, charts, and pictures.

This means that finding valuable information on the Web requires creativity, persistence, and the ability to guess the most likely places where the information might be found. This book shows you how to identify associations that might collect useful information, how to scour a company's Web site and financial filings for clues as to its viability and strategic direction, and how to find catalogs, portals, megasites, and other resources that collect the "best of the best" on financial and investment topics on the Web. Use the tools in this book as starting points, and see what gold you can mine from the Internet.

Acknowledgments

I would like to thank Laurie Kauffman of Net Worth Consulting, who many years ago first taught me how to make sense out of a financial statement. My perspective on the world of finance hasn't been the same since. Thanks, too, to John Temple, who encouraged me to write this book and helped me think through the topics to cover. Catherine Schwent of McGraw-Hill has been a patient and encouraging editor as this book has been written, and a friendly voice on the phone. And many thanks are due to Amy Pass, who once again has earned my undying gratitude for her assistance and Web-checking.

Writing a book involves more than simply putting words to paper—or word-processing a document. It also requires support and cheerleading from friends and family. So I also owe a great round of thanks to Reva Basch, writer extraordinaire and friend and colleague; Alex Kramer, one of the most multitalented people I know; my family, Flo and Pete Bates, Amy Grant, Sarah Van de Wetering, and Russell Bates; and, always, Dave.

Mining for Gold on the Internet

1
Internet 101

By now, it seems that everyone has been exposed to Internet addresses (also known as URLs—an acronym for Uniform Resource Locators). They're emblazoned on delivery trucks (www.FedEx.com), printed on soda cans (www.DietCoke.com), and featured in advertisements for hotels (www.embassy-suites.com). Anyone who's watched ESPN knows that they can get the latest sports scores and highlights at www.espn.com.

But there's more to finding information on the Net than knowing how to send email or get the results of last night's game. This chapter gives you some tips and pointers to help you find information, find it faster, and make the best use of your time on the Net.

First Things First: Getting Access to the Net

Many companies' employees have access to the Net on their desktop, usually through a high-speed line that makes navigation fast and relatively painless. For many of us, though, our Net use related to personal finance and investing will take place at home. That means that you will have to establish a separate account with an Internet service provider (ISP) in order to dial in to the Net at home.

Selecting an Internet Service Provider

The amount you pay for Net access and the Internet service provider you choose will depend on several factors:

- *Availability.* Do you need an ISP that offers local phone number access throughout the United States (useful if you travel extensively), or will you be using the Net just from your home?
- *Capacity.* The peak usage hours are usually during the evening. Some small ISPs do not have the capacity to handle all subscribers' calls during those hours. If you find that you are getting busy signals when you try to connect, or if you notice that the response time is consistently slow, consider changing to a larger ISP.
- *Speed.* Virtually all ISPs support regular dial-up access—that is, access through your PC's modem and your home phone line. The transmission speed depends on your modem and your ISP's equipment; most will support speeds up to 56K. However, if you have become accustomed to the blazing speed of your office Net connection, you may find modem access insufferably slow. There are several options for higher-speed connections—through your local cable company, wireless service from a small satellite dish mounted on your roof, or DSL (Digital Subscriber Line) service offered through your local telephone company or other ISP. You will probably need to buy specialized equipment to use these fast connections; the company providing you with the connection will usually sell and install the equipment.
- *Bells and Whistles.* Do you plan on setting up a personal Web page? Do you want an ISP that offers proprietary information—accessible only to subscribers—as well as just access to the Net? Does the ISP offer a spam filter (which detects and deletes most unwanted email advertisements)? Do you want or need 24-hour telephone customer support? Some ISPs offer these features; if you consider them important, be sure to ask about their availability.

If you stick to the regular dial-up connections, expect to pay $15 to $25 a month for unlimited usage. Cost for high-speed access is dropping as more competitors enter the field, but expect to pay $50 to $75 a month; some services cost significantly more. There are thousands of small ISPs that provide Internet access for a local community. Many advertise in newspapers and the Yellow Pages. If, on the other hand, you want to go with one of the nationwide providers, consult C|Net's ISP Guide at www.cnet.com. At the main page, click the [Find an ISP] link. See Figure 1.1 for the front page of C|Net's guide.

Some of the large ISPs that offer a full range of services are:

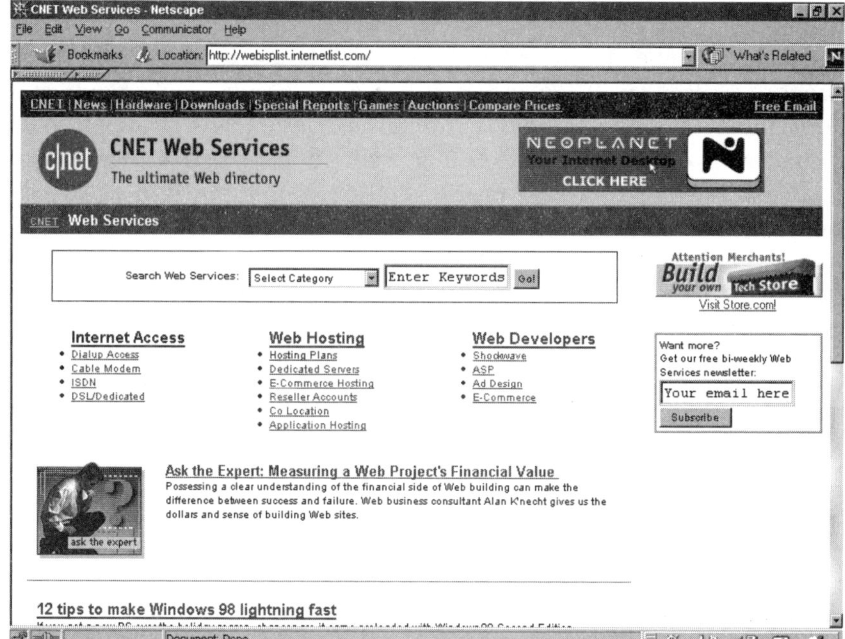

Figure 1.1. C|NET maintains a well-designed guide to Internet service providers.

- AT&T WorldNet
  www.att.com/worldnet
  (800) 967-5363
- EarthLink Network
  www.earthlink.net
  (800) 395-8425
- GTE Internet
  www.gte.net
  (800) 927-3000
- WorldCom
  www.wcom.com
  (800) 888-0800

Note, too, that a few ISPs are now offering free access in exchange for advertising on each screen. The price is right, but you tend to get what you pay for. If you want reliable access, particularly during busy periods, it probably makes more sense to pay for a regular ISP account.

Is AOL the Same as the Internet?

For many people, their first encounter with the Internet is through America Online (www.aol.com). AOL has succeeded in bringing millions of people onto the Internet through user-friendly software and the inclusion of America Online on many new personal computers. What may not be evident to these people, though, is that much of what they see on AOL is in fact information only accessible to them as subscribers. America Online began as a self-contained online service, offering discussion forums, email, and information sources on everything from business to sports and health. It still offers a rich collection of material, in well-organized *channels* for subscribers. See Figure 1.2 for a display of AOL's channels and the opening screen of the Personal Finance channel.

While each channel has its own look and feel, there is a degree of overall organization and structure to AOL—not to mention access to value-added information—that simply isn't available on the Internet. Of course, America Online subscribers can also go outside AOL's own service and

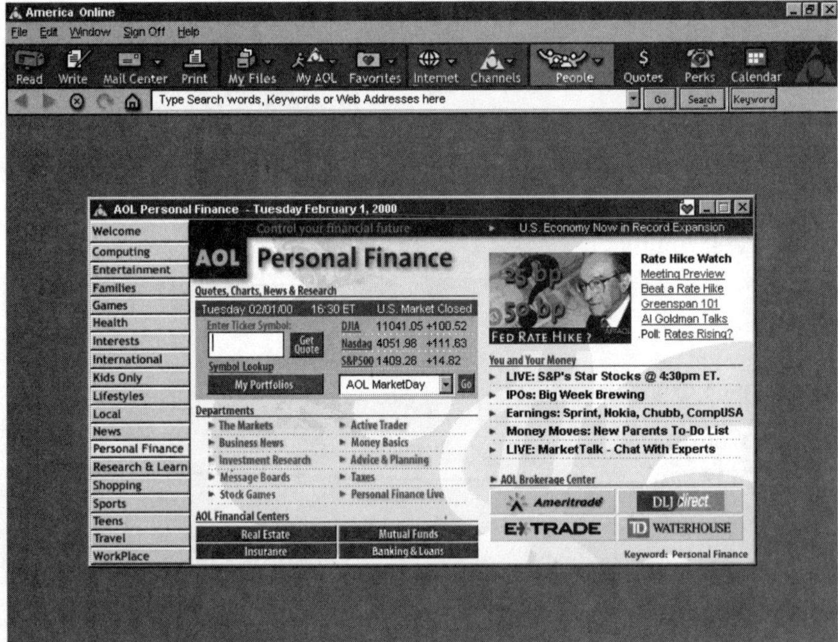

Figure 1.2. America Online organizes its information by channels, including a Personal Finance channel.

onto the Net, either by typing in a URL in the Keyword box at the top of the screen or by clicking the Internet icon.

If you are an AOL subscriber, keep in mind that this book focuses on information available to anyone on the Net, which means that it does not look at material that is only on AOL's proprietary service and thus not available to nonsubscribers. You can get from AOL to any of the Web sites described in here by typing in the address in the Keyword box. Note, too, that in the Personal Finance channel you have access to some of the same information that I describe elsewhere in the book. For example, stock quotes (delayed by 15 or 20 minutes) are available both on this channel and on a number of Web sites. (See Chapter 4 for more information on stock quotes and managing your portfolio.) America Online also contains links within its proprietary channels to Web sites that are publicly accessible, which is why some subscribers can get confused as to where AOL ends and the public Web begins.

CompuServe, Prodigy, and Microsoft Network

America Online has several competitors in the proprietary-content arena. The largest of these are CompuServe, Prodigy, and Microsoft Network (MSN). All offer at least some subscribers-only content, although none is even half the size of America Online. (CompuServe is owned by AOL, but operates as a separate unit.) Of these three, CompuServe has what most business users consider to be the richest collection of discussion forums and information resources. While Prodigy and MSN both concentrated on developing proprietary content when they began, both now focus more on simply providing Internet access, with some subscribers-only areas. You can get information about CompuServe through its Web site at www.compuserve.com.

CompuServe has always focused on the business and professional market. As a result, it highlights its personal finance and computer-oriented channels rather than its more consumer-oriented channels such as Health & Fitness or Shopping. The Personal Finance channel includes a good selection of information resources, including a link to Dow Jones Interactive (see Chapter 11 for more information on DJI), retirement guides, a portfolio management system, and financial news. CompuServe's personal finance discussion and investment forums are well-organized, populated by thoughtful participants, and moderated by people who ensure that the tone of the forums remains professional. See Figure 1.3 for the main Investors Forum page.

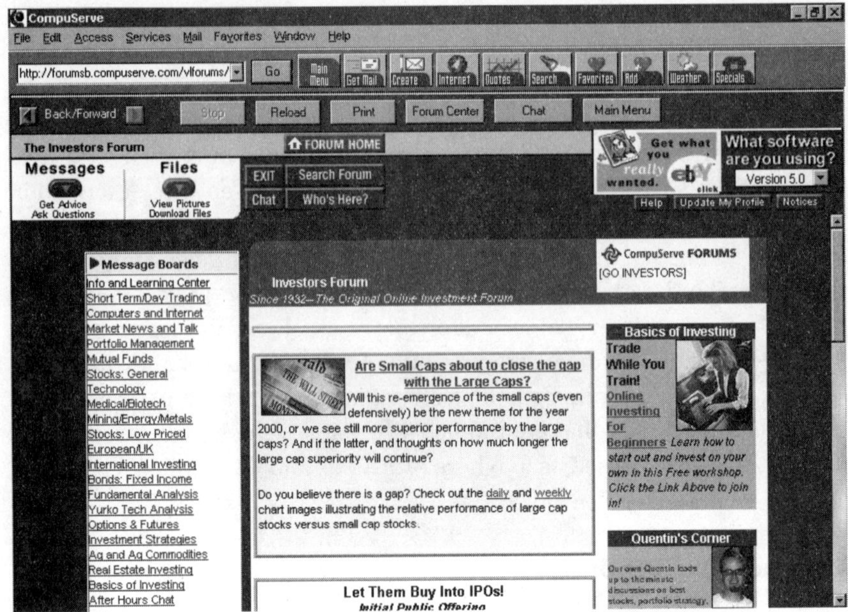

Figure 1.3. CompuServe offers discussion forums on personal finance and investment.

Tools for Finding Information on the Net

Later chapters in this book will look at specific tools to find investment information on the Net. But there are some basic research techniques that apply regardless of the type of information needed. In general, there are three ways to find information on the Net:

- Going directly to a Web page that you know will have useful information
- Using catalogs, vertical portals, and other human-organized guides to the Net
- Using search engines that attempt to cover the entire Net

Each of these methods has its advantages and disadvantages: The first is by far the most efficient if you know where you're going; the second is useful if you want a filtered view of the most likely sources for information; and the third is best when you are seeking an elusive piece of information and need to look in as many places as possible.

There are several caveats to keep in mind, though, as you use any of these tools. The most important is that no research tool is comprehensive or completely up to date. The Web is expanding so fast that no existing system can index it, and many areas of the Net block access by search engines. If you want to find information on an announcement that a company made yesterday, you will probably not be able to find pointers to the news in any of the catalogs or search engines; rather, you will need to go directly to a Web site that provides news stories. Likewise, if you want to find the latest software add-ons for your word processor, you probably won't find them by using one of the research tools; databases of software files, newspaper articles, or product specifications are generally not searchable except from within the Web site on which they reside.

Going Right to the Source

The most straightforward way of finding information, if you already know where you might find it, is to go directly to the source. If you want a copy of a company's press release describing its new CEO, the fastest way to get the release is to go to the company's Web site. But what if you don't know the URL? Guess! Most organizations want you to be able to find their site, so they make their address as simple as possible, within the limitations of the Web. Since most companies' Web addresses begin with *www.* and end with *.com,* try inserting the company name in the middle and see if that gets you to the right place. Esprit de Corp.'s address, for example, is www.esprit.com, and the address for *The Washington Post* is www.washingtonpost.com. Of course, this does not always work. United Technologies' Web site is www.utc.com rather than www.unitedtechnologies.com, and the address for *The New York Times* is not www.newyorktimes.com but www.nytimes.com. In sum, this research technique, while not perfect, is a way to get to many sites quickly.

Catalogs and Portals, or the Web with a Human Touch

What if you try guessing a site's address and strike out? The second-fastest way to find an address is often to use a Web catalog, such as Yahoo! (www.yahoo.com—and yes, the exclamation point is part of the trademarked name, although that is not included in the URL). The advantage of Web catalogs is that they are built by real people looking at Web sites and deciding what general category to which each site belongs. The disadvantage of Web catalogs is that while they are designed to include organized access to the significant sites on the Web, they do not capture information on every Web page in existence. Just as you could not use a library's card catalog to find every book that mentions the word *marathon,* likewise you could not use a Web catalog to find every Web page that mentions *marathon.* Use catalogs when you want pointers to the most relevant sites, not to every site.

Drilling Down in Yahoo! Yahoo! is one of the best-known and largest of the Web catalogs. See Figure 1.4 for the main Yahoo! page. You can look for information on Yahoo! in two ways: (1) by typing in a word or phrase in the search box, or (2) by *drilling down* from a broad category like Business & Economy to narrower and narrower subcategories.

The search box option works well if you want to find the URL for a specific site; to get the pointer to the Donaldson, Lufkin & Jenrette Web site, for example, type in *Donaldson Lufkin* in the search box and you will see a link to the company's home page (www.dlj.com). If, on the other hand, you want to see a list of companies offering Internet telephone software, you can work your way down the subcategory chain. Click [Internet] at

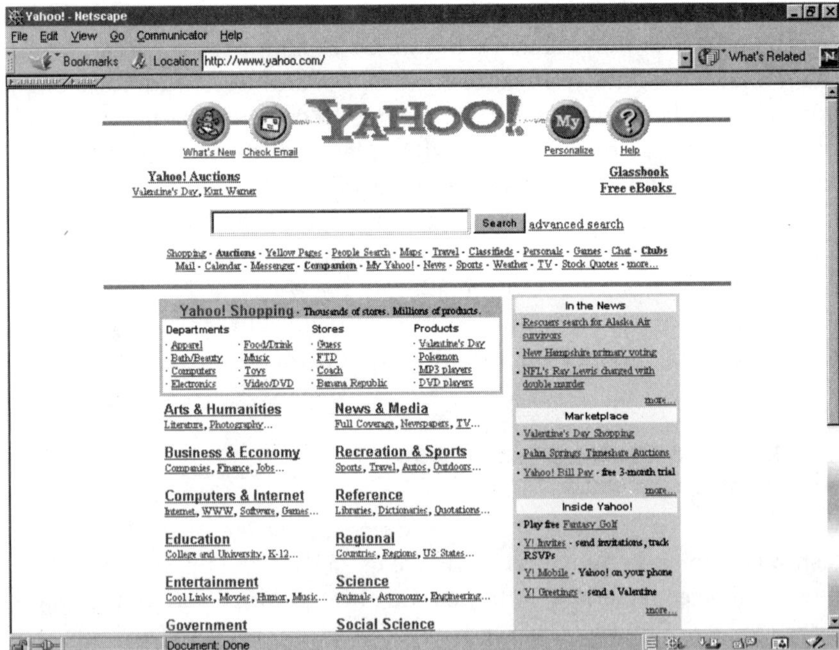

Figure 1.4. Yahoo! organizes its vast database of Web sites into categories and subcategories.

the main page (listed under Computers & Internet), then click [Internet Phone] at the next list of subcategories, and finally click the [Commercial Software] link to get a list of links to companies offering software that enables you to use the Internet to make voice telephone calls.

But what if you didn't know what category to start drilling down from? Say you had heard of Debt Busters International, a credit counseling service, and wanted to find other credit counseling services that have Web pages. You can use a reverse form of drilling down—call it drilling *up*—to find similar Web sites. First, type in the name of the organization in the Yahoo! search box. This will give you a listing for just the Debt Busters' site, as shown in Figure 1.5.

Note that just above the listing for Debt Busters is a link to the subcategory in which Debt Busters appears: *Business and Economy > Companies > Financial Services > Credit Services > Consumer Services > Credit Counseling*. If you click that link, you will see a list of all the Web sites in the Yahoo! database categorized as credit counseling, including Debt Busters International.

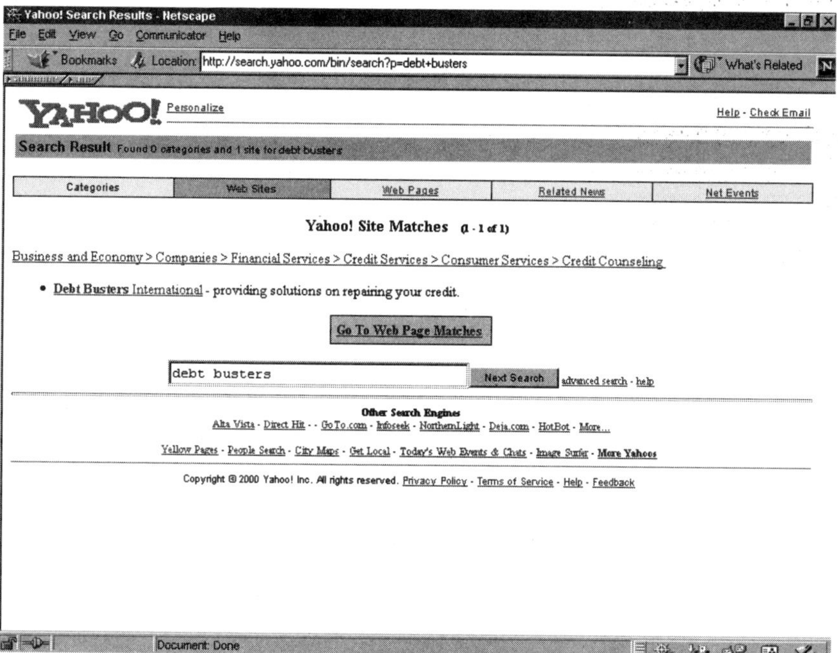

Figure 1.5. You can drill up from an individual Yahoo! listing to see related Web sites.

Portals, Virtual Libraries, and Authority Pages. While Yahoo! is the oldest and largest of the Web catalogs, there are a number of other human-organized guides to the Internet. The most common of these are *portals,* guides or gateways to the Net that help point you in the right direction. Many of the search engines, described in more detail later, are adding portals to their sites. These often closely resemble Yahoo! in format—they have broad categories such as News, Health, Sports, and so on, and each category includes a list of what are judged to be the best Web resources in that subject. See Figure 1.6 for an example of the portal on the Lycos search engine (www.lycos.com).

Another type of Net resource built by people is the *virtual library* or *authority Web site.* These sites often focus on specific industries or subjects and are built and maintained by people who are passionate about the topic. While they are far from comprehensive, they usually contain the best, most current, most authoritative sites. One of the best-known of the virtual library sites is, yes, the WWW Virtual Library (vlib.org/ Overview.html). As with Yahoo!, the library is broken down into categories—agriculture, humanities, engineering, and so on—and each sub-

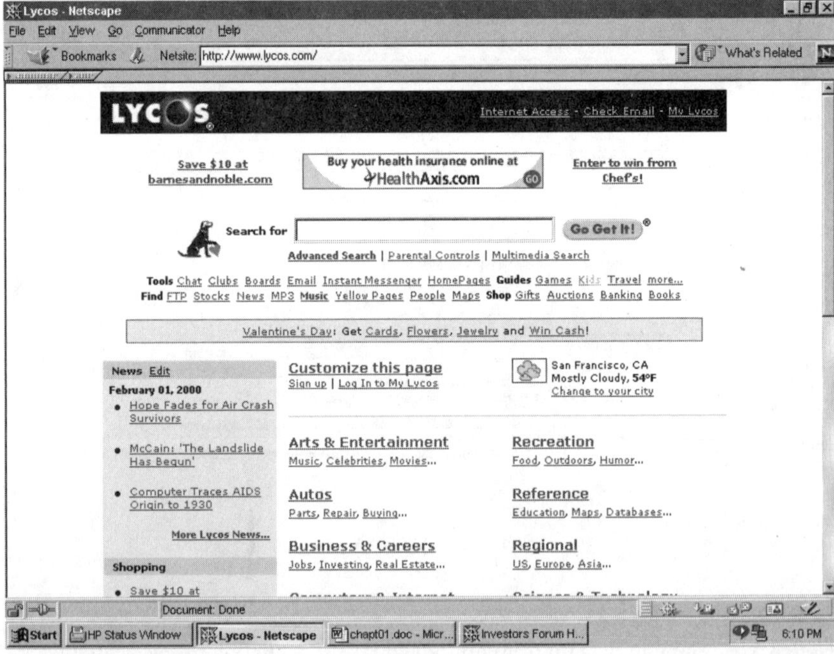

Figure 1.6. Lycos includes a portal or guide to selected Web resources.

ject area has its own list of top resources. Since a different librarian maintains each subject guide, there is no uniformity in their format. All are updated frequently, and they solicit comments and suggestions. They are often good starting points if you aren't sure what you are looking for.

Similar to virtual libraries but with a commercial bent, About.com (www.about.com) is an advertising-supported collection of *guide-sites* to a wide array of subjects. Unlike many other Web resources, the experts who maintain each site—the guides—are prominently featured, with their names and photographs displayed at the top of each site. The guides' compensation is based on the amount of traffic through their sites, so they have an incentive to develop and maintain top-quality guide-sites. See Figure 1.7 for the Financial Planning guide-site. Note that these sites include not only links to information resources but also discussion forums, chat areas, and full-fledged articles on the subject.

Less formal authority pages are often maintained by people who simply have a deep and abiding interest in a topic. You often learn about these through word of mouth; there is no centralized index or list of authority pages. While some of these sites are updated frequently, others have been

Figure 1.7. About.com's guide-sites offer collections of resources on finance and investment subjects.

allowed to grow stale. Be sure to look through the site carefully. When was it last updated? What are the credentials of the person who is maintaining the site? A well-organized site includes information on both the frequency of updates and background of the Web site owners.

Search Engines, or Searching for the Needle in the Haystack

Unlike catalogs and other selective Web indexes, the goal of most search engines is to offer access to as much of the Web as possible. There are some areas of the Web that are not captured by search engines, such as current newswires and archives of newspaper and magazine articles. In addition, it has been estimated that no single search engine covers more than 15 percent of the publicly-accessible Web. Given the current rate of expansion of Web pages, it is possible that no search engine can ever approach 100 percent coverage. For a good analysis and a report card of the scope and depth of coverage of the major search engines, check out the Search Engine Watch (www.searchenginewatch.com).

Use a search engine when you want as much information as possible on a subject, or when you are looking for data that you think might be buried deep in a Web site. For example, if you want to find any sites that mention a newly appointed executive, only a search engine will turn up relevant Web pages. Since search engines cover so much more ground than Web catalogs, the results of your search may stagger you. It is fairly common to see something like "we found 317,415 Web pages." Don't be alarmed; the Web pages are listed in descending order of probable relevance, so after about the first 50 listings the usefulness will probably drop off considerably.

Alta Vista. One of the early leaders in the race to index as much of the Web as possible is Alta Vista (www.altavista.com). Still one of the largest of the search engines, Alta Vista offers both basic and advanced search options, as well as a directory of key Web resources, organized by category and subcategory (see Figure 1.8). Alta Vista even lets you type in your search in the form of a question; some search engines require that you enter only the key words to search.

If you want to use advanced search techniques, some of which are described in the following section, click the [Advanced Search] tab to go to a new search screen. Note that in addition to its search engine, Alta Vista also has a catalog of selected Web sites, similar to Yahoo!'s. Click [Investing] to see a well-organized collection of resources, including investment guides, newsletters, retirement planning . . . even sites offering investment humor.

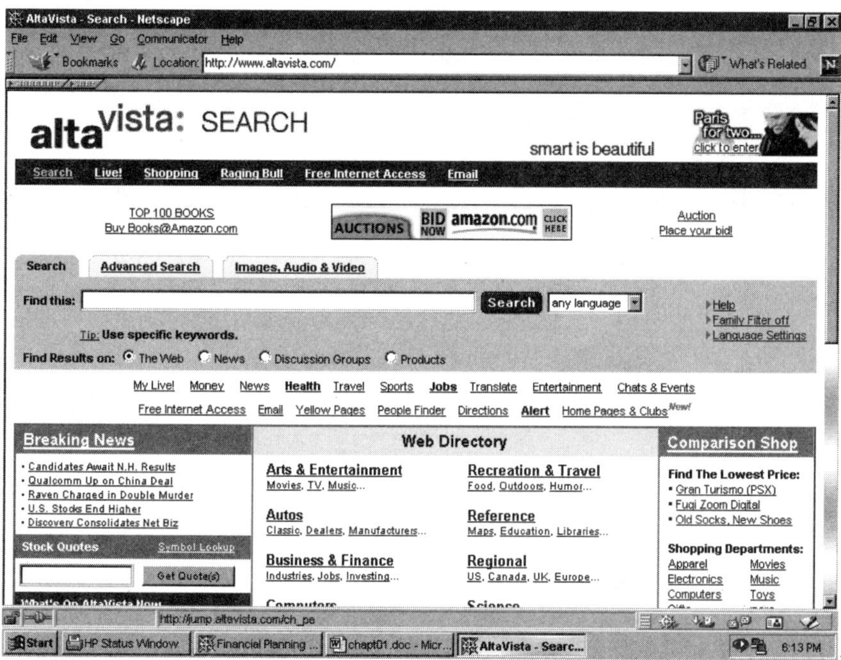

Figure 1.8. Alta Vista has both a search engine and a subject catalog.

HotBot. Put on your dark glasses before you head over to one of the other large search engines, HotBot (www.hotbot.com). There is a lot of neon green on this site, but it also offers some of the most powerful search options available. At the main site, click [Advanced Search] if you want the ability to look for information from specific Web addresses (e.g., look only in all the IRS Web pages), pages added or modified after a certain date (useful if you are monitoring a company's site on an ongoing basis), or for pages containing words related to your search terms (see Figure 1.9).

Like Alta Vista and many other search engines, HotBot has built a directory of the best sources of information on a wide range of topics. Click the [Investing] link at the main search page to get a list of subcategories, from *Brokerages* to *Women in Investing.* Like About.com, HotBot lists the names of the editors of each of its categories at the bottom of each category screen, and encourages users to submit additional sites for possible inclusion.

Search Engine Hybrids. Northern Light (www.northernlight.com) is an interesting example of a hybrid—part search engine and part electronic library. It competes directly with AltaVista in terms of total size of its Net

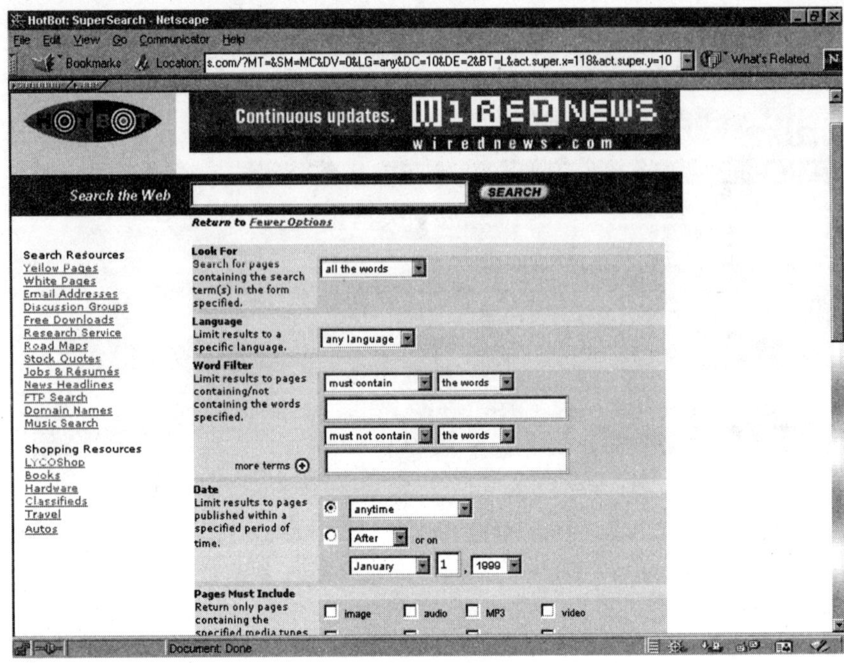

Figure 1.9. HotBot's advanced search feature lets you fine-tune your search.

index; both claim to have the largest search engine on the Net. But Northern Light also has a special collection of articles from magazines, trade journals, and newspapers, which you can purchase for a few dollars apiece. (See Chapter 11 for more information on Northern Light's Special Collection.)

One of Northern Light's distinguishing features is that, while it returns the results of a search in a single, relevance-ranked list as do most other search engines, it also compiles ad hoc Custom Search Folders of the results. For example, a search for *electronic retail* resulted in a single list of Web sites, sorted by relevance as well as the same sites sorted into folders such as retail industry, press releases, and electronic commerce. See Figure 1.10 for the search results page.

Power Tips for Online Researchers

Entire books have been written about how to do effective online research. The purpose of this section is to give you a few important tips to streamline and focus your online searches so that you can spend your time *using* information instead of looking for it.

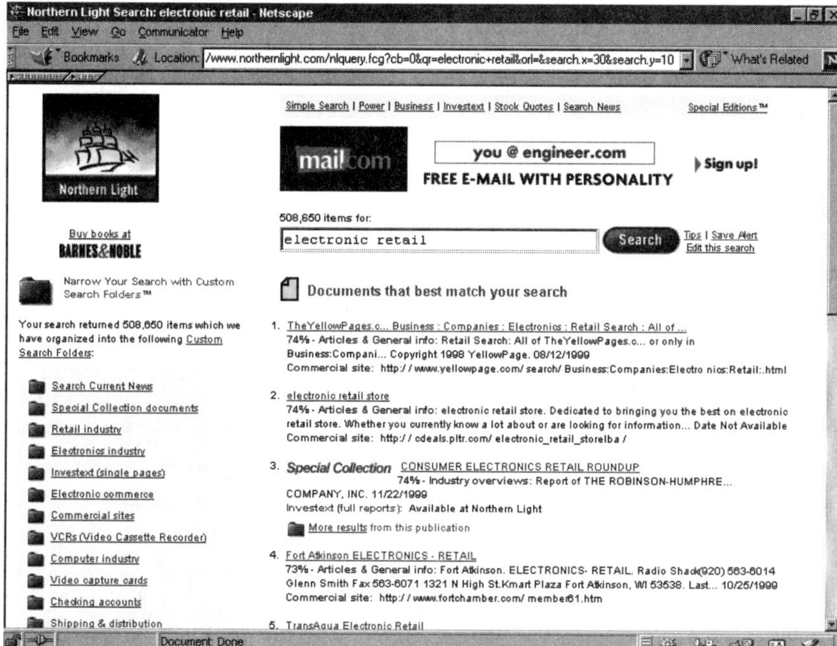

Figure 1.10. Northern Light categorizes search results on the fly into Custom Search Folders.

- *Evaluate each site for point of view, timeliness, and depth.* Most Web sites are fairly straightforward; they are maintained by a company, a government agency, or a well-known association. Be careful, though, if you do not recognize the source of the information. While the Citizens for Limited Taxation and Government (cltg.org) declares its orientation in its name, it is not clear where the Council for Responsible Nutrition (www.crnusa.org) stands. Look for links labeled [Who we are] or [More about us]; these usually will explain the organization's point of view. See if there is an indication of when the site was last updated. If the most recent press release is six months old, or if there are outdated links, you may not want to rely on the information contained at the site, since it would appear that it is not being maintained.
- *Look for external validation of the information.* Just as newspaper reporters are told never to rely on information that they cannot verify from an independent source, always try to verify information you find from a Web site. Likewise, try to gauge the reliability of the information source. One way of doing this (based on the assumption that referrals by peers is a good indication of respect) is to see how many Web sites link *to* the site you are reviewing. The oddly named Google search engine

(www.google.com) does a good job at displaying what it calls *back-links*—links from one site to another. In the search box, type *link:* and the URL of the site you are investigating (e.g., link:www.crnusa.org). See Figure 1.11 for the results of this back-link search.

- *Be persistent.* The fact that you could not find what you were looking for in your first attempt does not mean that the information is not there. Work from the assumption that what you want is available somewhere. The secret is figuring out who would care enough about your topic to compile the information and make it available. Is it something that a government agency regulates? Is it something that concerns a trade association? Would a nonprofit organization want to make information available about it? Think creatively about who or what group would be passionately concerned, and then use the research tools I've described in this chapter to find that person's or group's Web site.
- *Keep in mind George Bernard Shaw's observation that the British and Americans "are two countries separated by a common language."* Not only do we spell words differently but we use different words for the same concept. (My favorite example is *public school*—meaning a state-run school in the

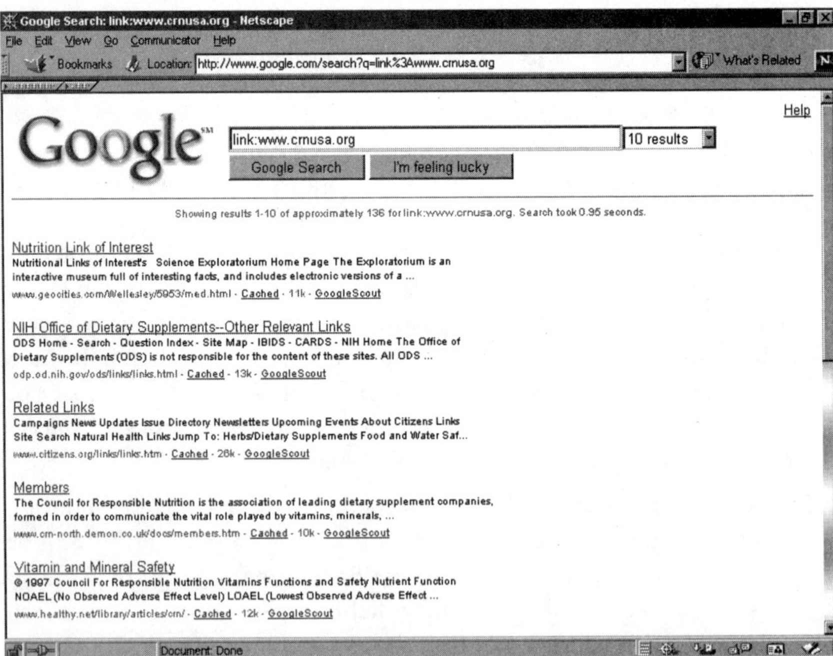

Figure 1.11. Google searches for Web sites that link to a particular site.

United States and a private school in the United Kingdom.) This issue is particularly important for Americans searching British publications or Brits searching American publications. Remember to look for both *organization* and *organisation, labor* and *labour, check* and *cheque, soccer* and *football.*

- *Always look at the [Advanced Search] and [Help] links on a search engine's site.* These files will tell you how to fine-tune your search. Options usually include truncation (for example, typing *fraud** to find *fraudulent, frauds,* and *fraud*), phrase searches (usually enclosing the words in single or double quotation marks), and Boolean logic (connecting two words with AND to indicate that both must appear in any retrieved site, or with OR to indicate that only one or the other need appear).
- *Be sure you have the software needed to accommodate non-HTML files.* Some organizations make many of their publications available in PDF files. These Portable Document Format files are essentially photocopies of the original documents, including any graphics, special formatting, and page breaks. You need an Adobe Acrobat *reader* to open and print these files. The software is available at no charge at Adobe's Web site (www.adobe.com/prodindex/acrobat/readstep.html). Most sites with PDF files include links to this download site. Once you have installed the Acrobat software, you can click on a link to a PDF document and Acrobat will be launched automatically and the document displayed.

2
Financial Basics Online

While most of this book focuses on sources of information for specific purposes—tracking stock prices, evaluating mutual funds, or digging up information on a specific company, for example—there are times when you need to find more basic information. This chapter shows you how to find well-organized collections of introductory material on finance and investing, sources for glossaries and tutorials, guidance on how to read an annual report or evaluate the relative risks of various investment vehicles, and how to take a more active role in managing your investments.

As noted in Chapter 1, remember to look at every information source critically, evaluating the site's purpose, point of view, timeliness, and depth. If you want to find some basics on various investment strategies, look for a site that does not espouse a particular point of view. Resource guides compiled by search engine sites, librarians, or nonprofit agencies are usually unbiased and well-maintained. Be wary of sites that denigrate a particular type of investor or investment strategy; odds are good those sites have a strong point of view and would not provide unbiased information on financial and investment fundamentals. Watch, too, for sites that promote books, tapes, seminars, or other products. The one exception to this caveat is that some brokerage houses maintain at least some basic information on their Web sites, including glossaries, retirement and college expense calculators, and general discussions of investment planning. You will still have to wade through some promotional material, but the more Net-savvy firms have learned that it pays to provide solid information to potential investors.

Catalogs of Basic Information Links

One of the most valuable features of the Internet is that it is essentially self-organizing. People and organizations not only make their own information available on the Net, but they try to catalog and create links to other sources of information as well. These catalogs of links are bibliographies, pointers to other resources rather than sources of information themselves. In addition to the publicly available sources listed on the following pages, America Online subscribers are reminded that there is an area within AOL that focuses on investment basics (Keyword: Money Basics). This area includes message boards, links to a number of public Web sites that provide basic information in investing and finance, and several tutorials on personal investment. See Figure 2.1 for the main Money Basics screen.

Evaluation Tips

Some catalogs are built by subject experts and are well organized, updated regularly, and pruned of outdated or dead sites. Other catalogs, alas, are

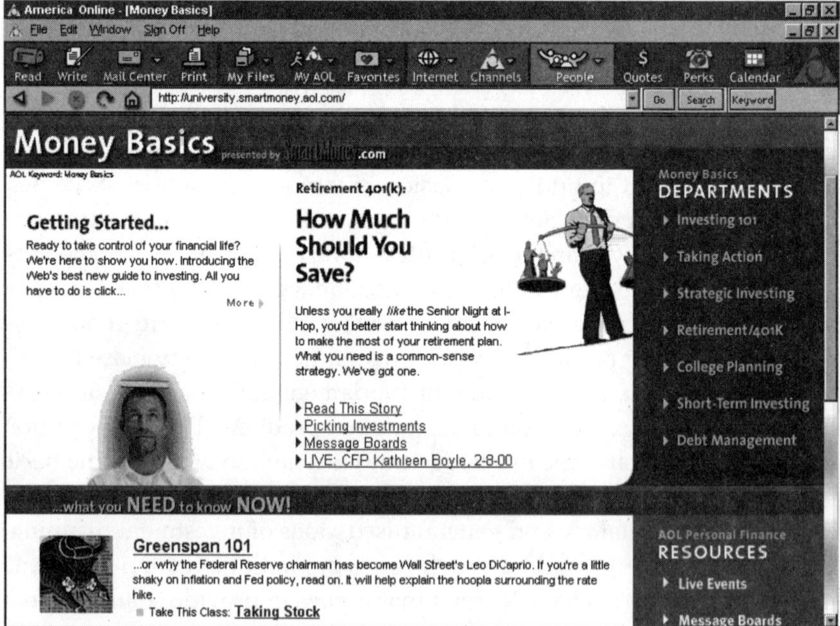

Figure 2.1. America Online has a subscribers-only area on money basics.

built on a whim and not maintained. Distinguishing the former from the latter is sometimes as simple as looking for a notation at the bottom of the Web page such as "Last updated on xx/xx/xx." If the catalog has not been updated within the past six months, you can assume that it has been allowed to go fallow; look elsewhere. If you find that many of the links point to nonexistent Web sites, you can also assume that the catalog is not being maintained regularly.

Look for a description of the Web site manager: is he or she someone who has longtime expertise in the field—or a student building a site for a course assignment? Are most of the links simply pointers to *other* catalogs of links, or do they point directly to resources you can use? Does the catalog appear to cover all the areas you are interested in, or is it too narrowly focused for your needs? Likewise, does it include resources at your level of expertise, or are the listed resources too basic or too advanced?

The catalogs and sources listed on the following pages have been designed by organizations with an interest in maintaining their credibility and reputation; hence, it is reasonable to expect that their links will be updated frequently. Most of these catalogs actively solicit your feedback and suggestions for new sites; be sure to contribute if you find a site you think should be included.

Search Engine Channels and Catalogs

"Channels? I thought we were talking about the Web, not television." Many of the major search engines offer more than merely a search of the entire Net; they also provide a selection of what they consider to be the best sources for particular types of information. Instead of having to type in a phrase such as *stock quotes* and reviewing the thousands of sites that the search engine retrieves, you can click on what are now called *channels* and see a structured and evaluated collection of investment-related sites, including sites that provide close-to-real-time stock quotes. The value of these channels or catalogs is that they are maintained by companies that want you to come back again and again—the search engine site is selling advertising based on the number of people who come to its site. That means that their channels and catalogs are more likely to be well-designed and updated regularly.

Yahoo! A few years ago, the only real catalog of Web-based resources was Yahoo! (www.yahoo.com). Rather than using *spiders* or software programs to automatically scour the Net for publicly available sites, Yahoo! is a selective list of sites, each one of which has been reviewed by a Yahoo! employee. The sites are organized into broad categories such as Business & Economy or Science, then into more and more specific subcategories. In a sense, Yahoo! is the granddaddy of channels, and its categories have more depth and breadth than any of the other search engines' offerings.

Yahoo!'s initial screen lists its top-level categories. You can either type in a specific topic—*investment glossary*, for example—or you can *drill down* the subcategories to the one you want. If you are typing in a search, remember that you are not searching the entire Internet; you are searching a selected catalog of sources. If, instead of searching, you want to drill down to the specific subcategory you want—investment glossaries, for instance—simply click on the [Business & Economy] category. You will see a new listing of all the categories within Business & Economy. Click on [Finance & Investment]. At the next screen, click on [References & Guides], and at the next screen, click on [Glossaries] (finally!). Here you will see a collection of glossaries, including Yahoo!'s own financial glossary. See Figure 2.2 for an example of Yahoo!'s subcategory on financial glossaries.

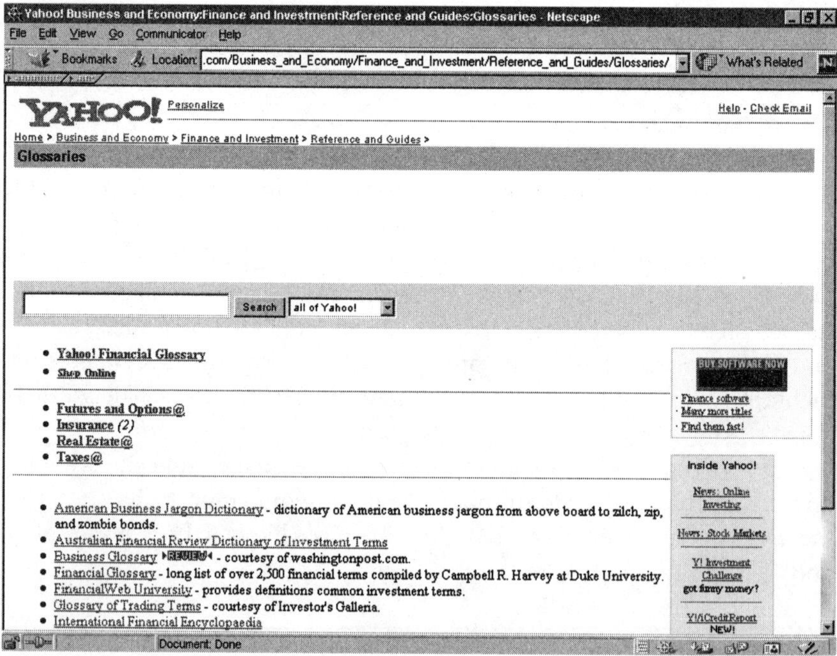

Figure 2.2. Yahoo! provides a list of financial glossaries.

AltaVista. One of the largest search engines, AltaVista (www.altavista.com), has a channel for Business & Finance, which contains selected sites along with brief descriptions. As with Yahoo!, AltaVista lets you drill down to more and more specific subcategories and lets you search within its channels for selected sites on a particular topic. To search within a category, click the category link, then type your key words in the [Find this:] box that appears on the screen.

To find a collection of basic financial guides in AltaVista using the drill-down technique, select the [Business & Finance] link at the main AltaVista page. You will then see a listing of the subchannels within Business & Finance. Select [Investing], then select [Investment Guides]. Note the descriptions of individual sites; some catalogs do not provide this much information on each site. See Figure 2.3 for the list of financial guides in AltaVista's finance channel.

HotBot. Another contender for the title of Largest Search Engine is HotBot. This search engine provides a channel for investment-related topics, including stock quotes, market statistics, and a good collection of finance-

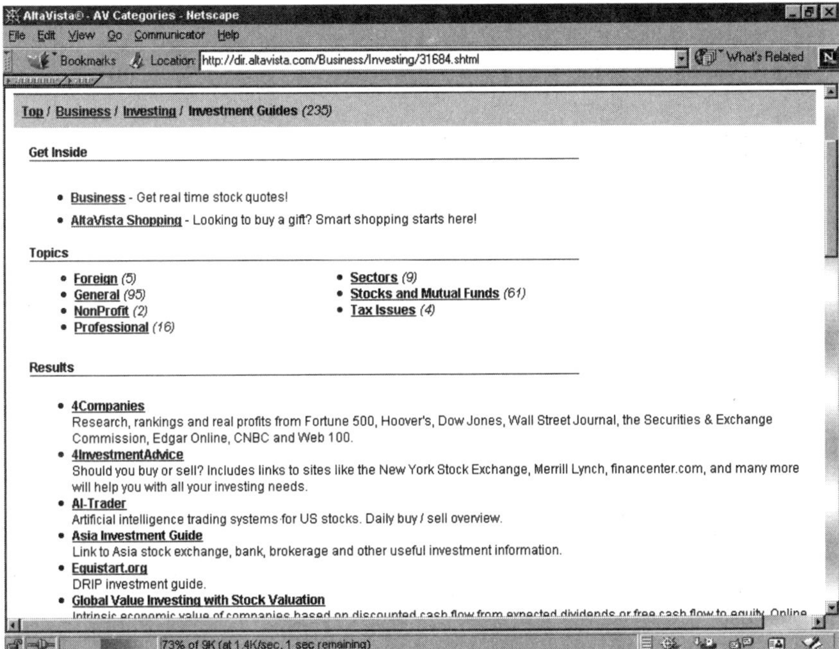

Figure 2.3. AltaVista's list of financial guides includes a useful description of each site.

and business-related resources. Unlike Yahoo! or AltaVista, this is a very selective guide to sources, and it includes fee-based services such as Wall Street Journal Interactive Edition (see Chapter 10 for more information about WSJIE, and Chapter 11 for more information about other fee-based information services). The descriptions are lengthy and entertaining. From the main HotBot Web page, click [Investing] to get to the investment channel.

Note in Figure 2.4 that this channel also lets you search the Hoover's company database (see Chapter 12 for a description of online directories of company information). Although it isn't obvious from the screen, HotBot also links to the LookSmart catalog that AltaVista uses; you can jump to that catalog by clicking on any of the categories listed under [More Business Sites].

Virtual Library Collections

In addition to the channels and catalogs built by search engines, there are many electronic reference collections on the Web built by information professionals. These can be of particular value because they are often main-

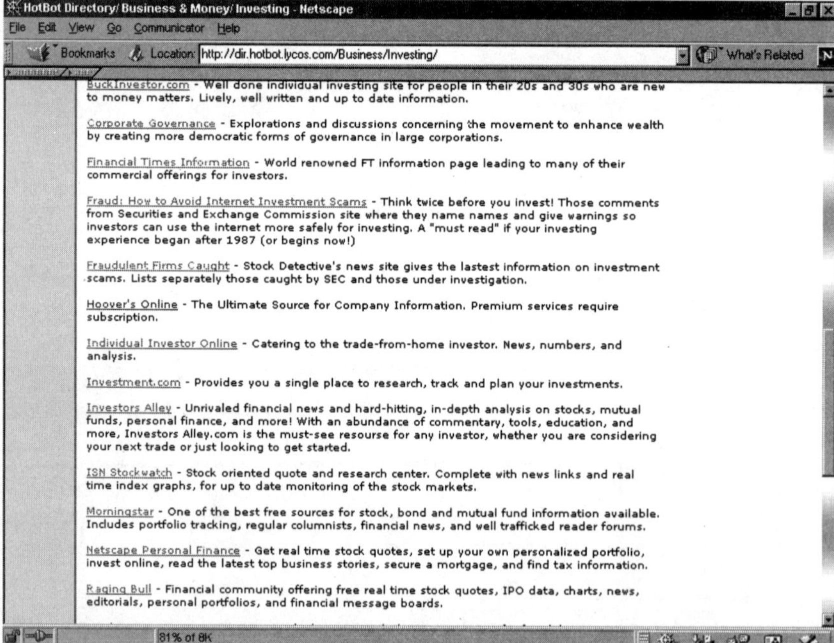

Figure 2.4. HotBot's Business channel has lengthy write-ups of recommended business sites.

tained by reference librarians who field the same basic business and finance questions day after day, so they know which sources answer the questions best.

As with any other site maintained by an individual, look carefully to see when the site was last updated. Be prepared for a site that is low on graphics and glitz; many virtual library collections are designed for the lowest-common-denominator browsers, which means that these sites often are very plain and text-oriented. While they may not look as visually appealing as their flashier competitors, they load fast and are usually simple to navigate.

Internet Public Library. The Internet Public Library (www.ipl.org) is an interesting combination of Web-based collections of sources and a network of real live librarians. Just as in a bricks-and-mortar library, there is a reference collection of information; if you can't find what you want there, you can ask a librarian for help in finding the answer. At the main IPL screen, click on [Reference], select the [Business & Economics] link, then select the [Finance] link. At this point, check out the [Investments] and [Personal Finance] sections; both have useful collections of resources.

As you can see from Figure 2.5, each IPL item lists the various categories in which the item appears. In this example, you can see that The Insider is listed under both the Business & Economics–Finance–Personal Finance, and Business & Economics–Finance–Investments subject categories.

WWW Virtual Library. Unlike the Internet Public Library, which is a single site that tries to follow the model of a real library, the WWW Virtual Library (vlib.org/Overview.html) is a more casual collection of individual Web bibliographies. Each subject specialization is handled by a different volunteer and housed on a different site. The WWW Virtual Library's Finance collection is maintained by the business school at Ohio State University (www.cob.ohio-state.edu/dept/fin/overview.htm).

The Virtual Finance Library site is well-organized and easy to use. For example, it has separate sections for researchers, investors, and executives. The For Investors area contains links to investment FAQs (Frequently Asked Questions files), glossaries of financial terms, and several guides to basic investment strategies.

About.com. An alternative to the library model is About.com (www.about.com), an advertiser-supported site that is built by subject *guides*, similar to the IPL and WWW Virtual Library. The main distinction is that About.com guides are paid a portion of the ad revenue generated by the

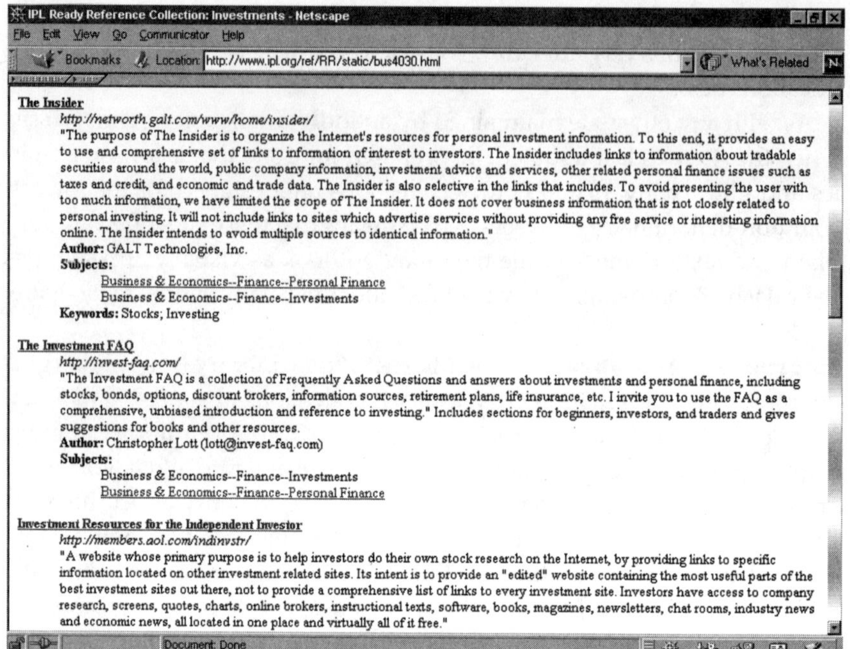

Figure 2.5. Internet Public Library listings are low on graphics but high on content.

site. The site has a more cluttered feel to it than other sites, due to the number of advertising links. On the other hand, it is well-maintained and simple to use. As with Yahoo!, you drill down to the area you want, starting with the [Finance/Investing] link on the main page. See Figure 2.6 for the Stocks page.

Finance and Investing 101

While the catalogs and research guides listed at the beginning of this chapter will point you in the right direction, you may just be looking for a tutorial on managing your investments, a guide on how to read a company's annual report, or a way of calculating how much you need to save in order to retire comfortably.

The best way to find this kind of information is to think about who would care about it, compile it, maintain it, and make it available to the public. Would a government agency be likely to provide this information? Are there nonprofit consumer advocacy organizations involved in finance

Figure 2.6. About.com has *guides* who maintain each section of its Web site.

and investment issues? What about for-profit companies that would make introductory information available on their Web sites in order to attract potential customers?

This section will explore all of these avenues of finding basic information. As useful as the examples are, keep in mind that they are simply illustrations of what can be found on the Net. As you read the newspaper, listen to the radio, or watch TV, think about whether an advertiser or quoted source might be a good resource for financial information on the Web.

Consumer-Focused Organizations

Some of the first places that experienced researchers go to for unbiased information are government and nonprofit organizations focused on the subject at hand. For our purposes, that means identifying what agencies, associations, or other groups are concerned with investment information and consumer finance. Groups that target beginning investors will be particularly useful if what you want is basic, introductory material.

Government Agencies. The U.S. Securities and Exchange Commission was formed after the stock market crash of 1929; as noted on its Web site (www.sec.gov), employees of the SEC "are the investor's advocate." The SEC regulates companies whose stock is publicly traded, brokerage firms, investment advisers, and other market participants. See Chapter 9 for more detailed information on the information filed with the SEC.

One of the SEC's roles is to educate individual investors and protect them from fraudulent securities practices. You can find a collection of clear, well-written publications by clicking the [Investor Assistance & Complaints] link at the SEC's main page. Within this section, there is a list of recent SEC publications. See Figure 2.7 for a sample of available fact sheets.

Other federal government agencies that provide information to new investors include the U.S. Federal Trade Commission (www.ftc.gov), the Social Security Administration (www.ssa.gov), and the Federal Deposit Insurance Corporation (www.fdic.gov). Your state government probably has an agency that deals with securities regulation. One example of a useful state government site is Michigan's Corporation, Securities and Land Development Bureau (www.commerce.state.mi.us/corp/invested.htm).

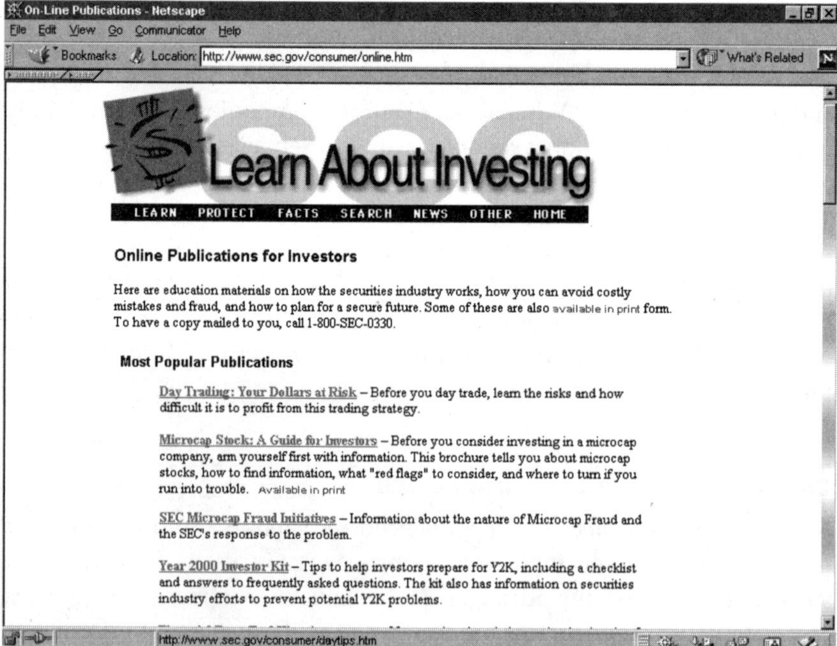

Figure 2.7. Basic financial publications are available through the U.S. Securities and Exchange Commission's Web site.

Nongovernment Organizations. Investment-related professional and trade associations often provide information on their Web sites directed to the beginning investor. Be mindful of the possibility that an organization may have a point of view or slant in its advice. This is not to suggest that the information is untrustworthy, but simply to remind you that, for example, an association of investment brokers may be more enthusiastic about investing in the stock market than would a group focused on consumer credit counseling.

As always, think about what associations or trade groups would be interested in providing basic investment information. Some that might come to mind are the National Association of Securities Dealers (www.nasd.com), the Securities Industry Association (www.sia.com), the American Association of Retired Persons (www.aarp.org), and the American Association of Individual Investors (www.aaii.com). See Figure 2.8 for an example of the information available on the NASD site targeted to individual investors.

Look through the sites for areas titled *Publications, Reference,* or *Resource Guide.* You can also try the [Search this Site] feature, if the site offers this option, and type in a term such as *information, investors,* or *publication.* If

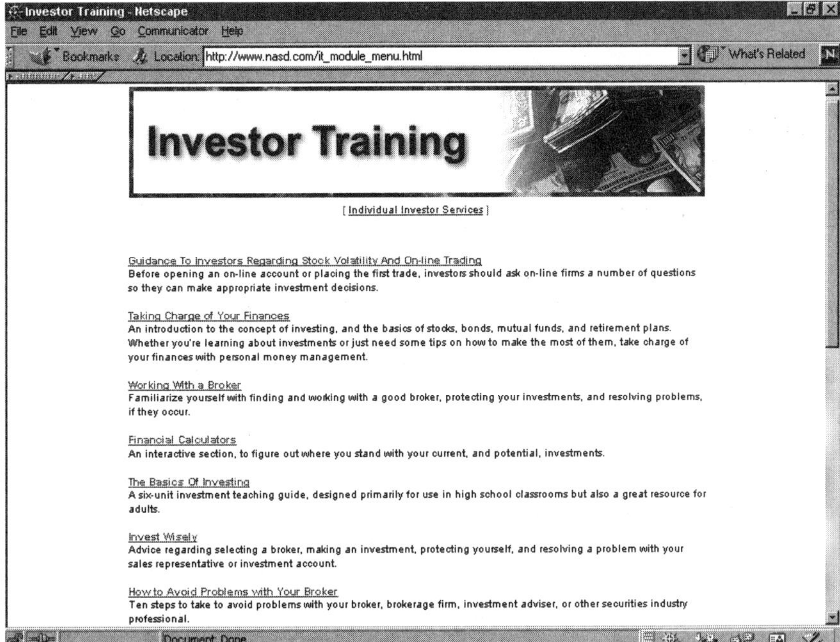

Figure 2.8. The National Association of Securities Dealers makes many of its publications for individual investors available on its Web site.

you need help identifying likely associations or other professional groups, contact your local library and ask a reference librarian to check the *Encyclopedia of Associations* for possible organizations. The *Encyclopedia* may contain the organization's Web address; if not, search for the name or acronym in Yahoo!.

Keep your eyes open as you browse; many sites include links to related information sources. A number of the sites described in this section, for example, include references or links to the American Savings Education Council (www.asec.org), which is a sponsor of the "Choose to Save" program. This education program contains a wealth of information (no pun intended) on planning for retirement, saving and investment strategies, and related information. See Figure 2.9 for a listing of some of the material available on its site.

As just noted, it is important to identify the organizations responsible for the site. Fortunately, the ASEC site has a clear link to [Partners], which lists the members of the Council. These range from the American Bankers Association to the U.S. Securities and Exchange Commission and PaineWebber. With a coalition this broad, you can be reasonably sure that the

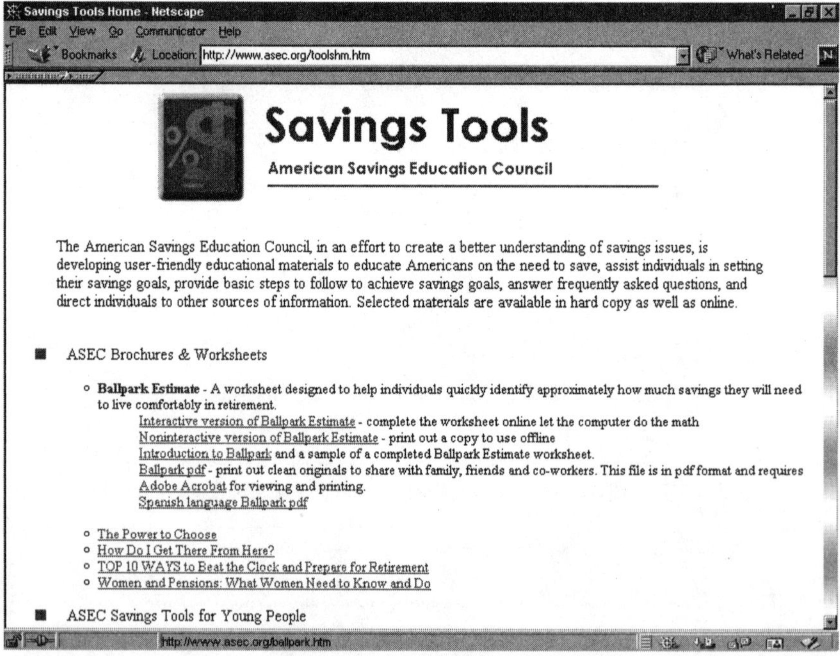

Figure 2.9. The American Savings Education Council's Choose to Save program encourages individuals to establish savings goals.

information on its Web site will not promote a single organization's agenda.

Commercial Organizations

Brokerage firms, stock exchanges, and companies that sell financial and investment information maintain Web sites with at least some basic financial information. The quality and depth of the information varies, and the amount of promotional material and hype is inevitably greater than you find in nonprofit organizations' Web sites. Use these resources with a grain of salt.

The New York and NASDAQ-Amex stock exchanges both provide information on how the stock market operates, how to read an annual report, how to interpret a stock table, and how to develop an appropriate investment strategy . . . along with plenty of information on why one stock exchange or the other is preferable. For the NYSE, go to www.nyse.com, select the [About the NYSE] link, then click [Education], and then [Educational Publications]. For the NASDAQ-American Stock Exchange, start at www.nasdaq.com and click [Investor Resources].

Commercial organizations that sell financial and investment information provide a limited subset of their material for free on their Web sites. Don't expect to get access to their value-added information; you can, however, often find basic investment advice. Some of the major financial information companies are Disclosure Inc. (www.disclosure.com—select [Public Sector Resources]), ValueLine Inc. (www.valueline.com—free registration required), and Standard & Poor's (www.standardandpoors.com). S&P also offers a Personal Wealth site (www.personalwealth.com), for which you have to register. Within that area, select [Basics] for tutorials, bibliographies of financial planning books, and articles on tax issues. Remember, you can identify the names of the top financial information companies by asking a business reference librarian at your local public library.

As expected, some brokerage houses offer basic investment information along with the usual promotional material on their sites. Fidelity Investments has an unusually rich collection of personal investment tutorials. Start at Fidelity's Personal Investing site at personal300.fidelity.com, and click [Planning]. Figure 2.10 shows an example of information available on Fidelity's Personal Investing planning page.

Other investment houses that offer some straightforward financial advice and tools include Prudential Securities (www.prusec.com), A.G.

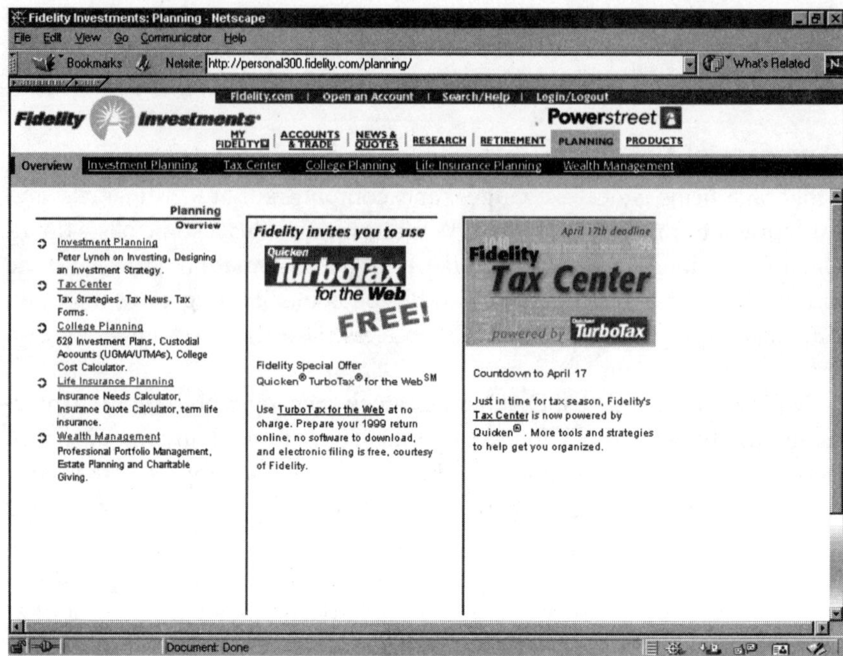

Figure 2.10. Fidelity Investment's personal investment guide provides basic investment information as well as highlights to its own services.

Edwards (www.agedwards.com), and Salomon Smith Barney (www.smithbarney.com). As already noted, keep in mind that these resources are provided by organizations that have a vested interest in encouraging you to use their services.

Games and Other Painless Learning Tools

Risking your own money is certainly one of the best ways of focusing your attention on investment skills; a less painful way of learning how to judge stocks is by "investing" in one of the fantasy stock portfolios available on the Web. Many start you off with a portfolio of $100,000 in fantasy money; you make fantasy trades of publicly traded stock, and you see how well you do in relation to other players. Think of this as the financial equivalent of rotisserie baseball. These are educational tools to help you learn how to monitor the market, evaluate a company's prospects, and compare your skills to the market average . . . all without risking any of your own money.

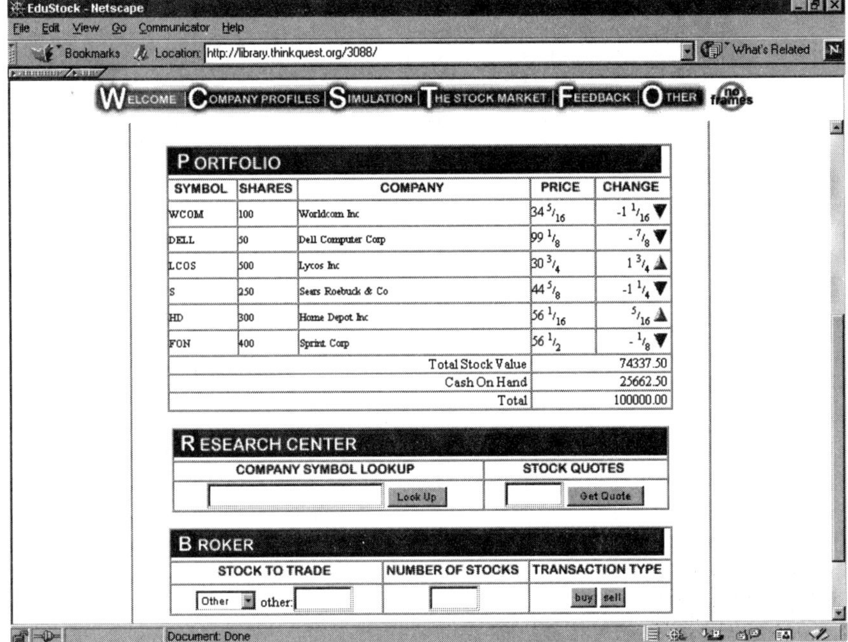

SYMBOL	SHARES	COMPANY	PRICE	CHANGE
WCOM	100	Worldcom Inc	34 5/16	-1 1/16 ▼
DELL	50	Dell Computer Corp	99 1/8	-7/8 ▼
LCOS	500	Lycos Inc	30 3/4	1 3/4 ▲
S	250	Sears Roebuck & Co	44 5/8	-1 1/4 ▼
HD	300	Home Depot Inc	56 1/16	5/16 ▲
FON	400	Sprint Corp	56 1/2	-1/8 ▼
			Total Stock Value	74337.50
			Cash On Hand	25662.50
			Total	100000.00

Figure 2.11. EduStock's simulated stock portfolio page makes construction of a portfolio easy.

The Web catalog Yahoo! has a fantasy portfolio in its Finance category (quote.yahoo.com/t1) You start with $100,000 in your portfolio; at the end of the month, the three participants with the highest portfolio value win real cash. Free registration is required in order to participate.

The Virtual Stock Exchange (www.virtualstockexchange.com) starts you out with $500,000 in VSE dollars, once you register. Not only can you hone your stock-picking skills, you can also participate in electronic discussions with other investors. As with Yahoo!'s fantasy trading, you have to register to access this free site.

EduStock (library.thinkquest.org/3088/) is a stock-trading site designed to teach students about the stock market. Its educational focus is clear from the site design—it has plenty of navigational aids; it has a well-written tutorial on the stock market; and it provides a clear explanation of how to read a company profile. See Figure 2.11 for an example of EduStock's portfolio page.

3
Financial Planning Online

Financial planning means more than simply knowing what your income is and what your retirement needs are. It also involves understanding and managing your creditworthiness, getting out from under excessive debt, and saving for specific major expenditures such as real estate purchases. This chapter examines each of these areas of financial planning and looks at how to find information online to help you plan and manage your financial future.

What *Is* My Net Worth?

Before you can design a savings and investment plan that will meet your financial goals, you need to know what you're worth. Think about all your assets and possible sources of income, both now and after you retire. These might include:

- A pension from your employer
- Individual retirement accounts and other tax-deferred savings
- Social Security retirement benefits
- Savings accounts

It is easy enough to figure out the current value of most of your assets. Your pension fund often has a set pay-out—assuming you will be working for the same employer long enough to qualify for the pension when you retire. And see Chapter 9 for information on how to get a Social Security Statement from the Social Security Administration. This report will tell you how much to expect in retirement benefits from Social Security, based on what you have paid in so far and how long you expect to continue working.

But what will your other assets be worth when you need them? How much should you be putting into certificates of deposit (CDs), mutual funds, savings accounts, and individual retirement accounts to ensure that you will be able to live comfortably when you retire? Part of the answer is how optimistic you are about the direction of the stock market and the economy between now and when you retire, and how aggressive you are in your investment philosophy. Obviously, the rate at which your retirement nest egg grows will be a lot lower if you put it all in a savings account with three percent interest than if you invest in a high-risk but high-return stock portfolio. On the other hand, a portfolio heavy on high-risk investments may actually lose money. As with much of life, the best path is usually one of moderation and diversity.

Many of the investment services on the Net have tools that help you calculate what you can expect to retire with, based on your current assets and

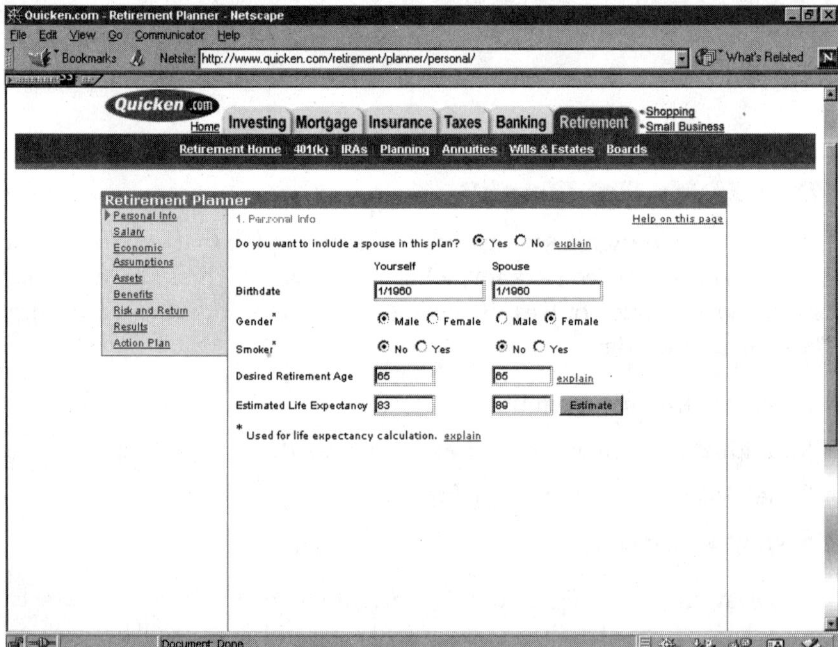

Figure 3.1. Quicken.com has a seven-step retirement planner to help you meet your retirement income objectives.

investment strategy, adjusting for inflation. Quicken, one of the more popular financial management software packages, has a step-by-step Retirement Planner at its Web site (www.quicken.com/retirement/planner) that walks you through the process. Figure 3.1 shows the beginning of the questionnaire.

Keep in mind that none of these tools take the place of a professional financial planner. Each Web-based planner includes certain assumptions, not all of which may be explicitly stated. Your after-retirement spending may be higher than the average; you may disagree with the program's assumptions of future inflation rates; you may have sources of postretirement income that do not fit neatly into the program's options. Use more than one of these online calculators to ensure that you have a fairly reliable indicator of how well you will be able to meet your retirement goals.

And remember that if you have special investment needs, such as caring for a disabled child or starting a business when you retire, your investment strategies will be significantly different from the average. For a discussion of dealing with college expenses—hardly an unusual investment goal for most families—see Chapter 14.

Planning for Retirement, or, Financing Your Life After Paychecks

Once you have used one of the financial planning tools to establish how much you will need to have on hand in order to retire, how do you set about building your assets? The Web is full of sources of advice, some of which may be biased toward the interests of the site owner. Caveat emptor—and be sure to get advice from a number of sources.

One well-designed site with a collection of retirement planning resources is maintained by InvestorGuide at www.investorguide.com/Retirement.htm. In addition to a good collection of links, it includes descriptions of each site referenced. See Figure 3.2 for an outline of what its retirement guide contains.

Pension Plans for Today

Ask many people who are retired today about where their current income is coming from, and you will often hear about wise investments, Social Security benefits, and a pension plan. While wise investing will always be a significant part of anyone's retirement planning, Social Security benefits may not be as sure a likelihood in years to come, and an employer's pen-

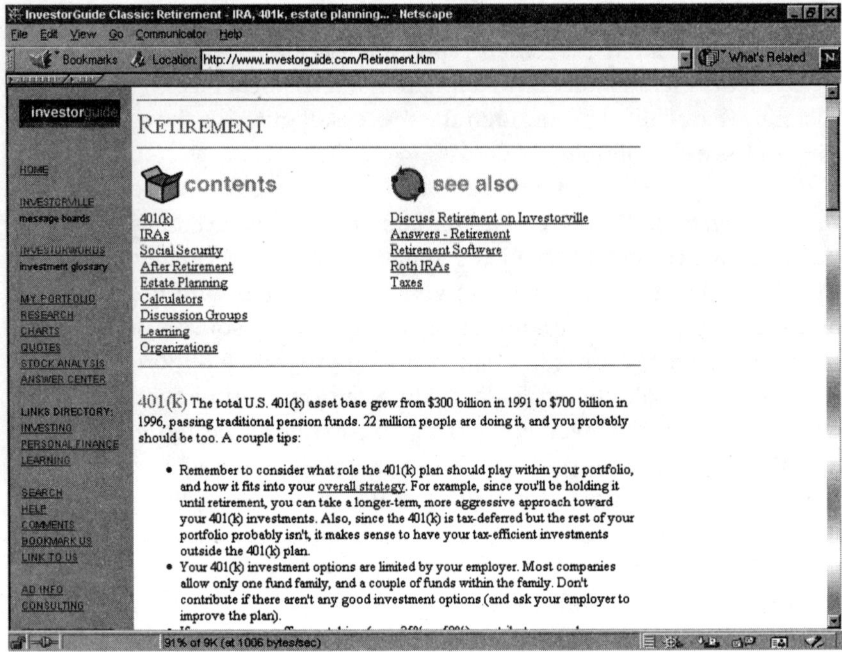

Figure 3.2. InvestorGuide's Retirement Guide is a collection of Web resources on retirement planning, along with descriptions of each site.

sion plan may be even less probable. Fewer people today stay with the same employer all their working life, and many employers are moving away from the guarantee of a job for life and a pension for retirement. Instead, the trend is toward changing employers—and indeed, careers—several times during your lifetime. That means that the responsibility for building that retirement account rests much more heavily on you than it did when the current retirees were in the prime of their careers.

Any financial planner will tell you that employer-sponsored 401(k) plans are like free money. These alternatives to traditional pension plans allow you to put aside a portion of your income into a tax-deferred retirement account, immediately reducing the amount of income you pay taxes on and increasing the value of your contribution (since the entire amount of your contribution goes to the retirement account, rather than the amount minus income taxes).

But the "free money" feature of 401(k) plans is most notable if your employer offers a matching contribution as an incentive for you to join the retirement plan. Often the company will contribute a set percentage of your contribution, from $.25 for every dollar you put into the plan up to matching your contributions dollar for dollar. If your employer does offer this matching, it makes sense for you to contribute up to the maximum allowed, since this way you maximize the amount your employer contributes to your retirement account.

Employees are expected to take more responsibility for their 401(k) accounts than they do with a traditional pension plan. Useful information specific to 401(k) investments is often available from financial advisors; there are also plenty of Web sites that focus on 401(k) plans. Start with the 401Kafé (www.401kafe.com), which includes discussion groups for employees managing their own 401(k) accounts, basic information on topics such as how much you can contribute to and under what circumstances you can withdraw money from a 401(k) account, and a tutorial on 401(k) plans. See Figure 3.3 for a summary of some of the information available on 401Kafé.

You can find additional resources by using any of the Web search engines and catalogs described in Chapter 1. Be mindful of the various ways in which the term 401(k) would appear, and check to see how each of the search engines handles parentheses. See Table 3.1 for suggested searches in some of the Web search tools.

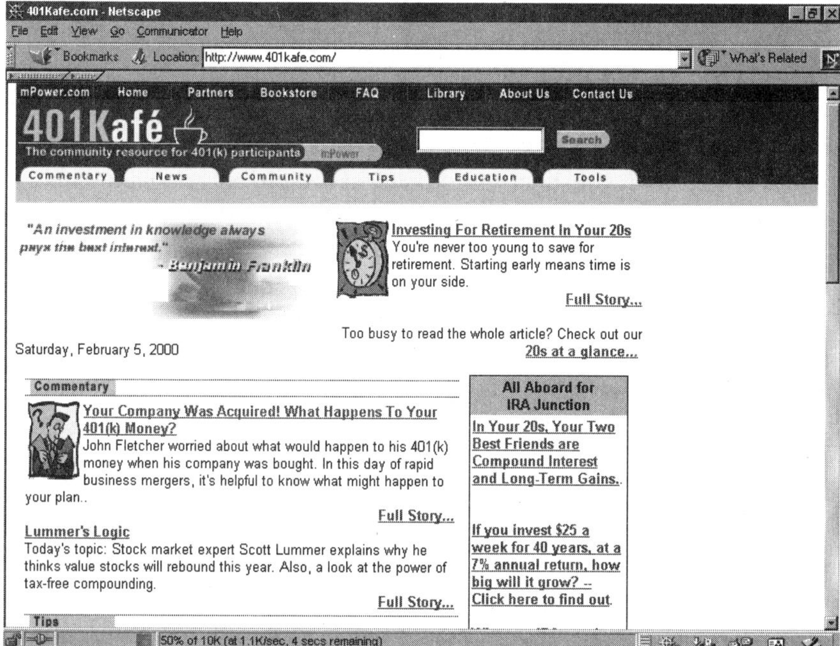

Figure 3.3. The 401Kafé is a useful source for any investor who wants to understand how 401(k) plans work and how to best manage them.

Table 3.1. 401k/401(k) Searches Using Web Search Tools

AltaVista (www.altavista.com)	Excite (www.excite.com)	HotBot (www.hotbot.com)	Northern Light (www.nlsearch.com)	Yahoo! (www.yahoo.com)
401k "401(k)" (Run two separate searches)	401k OR "401(k)"	401k "401(k)" Select [Any of the Words] in the pull-down menu	401k or "401(k)"	401(k)

IRAs, SEP/IRAs, Roth IRAs, and More

It feels like alphabet soup sometimes, when you attempt to sort out the various available Individual Retirement Account options. All of these IRAs offer some form of tax-deferred or tax-free retirement savings, apart from any employer-sponsored pension plan or 401(k) plan you may have in place. Which IRA you chose will depend on your situation—Education IRAs enable you to put money away for a child's education; the self-employed may want to establish a Simplified Employee Pension (SEP) IRA; Roth IRAs require that you pay income tax on the money you contribute, but your subsequent withdrawals are tax-free; and so on.

Most investment firms have tutorials on IRAs on their Web sites. These constitute one of the more confusing retirement investment vehicles, so you should expect to find FAQs (Frequently Asked Questions . . . and answers) as well as basic descriptions of your options. This sometimes takes persistence, as tutorials are usually not posted at the top of a firm's Web page. However, it is often worth the effort, as most investment companies understand that in order to attract and keep clients they need to educate investors about the various retirement account options. The Vanguard Group's site (www.vanguard.com) is a good example. At the main page, click [Education, Planning & Advice]. This will take you to a catalog of resources, including the Retirement Resource Center, which has loads of information on the various forms of IRAs, decisions you have to make when changing employers, and managing your assets once you retire.

Since IRAs were created as a result of U.S. Internal Revenue Service regulations, it makes sense to assume that that agency's Web site would have some guidance on IRAs. Head over to the IRS (www.irs.ustreas.gov) and look at the friendly Digital Daily page. Down at the bottom of the page are links to all the areas within the IRS site, including [Taxpayer Help & Education], [Tax Info for You], and [Forms & Publications]. While any of those links may eventually get you to where you want to go, the simplest way of finding out what IRS publications you want is to use the [Search] feature, at the very bottom of the Web page.

At the [Search] page, type *IRA* in the search box; you will get back a list of links to IRS publications. By skimming through the list, you will see a number of references to two publications, Publication 590, *Individual Retirement Arrangements,* and Chapter 18 of Publication 17, *Your Federal Income Tax, Individual Retirement Arrangements.* Now that you know the two publications you want, use your browser's [BACK] button to return to the main Digital Daily page, and click the [Forms & Pubs] link. Click on [Publications & Notices], then scroll down the list of publications until you find the ones you want. See Figure 3.4 for the screen listing available IRS publications. You can select more than one publication at a time by holding down the [Ctrl] key when clicking on the publication titles you want. When you have selected Publications 17 and 590, click [Retrieve Selected Files].

The Web site will return those two titles to the screen, and you can click on them one at a time to retrieve the PDF file. (For help with downloading and reading PDF files, see Chapter 1.) All of this is a somewhat cumbersome process, but it beats trying to get the publications from your local IRS office.

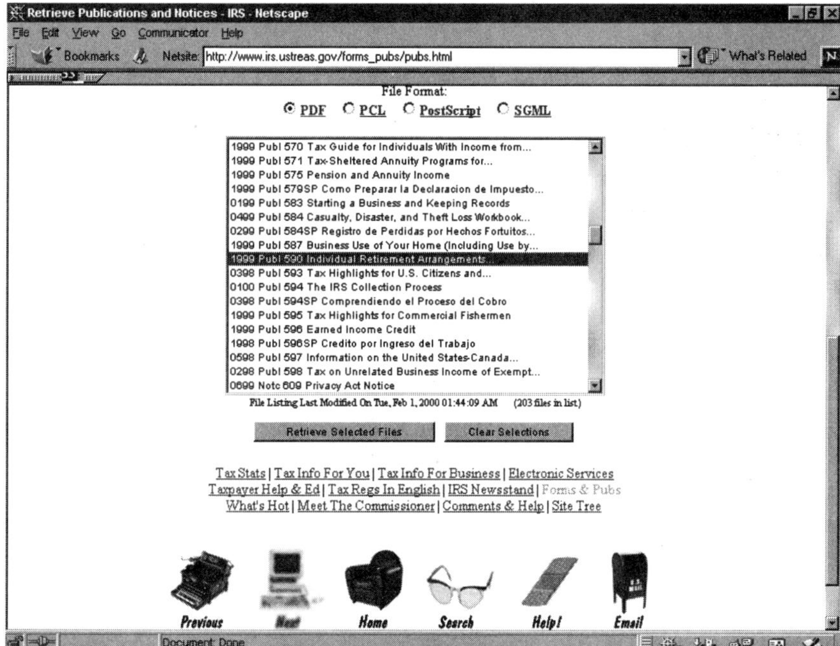

Figure 3.4. You can select several IRS publications at once by holding down the control key when clicking on the titles you want.

Managing Credit

Just about everyone has a wad of credit cards in their wallets, and often a few department store charge cards stashed away in a drawer somewhere. You don't usually think about all the institutions that have granted you credit, nor do you need to most of the time. But what about when you are getting ready to apply for a car loan or a home mortgage? You know that the lender will be looking through your credit report to see what kind of history you have, whether you have been late paying your bills, whether you have a large outstanding debt, and so on. Before you put yourself in the position of having the lender check you out, it is a good idea to look yourself and see what your credit report says about you. Did that disputed bill you had with the hardware store four years ago get removed from your profile, or are they still reporting it to the credit bureaus as an unpaid balance? Is that college loan you paid off years ago still showing up on your credit report? The only way you will be able to correct any errors in your credit profile is by reviewing it regularly and reporting any mistakes to the credit bureau.

Ordering Your Own Credit Report

The major providers of consumer credit information are Experian (formerly part of TRW), Equifax, and TransUnion, and they all have sites on the Net where you can order a copy of your credit report. In fact, it is a good idea to look over the information that each company has on you once a year just to catch any discrepancies.

Finding the Web sites for the credit bureaus is as straightforward as plugging in the company names in the standard Web address format. Equifax's consumer credit information is at www.equifax.com; Experian's is at www.experian.com; and TransUnion's is at www.transunion.com. Each one has an easy-to-find option for ordering your credit report online.

Some states regulate how much a credit bureau can charge you for a copy of your credit report; some states even require that you be given a copy of your credit report once a year at no charge. Table 3.2 shows how much your credit report costs in selected states, to give you an idea of what the charges are.

In addition, if you've been denied credit based on a credit bureau's report, you are entitled to a free copy of your credit report from that company. Credit companies may also give you a free report if you are unemployed or on public assistance, or if you think you have been a victim of credit card fraud.

Table 3.2. Credit Report Costs in Selected States

State	Equifax	Experian	TransUnion
California	$8	$8	$8
Connecticut	$5	$5 plus tax ($7.50 for additional copies)	$5
New Jersey	$8 (You are entitled to one free report a year)	$8 (You are entitled to one free report a year)	Free if ordered by phone or mail
New York	$8	$8 plus tax	$8

Have You Shopped 'Til You Dropped?

Many people were sent their first credit cards when they were still in college. The idea of being able to spend money—even if you don't have cash in your wallet—can be attractive, particularly if you haven't yet learned about the impact of 18 percent interest on the unpaid balance. And, reminiscent of the old joke, "I can't be out of money . . . I still have checks left," some people assume that if a credit card company sends them an application, then surely they must be able to handle the additional debt. I mean, don't banks know already how much I make?

The credit bureaus can be excellent sources of information on managing credit and getting out from under credit card debt. This makes sense—keep in mind the discussion in Chapter 1 about the golden rule of finding information on the Internet: "Who would care about this?" Credit bureaus—and their clients, the credit-granting institutions—are acutely aware of the possibility of a borrower becoming delinquent on payments or declaring bankruptcy. They have a strong incentive to make information readily available on how to manage debt wisely. See Figure 3.5 for an example of the type of credit management information available on Experian's site. As expected, the FAQs and brochures are clear, informative, and written in a style that any consumer can understand.

Remember to dig down into each site for additional leads. By reading a few of the online brochures at Experian's site, you can find links to other credit management services. Among the links provided are:

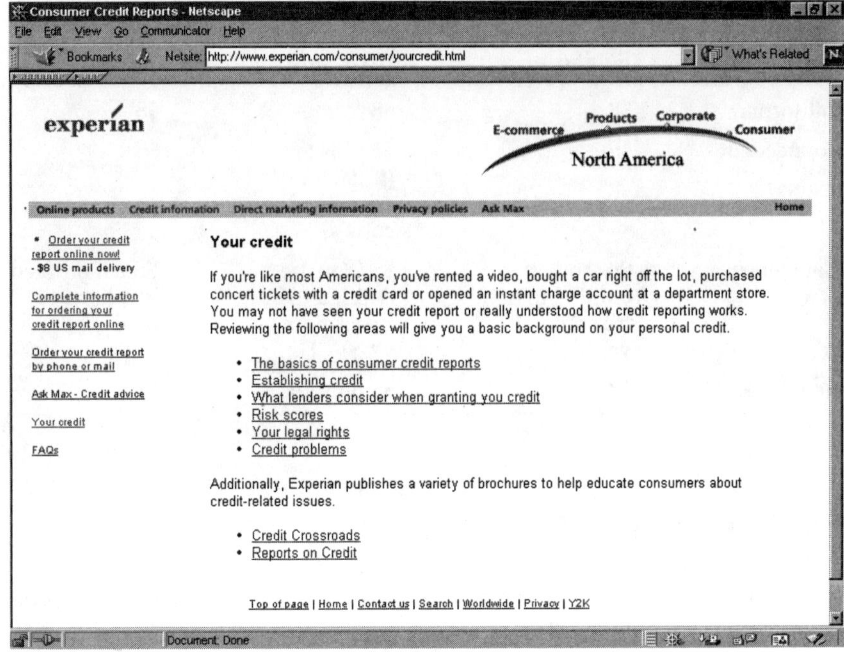

Figure 3.5. Experien's Web site makes it easy for you to request a copy of your credit report.

- National Foundation for Consumer Credit

  Help in budgeting and negotiating with creditors to pay bills.

  1 (800) 388-2227

  www.nfcc.org

- Call For Action

  An international network of volunteers who work hotlines at radio and television stations to assist, educate, and solve problems for consumers and small businesses.

  (301) 657-7490

  Also available is a list of Call for Action affiliates at www.experian.com/customer/action.html

- Debt Counselors of America

  A nonprofit group that assists consumers across the country and around the world via the Web. The site provides useful information, free publications, shareware, and a debt forum where you can ask questions for counselors to answer. Special programs also are available to help consumers get out of debt.

  www.dca.org

These sources look pretty useful, but you know there must also be other reliable sources of information on managing credit. To find other sources, use the principle of working back up the stream, described in Chapter 1. Take one of the resources just listed—say, Debt Counselors of America—and head over to Yahoo!, the organized catalog of Internet sites (www.yahoo.com). Type *Debt Counselors of America* in the search box. See what Yahoo! category this organization appears in, and click on that category to see more listings of related companies. Debt Counselors of America is categorized under [*Business and Economy: Companies: Financial Services: Credit Services: Consumer Services: Credit Counseling: Organizations*]. Clicking on that category will take you to a list of all the credit counseling organizations in Yahoo!, including Debt Counselors of America. See Figure 3.6 for the Yahoo! credit counseling organizations category.

Browse through the listing for other sites that look useful. One of the links will be for the local offices of the Consumer Credit Counseling Service, one of the leading nonprofit organizations that provide credit counseling. CCCS is funded primarily by credit-granting organizations

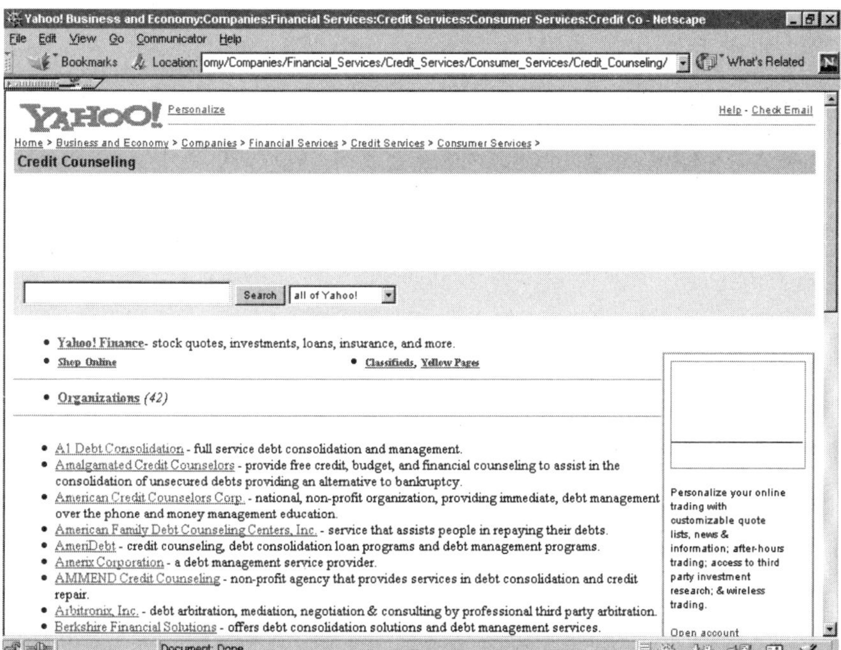

Figure 3.6. Yahoo! has a category specifically for consumer credit counseling organizations.

and is designed to help consumers manage their credit and avoid having to declare personal bankruptcy. If you are having problems paying off debt, the local CCCS office can help develop a Debt Management Plan by which you pay an agreed-upon amount to your creditors each month, and your creditors agree to waive or lower the interest rate while you are on the plan.

4
Wall Street Hits the Web

This chapter gets down to the nitty-gritty of managing your portfolio on the Internet—finding information about stocks, learning what analysts say about them, and using Web sites and Web software to track your investments. One note of caution: There are plenty of Web sites that offer guides to investing, stock tips, weekly news delivered to your email account, and so on. Before relying on any of these sources of free advice, be sure to find out who's providing the commentary. How aggressive is their strategy, and how risky are their recommended investments? To find this out, do some snooping around the site. Often there is a link labeled [Who We Are] or [About Our Company]. If you cannot find any general statement of investment philosophy, email the owner of the site and ask. If no contact information is clearly listed, that in itself should be a warning flag that the site may not be completely legitimate. Remember, investing based solely on advice from strangers on the Web is like shopping at a used car lot with the "assistance" of a stranger. Sure, there may be some great deals there—and there may also be some real lemons.

Finding Online Stock Quotes

Fortunately for investors, most Web search engines and portals now offer online stock quotes as an enticement to visit the site. (See Chapter 1 for a discussion of search engines and portals.) As it turns out, many sites license the same data from a few well-established sources—Zacks Investment Research (www.zacks.com), Market Guide Inc. (www.marketguide.com), Edgar Online (www.edgar-online.com), and FirstCall Corp. (www.firstcall.com), among others. Although these investment news sources license some of their information for free distribution, they are primarily in the business of providing value-added financial information to subscribers for substantial fees. What you see on the Web is the equivalent of those free crackers and dip handed out in the aisles of supermarkets—the first bite is free, but you have to buy the box if you want your appetite sated. One distinction between the information available for free and what the subscribers get is the timeliness of stock quotes. The publicly accessible stock quote figures are usually embargoed for at least 15 minutes; subscribers can often get access to real-time quotes.

America Online subscribers are reminded that they can also get delayed stock quotes by typing Keyword: Snapshot (for the AOL Investment Snapshot service).

Portals for Stock Information

While you could go directly to these information providers' sites, it often makes sense to find a portal site you like and use its collection of information sources. A well-designed Web site will provide a good selection of basic information on a particular stock:

- Current stock quotes
- Day and year price range
- Recent news on the company
- A consensus of the company's anticipated earnings
- Basic financial information on the company, extracted from its Securities & Exchange Commission filings
- Link to the company's Web site

Yes, you could get each of these pieces of information from the sources themselves (Zacks, Market Guide, the SEC's EDGAR site, and so on). But it sure is easier to find all the information in one place.

AltaVista. One of the better-designed financial portals among the Web search engines is the [Stock Quotes] section of the AltaVista search engine. Start at the main Alta Vista Web site (www.altavista.com), click [Money], then type in the ticker symbol of the stock you want. Figure 4.1 shows the result of a search for Sprint Corporation (stock symbol FON). Note the

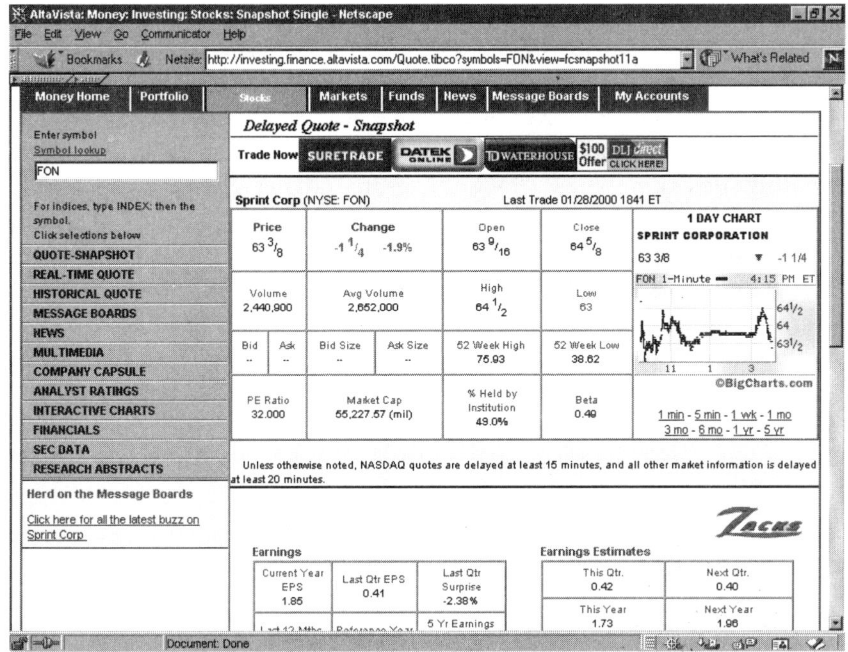

Figure 4.1. AltaVista's stock information page combines material from a number of sources in an easy-to-read format.

tabs on the left side of the screen; if you want more detailed financial information, historical stock prices, or earlier news items, you can click on the appropriate link.

What is particularly appealing is that AltaVista, like other portals that provide this type of service, has compiled access to several sources in one Web page. Instead of having to jump from site to site (and having to remember the tricks for conducting a search in each of those sites), the information is aggregated into a single Web page.

Wall Street Research Net. Another useful compilation of information from a number of sources is the Wall Street Research Net, or WSRN (www.wsrn.com). Unlike AltaVista, it does not offer a Web search engine—it focuses on providing access to financial information from a variety of selected sources. WSRN provides both free and fee-based information; a monthly subscription of $4.95 to $9.95 entitles you to detailed historical stock information and company profiles. Analysts' reports can be purchased for an additional $2 to $150, depending on the depth of the report. One big advantage of WSRN is that it clearly labels the sources of its information, enabling you to learn where to go to get the information directly.

The variety of information available on WSRN is almost overwhelming; this really is the equivalent of a well-stocked supermarket for investors. See Figure 4.2 for an example of the information available on AMR Corp.

Most of the sources listed in WSRN are accessible at no charge. The fee-based options are indicated with a dollar sign ($) and either require a monthly subscription to WSRN or a one-time charge for a particular report.

Stock Ratings on the Web

One of the purposes of this book is to help you find the tools you need on the Internet to make your own decision on whether to buy or sell a stock. However, stock prices are often affected by the recommendations of investment analysts, so it makes sense to monitor the consensus of Wall Street, even if you do not intend to follow the conventional wisdom.

You can, of course, go to the Web sites of individual Wall Street analysts and brokerage houses to see their listings of what they consider today's hot stock picks. One disadvantage of this approach is that an analyst's recommendation on a specific stock may not be available on the Web site—if

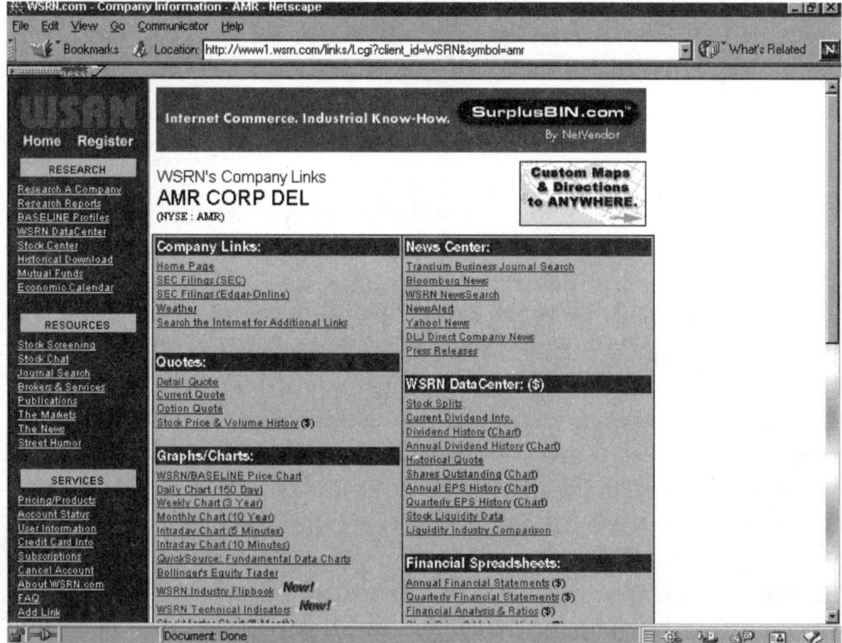

Figure 4.2. The catalog of information available on Wall Street Research Network can be almost overwhelming.

you are interested in what the analysts think of Wal-Mart Stores (WMT) in particular, for example, you may be out of luck because that is not considered the best-performing or most exciting stock today.

Fortunately, there are several financial information companies that compile brokers' buy/hold/sell recommendations and provide a scorecard on individual stocks. One of the better known of these services is Zacks Investment Research (www.zacks.com). From the main Web page, type the ticker symbol in the search box, click the button for [Estimates,] and then click [Go]. See Figure 4.3 for a Zacks report of Wall Street recommendations on Wal-Mart.

Not only do you get a count of the numbers of brokers recommending each buy/sell position, but you also can see whether the consensus is heading up or down, and how well the company fares in relation to other companies in the same industry. Granted, this doesn't tell you, for example, why a certain analyst rated the stock a strong buy. For that, you need access to the investment house reports, which will be covered later in this chapter.

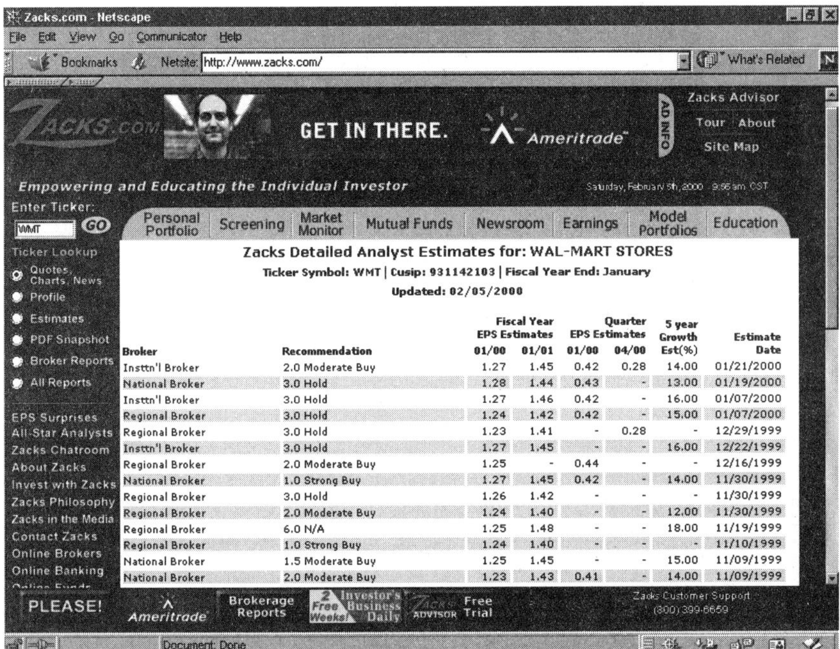

Zacks Detailed Analyst Estimates for: WAL-MART STORES

Ticker Symbol: WMT | Cusip: 931142103 | Fiscal Year End: January

Updated: 02/05/2000

Broker	Recommendation	Fiscal Year EPS Estimates 01/00	Fiscal Year EPS Estimates 01/01	Quarter EPS Estimates 01/00	Quarter EPS Estimates 04/00	5 year Growth Est(%)	Estimate Date
Insttn'l Broker	2.0 Moderate Buy	1.27	1.45	0.42	0.28	14.00	01/21/2000
National Broker	3.0 Hold	1.28	1.44	0.43	-	13.00	01/19/2000
Insttn'l Broker	3.0 Hold	1.27	1.46	0.42	-	16.00	01/07/2000
Regional Broker	3.0 Hold	1.24	1.42	0.42	-	15.00	01/07/2000
Regional Broker	3.0 Hold	1.23	1.41	-	0.28	-	12/29/1999
Insttn'l Broker	3.0 Hold	1.27	1.45	-	-	16.00	12/22/1999
Regional Broker	2.0 Moderate Buy	1.25	-	0.44	-	-	12/16/1999
National Broker	1.0 Strong Buy	1.27	1.45	0.42	-	14.00	11/30/1999
Regional Broker	3.0 Hold	1.26	1.42	-	-	-	11/30/1999
Regional Broker	2.0 Moderate Buy	1.24	1.40	-	-	12.00	11/30/1999
Regional Broker	6.0 N/A	1.25	1.48	-	-	18.00	11/19/1999
Regional Broker	1.0 Strong Buy	1.24	1.40	-	-	-	11/10/1999
National Broker	1.5 Moderate Buy	1.25	1.45	-	-	15.00	11/09/1999
National Broker	2.0 Moderate Buy	1.23	1.43	0.41	-	14.00	11/09/1999

Figure 4.3. Zacks provides a summary of Wall Street recommendations regarding Wal-Mart stock.

Analysis on the Web

Clichés about information overload on the information superhighway aside, one thing the Web is not lacking for is opinion. Individual investors are congregating in Web chat rooms to discuss the next hot stock. Brokerage firms are selling their reports online. And what might be called *hybrid* Web sites are springing up, supported by advertising and offering investment advice, stock quotes, and portfolio management tools. While keeping in mind that free advice on the Web is worth about what you paid for it, let's examine some of the sources of Wall Street analysis on the Net.

Investment Analysts' Reports

While one of the points of Web-based research is to eliminate, or at least supplement, the research services of full-service brokers, you may decide that you want some in-depth information on a company before making an investment decision. A number of investment houses sell their research on the Web on a pay-as-you-go basis. The simplest way to find and buy these reports is to use one of the aggregators that compile research from a variety of companies. As with investment portal sites, they often offer some information for free, but the focus here is on high-value information, priced accordingly.

Multex. Although somewhat focused on corporate investors and high-powered research companies, Multex (multex.multexinvestor.com) also offers services of interest to individual investors. You must register to get access to the information; registration is free. Once you have registered, click [Log on] at the bottom of the main Web page and type in your ID and password. You can read newsletters and columns from investment analysts, join in discussions of market trends or share research tips, and download market reports. Multex provides a free *consensus estimate* similar to the Zacks Wall Street recommendations shown in Figure 4.3; the Multex report also includes a discussion of *why* analysts view the stock the way they do. You can search for reports by ticker symbol. See Figure 4.4 for an example of some of the Multex reports available.

Multex also sells reports from brokerage houses and from third-party information services. These range in price from a few dollars to $150, depending on the source and the length of the report.

Wall Street on Demand. Wall Street on Demand (www.wallst.com) provides a similar service, although it does not offer any free reports as an enticement to drop by. Its reports are priced per *unit*—a unit costs between

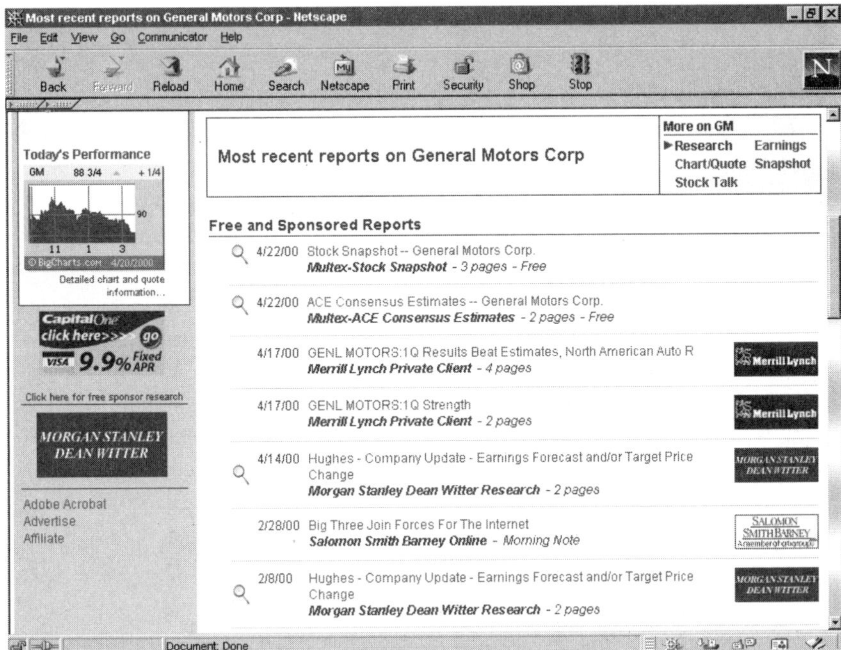

Figure 4.4. Multex offers a number of analysts' opinions regarding General Motors stock.

$1.50 and $3, depending on whether you commit to purchasing a certain number of reports or you simply buy reports on an ad hoc basis. Reports cost between one and three units and are delivered in PDF (Adobe Acrobat) format. (See Chapter 1 for a description of how to read PDF files.) Wall Street on Demand also sells consensus earnings estimates (one unit) and industry reports (one to two units), which enable you to compare a company's performance with that of the industry as a whole. Among the sources included in Wall Street on Demand's collection of reports are Standard & Poor's, Argus, Baseline, and Vickers Inside Trading Report. See Figure 4.5 for a list of reports available on Apple Computer (AAPL).

Also, don't forget the Wall Street Research Net site (www.wsrn.com); it provides links to a variety of research reports and spreadsheets of companies' financial statements going back 10 years.

Picks and Pans of the Stock Market

In addition to expert analysis from investment houses, the Web is rich with sites offering advice on stocks. (See Chapter 15 for a discussion of

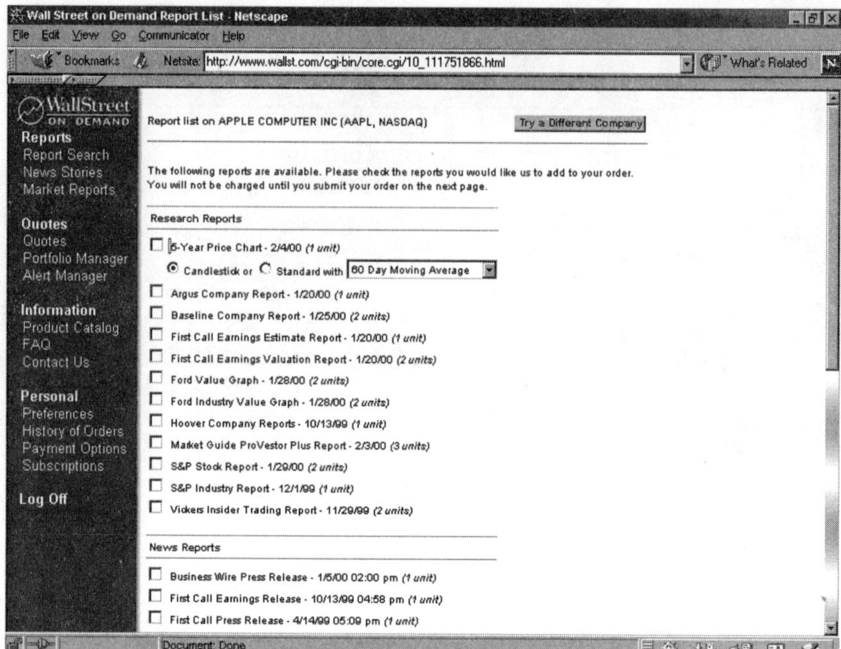

Figure 4.5. Wall Street on Demand offers a variety of analysts' reports on Apple Computer.

how to watch for scams and misleading stock tips.) As just noted, many investment portal sites offer discussion areas in which subscribers can post messages about individual stocks. But there are also a number of sites, usually advertiser-supported, that provide opinions and stock picks. Be sure you understand the investment philosophy of the advisors or columnists; some sites tend to favor long-term investments, others focus on undervalued stocks, and still others look at small-growth stocks. Try several of these discussion and advice sites to see which one best reflects your own investment strategy.

Armchair Millionaire. The Armchair Millionaire (www.armchair-millionaire.com) approaches investing as a long-term process, so the discussions cover topics such as understanding the fundamentals of investing, reducing personal debt, and investing regularly in mutual funds. It is a nice place to start if you want information on managing finances, living within your means, starting an investment program, and so on. However, since it is not designed for the advanced investor, do not expect to find much help in managing your portfolio or evaluating a stock. See Figure 4.6 for a sample of the topics covered in the Armchair Millionaire.

The Motley Fool. Started as a small discussion group in America Online, The Motley Fool (www.fool.com) has grown into a well-known financial Web site, and its creators have published several books on their investment philosophy. They encourage investors to research companies before investing in them, to learn how to use stock-screening tools, to watch for small and emerging companies, and to maintain a diverse portfolio. They work investors up from the basics to more complex investment strategies. As you can see from the main Web page (Figure 4.7), The Motley Fool is much more focused to the serious investor than is the Armchair Millionaire. In addition to columns on various market issues, this site also has a portfolio management feature, access to current stock quotes, and an amazingly lively bulletin board area.

TheStreet.com. There are times when all you want is financial commentary. No discussion areas, no back-to-basics guides on managing your

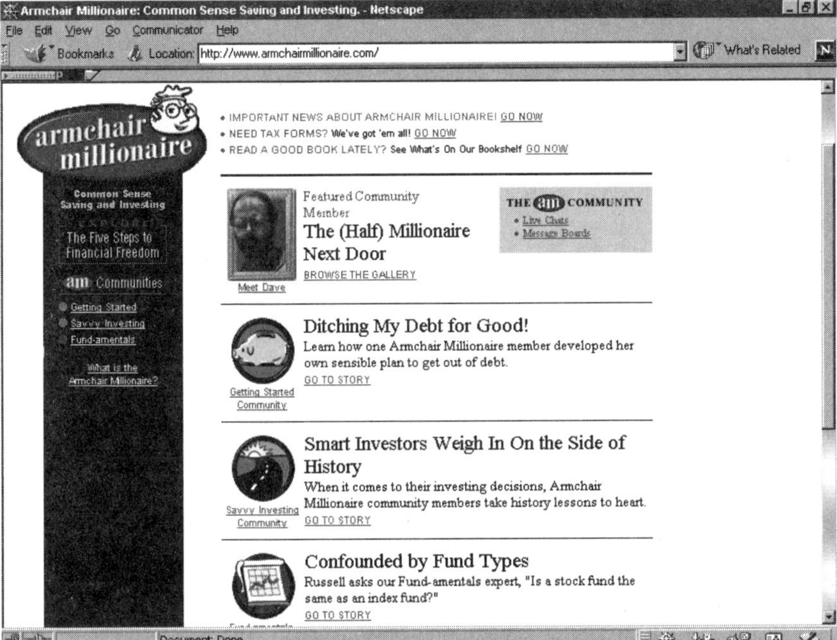

Figure 4.6. The Armchair Millionaire offers basic advice on investment and personal financial management.

Figure 4.7. The Motley Fool offers resources for both beginning and more advanced investors.

credit card balances, no suggested portfolios, just financial analysis and news. If that's the case, try TheStreet.com (www.thestreet.com), a collection of columns and news reports on finance and investing. It is strong on analysis and market perspectives, and covers a wide range of topics, from mutual fund performance to Internet stocks to commentary on the international markets. This is serious news, and while the articles are engaging, they are not necessarily written for the beginning investor. See Figure 4.8 for an example of one day's news. Note that some areas of the site are restricted to subscribers only; premium subscriptions are $9.95 per month or $99.95 per year.

Managing Your Portfolio on the Web

One of the challenges for new investors is keeping track of their portfolios. Am I actually making money? At what price did I tell myself I would sell

Figure 4.8. TheStreet.com provides daily news and commentary.

those shares? Are my investments meeting the performance goals I set? Answering these questions means either having a broker manage your investments for you (and if that were your solution, you probably wouldn't be reading this), or taking advantage of one of the many portfolio management sites on the Web.

Most of the financial portal sites described in this chapter offer online portfolios. These will let you monitor prices of stocks, mutual funds, and indexes (e.g., Dow Jones Industrial Average, Standard & Poor's 500). Separately, you can also keep track of your trades, purchase price per share, commissions paid, and notes about the purchase. These sites usually also provide you with the ability to monitor stock prices, and notify you if the price reaches a preset high or low price. America Online subscribers can type Keyword: My Portfolios to use the members-only portfolio service.

Most portfolio management sites let you download your data in a format that can be easily imported into a spreadsheet or a budgeting software package such as Quicken. To download the information into a spreadsheet such as Microsoft Excel, you will usually click a button at the site labeled [download spreadsheet format] or something similar. You will be prompted to indicate to what directory on your computer you want the information put; most people either use the Windows default directory called My Documents, or they put the file in the directory where the Excel program resides.

Even novices who want to practice investing without actually risking funds may find that these basic portfolio management sites work as well as the game or fantasy stock portfolio sites described in Chapter 2. While the sites designed for actual investors do not include some of the explanatory material provided in the fantasy stock portfolio systems or help in calculating commissions, for example, they do let you create virtual portfolios that you can monitor just as if you had actually invested your money.

Yahoo! Finance. One example of a basic financial portal site's portfolio tracking service is that of Yahoo! From the main Yahoo! site (www.yahoo.com), click on [Stock Quotes], then select [Create New Portfolio]. (You have to register to gain access, but there is no charge for the service.) At the next screen, you will be prompted to add the stocks you own or want to track, information on number of shares owned, trade date and purchase price, commissions paid, and so on. See Figure 4.9 for a display of a sample portfolio in Yahoo!'s Finance Web site.

Note that this portfolio management site lets you combine information on stocks you are following but do not currently hold a position in (Lucent Technologies—LU—in this example), market indexes (such as the Dow Jones Industrial—DJI) and the stocks and funds you own. This combination lets you watch a company you are considering investing in; just add that stock symbol to your portfolio profile but leave the information on shares owned blank. Figure 4.9 shows the Performance view of the stock data. By clicking on [Basic], [Day Watch], [Fundamentals], or [Detailed], different elements would be displayed, including 52-week or the current day's price range, market capitalization, average volume, price/earnings or earnings/share ratios, and so on.

Other investment sites that offer free portfolio management in addition to other financial information include AltaVista (money.altavista.com), WallSt.com (www.wallst.com), and The Motley Fool (www.fool.com). In addition, commercial sites often offer portfolio tracking as part of their

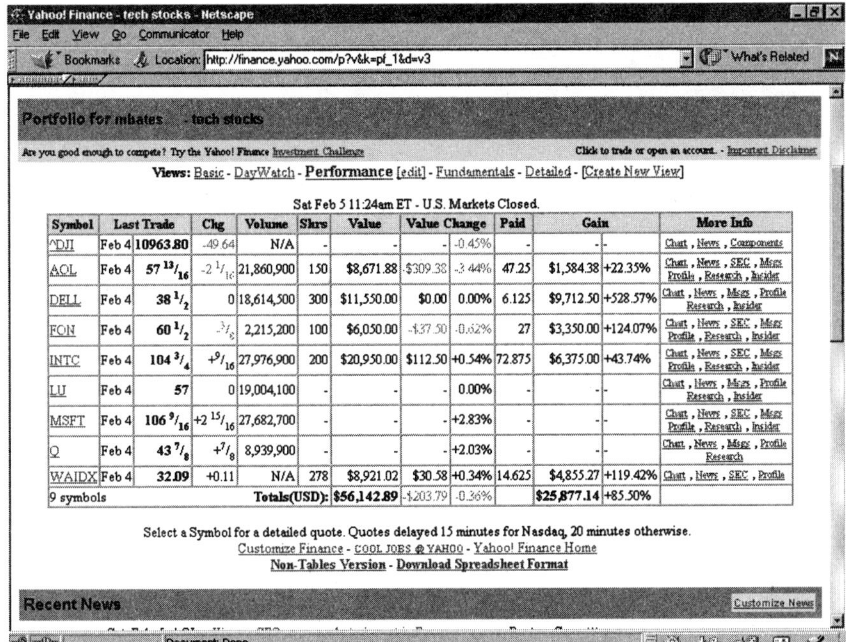

Symbol	Last Trade		Chg	Volume	Shrs	Value	Value Change		Paid	Gain		More Info
^DJI	Feb 4	**10963.80**	-49.64	N/A	-	-	-	-0.45%	-	-	-	Chart, News, Components
AOL	Feb 4	**57 13/16**	-2 1/16	21,860,900	150	$8,671.88	-$309.38	-3.44%	47.25	$1,584.38	+22.35%	Chart, News, SEC, Msgs Profile, Research, Insider
DELL	Feb 4	**38 1/2**	0	18,614,500	300	$11,550.00	$0.00	0.00%	6.125	$9,712.50	+528.57%	Chart, News, Msgs, Profile Research, Insider
FON	Feb 4	**60 1/2**	-3/8	2,215,200	100	$6,050.00	-$37.50	-0.62%	27	$3,350.00	+124.07%	Chart, News, SEC, Msgs Profile, Research, Insider
INTC	Feb 4	**104 3/4**	+9/16	27,976,900	200	$20,950.00	$112.50	+0.54%	72.875	$6,375.00	+43.74%	Chart, News, SEC, Msgs Profile, Research, Insider
LU	Feb 4	**57**	0	19,004,100	-	-	-	0.00%	-	-	-	Chart, News, Msgs, Profile Research, Insider
MSFT	Feb 4	**106 9/16**	+2 15/16	27,682,700	-	-	-	+2.83%	-	-	-	Chart, News, SEC, Msgs Profile, Research, Insider
Q	Feb 4	**43 7/8**	+7/8	8,939,900	-	-	-	+2.03%	-	-	-	Chart, News, Msgs, Profile Research
WAIDX	Feb 4	**32.09**	+0.11	N/A	278	$8,921.02	$30.58	+0.34%	14.625	$4,855.27	+119.42%	Chart, News, SEC, Profile
9 symbols					**Totals(USD):**	**$56,142.89**	-$203.79	-0.36%		**$25,877.14**	+85.50%	

Figure 4.9. Yahoo! Finance's portfolio tracking service offers a number of ways to view the information.

value-added services. Some sites charge for this service; your call will be in deciding whether the added features are worth the cost.

Wall Street Journal Interactive Edition. *The Wall Street Journal* is the granddaddy of financial news sources. Dow Jones, the publisher of the Journal, supports a heavy-duty online news and finance service called Dow Jones Interactive. See Chapter 11 for more information on the service in general. One of the features of this service is its Wall Street Journal Interactive Edition (www.wsj.com). Not only can you get your own customized version of the *Journal* delivered to your email every morning, but you can also take advantage of the site's portfolio tracking service. The cost for access to WSJIE is $59 per year. See Figure 4.10 for the portfolio display screen from WSJIE.

The icon next to each listing links you to news items from the Dow Jones Newswire and *The Wall Street Journal* on that company. The advantage of the WSJIE portfolio tracking service is that it includes access to the *Journal* as well as to an enormous database of articles from thousands of

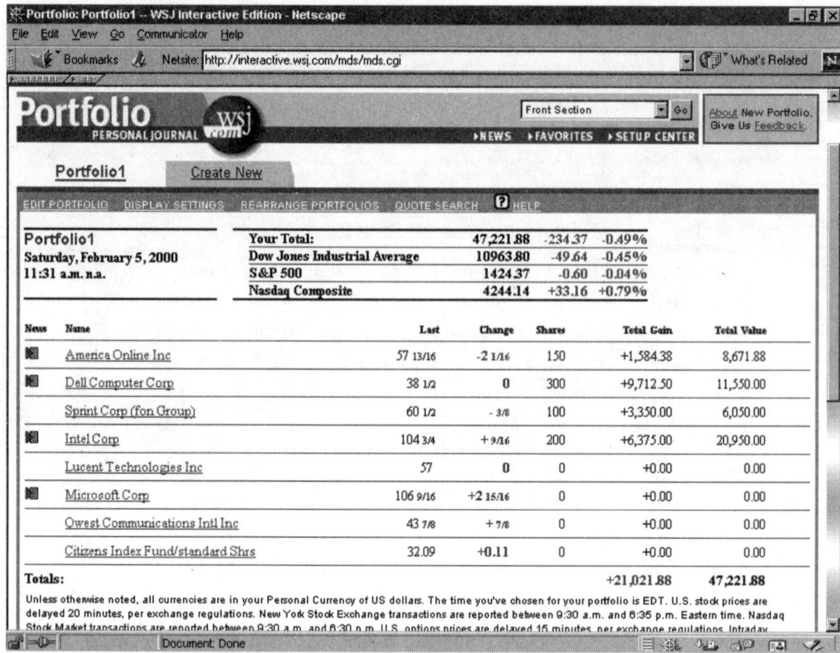

Portfolio1
Saturday, February 5, 2000
11:31 a.m. n.a.

Your Total:	47,221.88	-234.37	-0.49%
Dow Jones Industrial Average	10963.80	-49.64	-0.45%
S&P 500	1424.37	-0.60	-0.04%
Nasdaq Composite	4244.14	+33.16	+0.79%

News	Name	Last	Change	Shares	Total Gain	Total Value
	America Online Inc	57 13/16	-2 1/16	150	+1,584.38	8,671.88
	Dell Computer Corp	38 1/2	0	300	+9,712.50	11,550.00
	Sprint Corp (fon Group)	60 1/2	- 3/8	100	+3,350.00	6,050.00
	Intel Corp	104 3/4	+ 9/16	200	+6,375.00	20,950.00
	Lucent Technologies Inc	57	0	0	+0.00	0.00
	Microsoft Corp	106 9/16	+2 15/16	0	+0.00	0.00
	Qwest Communications Intl Inc	43 7/8	+ 7/8	0	+0.00	0.00
	Citizens Index Fund/standard Shrs	32.09	+0.11	0	+0.00	0.00
Totals:					+21,021.88	47,221.88

Unless otherwise noted, all currencies are in your Personal Currency of US dollars. The time you've chosen for your portfolio is EDT. U.S. stock prices are delayed 20 minutes, per exchange regulations. New York Stock Exchange transactions are reported between 9:30 a.m. and 6:35 p.m. Eastern time. Nasdaq Stock Market transactions are reported between 9:30 a.m. and 6:30 p.m. U.S. options prices are delayed 15 minutes, per exchange regulations. Intraday

Figure 4.10. Wall Street Journal Interactive Edition's portfolio management service includes links to *Wall Street Journal* articles.

magazines, newsletters, and newspapers. The downside is that you do not have some of the features available on many other portfolio management sites. You won't be notified if a stock hits a specified high or low price point. The display options are somewhat limited; you cannot get the detailed historical charts of your stock's performance, the 52-week range of prices, financial ratios, or other features common in most portfolio tracking sites.

Fortunately, much of this information is available elsewhere at the WSJIE site. From the home page, select [Briefing Books]. From here you can get detailed information on a specific company—a financial overview, stock charts, analysts' estimates of the company's earnings and stock performance, and other company information. Figure 4.11 shows the table of contents of the Briefing Book for Johnson & Johnson.

Quicken. Intuit, Inc.'s financial management software package, Quicken, is one of the more popular tools for managing your household finances. It is no surprise that they maintain a robust financial information

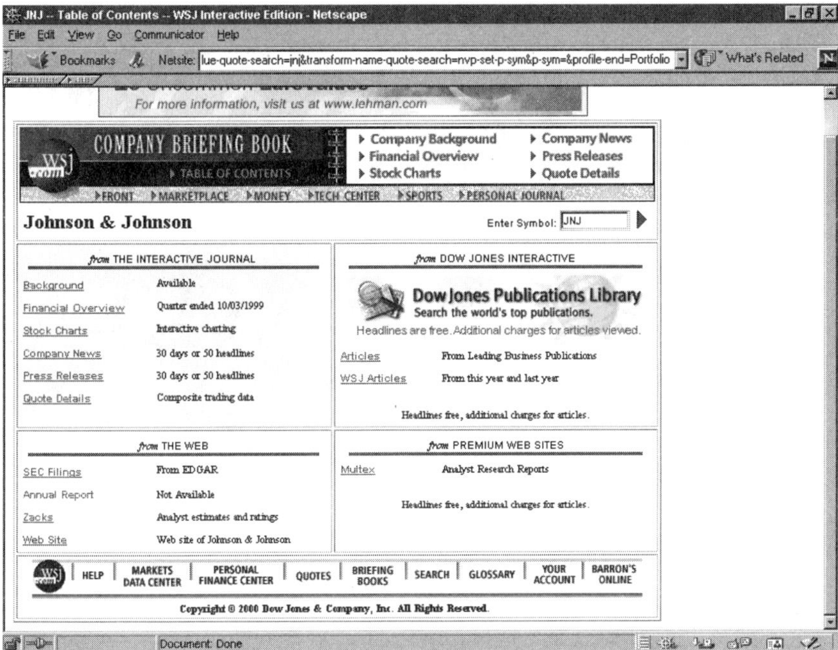

Figure 4.11. WSJIE's Briefing Books are well-formatted collections of company information.

site on the Web, too (www.quicken.com). You need to register to get access, but there is no charge for registration. Once you have access, click [Your Portfolio] at the main Web site page. The portfolio tracking tool on Quicken's site offers the usual features—current price, change from the previous trading day, stock charts, and so on. Interestingly, unlike most other portfolio tools, Quicken can import your account holdings directly from a broker as well as allow you to input it manually.

There are more steps involved in creating your portfolio profile yourself than in most other Web-based portfolio tracking sites, and Quicken.com does not handle multiple purchases of the same stock at different prices as well. On the other hand, it offers an interesting [Analyze Portfolio] feature that looks at your holdings and determines what percentage of your portfolio is in large-cap and small-cap stocks, bonds, and money markets. It also lets you see how diversified your portfolio is with respect to industry sector; it even offers a model allocation chart. A unique feature of Quicken.com's portfolio tracking sites is that it provides discussions of

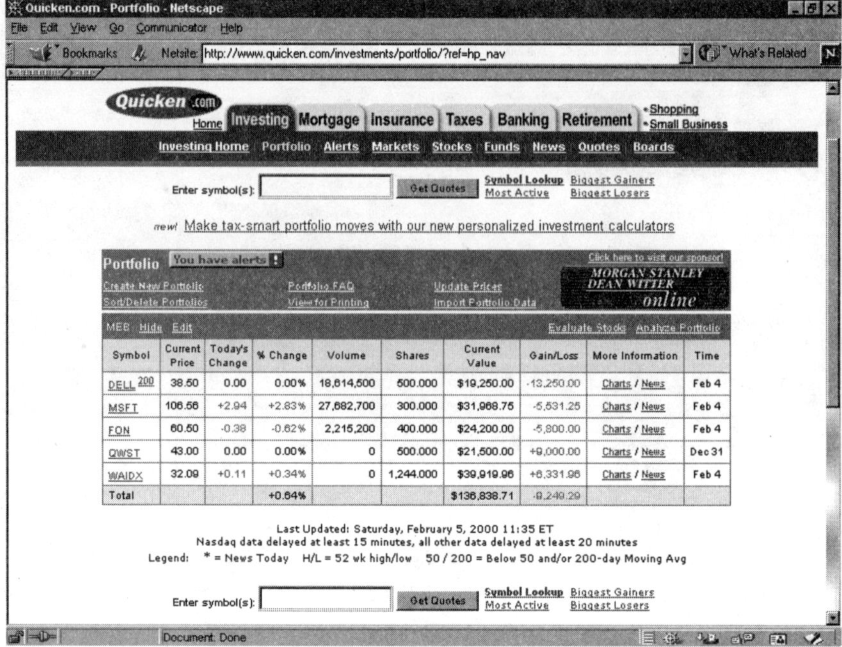

Figure 4.12. Quicken.com's portfolio management site provides a number of tools to evaluate your holdings.

how your selection of holdings compares with historically successful allocations. See Figure 4.12.

Which portfolio management tool you use will be determined by your own investment information needs—complex tracking, analysis of your holdings, ability to export into a specific software package, and so on.

5
Stock Screening on the Web

Stock screening is the process of reducing the universe of possible companies to invest in down to a manageable size. I'm assuming that you intend to research a company before investing in it; do you want to face the daunting task of researching 20 or 30 companies—or would you prefer to have a filtered list of the 6 or 8 companies that you are most likely to be interested in? I thought so!

But how do you narrow down your choices? Stock screening tools enable you to pull out a list of stocks that are at least potentially within your sphere of interest and familiarity. If you are already familiar with the computer hardware industry—that is, you understand not only the products themselves but the industry as a whole—then you might want to use a stock screening tool to identify hardware companies of a certain size, that pay a dividend, or that show a particular growth in earnings. Remember not to confuse your familiarity with the products or services of a company or industry with the investment potential of that company or industry. I may be a great fan of or even own solar-powered vehicles, but that doesn't necessarily mean that investing in a company specialized in solar-powered cars is a prudent investment for me.

Other stock screening tools let you filter for stocks that show a sharp rise in trading volume; that have increased significantly in value over the past week; or that have shown larger than average trading by company insiders. Remember that stock screening tools are only the first step in the process of selecting a new stock in which to invest. After you have identified possible companies, you can focus on researching each one, using the tools described in Chapter 12.

This chapter looks at Web sites that provide stock screening tools or are good metasites—collections of links to stock screening tools on other sites. Most electronic brokerages provide some form of a stock screening tool; other sites that focus on the individual investor do as well. The tool you select will depend on the level of sophistication or simplicity offered by the site, the degree of customization available, additional resources provided, and whether you already subscribe to a Web site's fee-based service.

Tutorials on Stock Screening

You may be looking for the stocks that Will Rogers recommended: "Take all your savings and buy some good stock and hold it 'til it goes up, then sell it. If it don't go up, don't buy it." Unfortunately, stock screening tools won't help you identify those stocks that will "go up"—if they did we'd all be rich. Some aspects of stock screening are pretty intuitive—you probably know that you want to limit your investing to a specific industry category, or companies of a certain size, or a growth rate of a particular range. But what about the more sophisticated screens, based on valuation, momentum, or stochastics? Some of the resources in Chapter 2 provide background on stock screening. There are other resources on the Net that specifically address this topic.

Intellifact

Intellifact.com (www.intellifact.com) is a business information source that, among other things, maintains a collection of tutorials on how to find information about stocks. Go to the main Intellifact.com Web page and click the [Tutorials] link to find the list of available tutorials. There are several that focus on stock screening, including [Understanding Stock Screening], [Utilizing "Pre-defined" Tools], and [Utilizing "User-defined" Tools]. It also has a link to download StockQuest, a PC-based stock screening program offered by MarketGuide.

Money Magazine

Money magazine has a useful set of tutorials on investing, titled Money 101, that you can review at its main site at www.money.com. In addition,

Money hosts interviews with investment experts, using the Yahoo! chat facility. To find the interview pertaining to stock screening, click the [MoneyLive Chat Center] at the main Web page, then pull down the menu of topics from the [What's in the Archives?] link. Select [Stock Screens] and you will be taken to the archive of an interview with Brian Murphy, a *Money* magazine reporter, about Web sites that screen stocks. See Figure 5.1 for the main MoneyLive screen.

About.com

For a rather lighthearted description of stock picking, head over to the About.com site (www.about.com) and type in the phrase *stock picking* in the search box at the main screen. Among the links that will be displayed in the search results screen will be one to [Stock Picking Suggestions, Part II], for which the description is "Stock screening is covered in this, the second part of the, um, critically acclaimed series, from your About.com Guide." You can also find this write-up by drilling down from the main About.com screen, clicking on the [Finance/Investing] link, then [Day

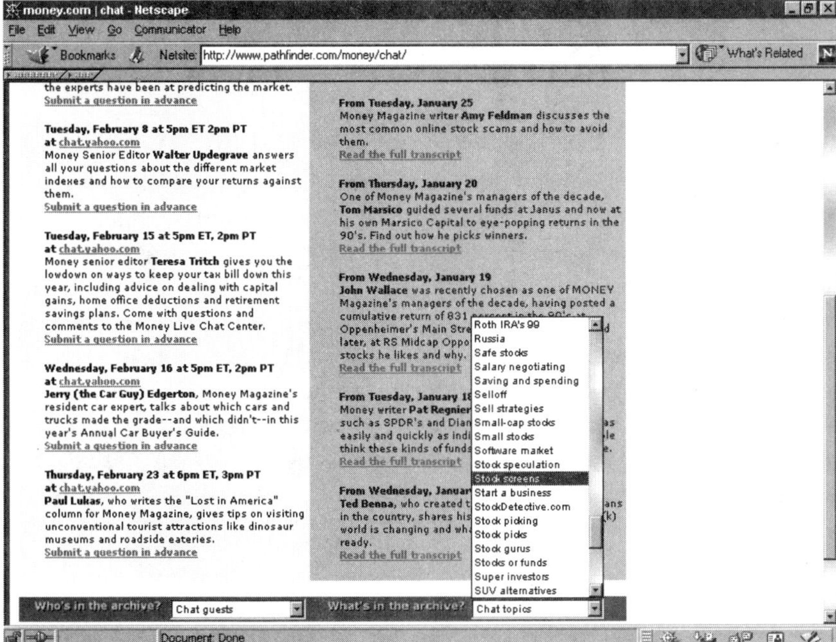

Figure 5.1. *Money* magazine hosts frequent interviews with finance or investment experts.

Trading] (not where I would have expected to find this tool), then [Articles]. While many of the articles are about day trading in particular, the one from March 15, 1998 focuses on stock screening tools.

Metasites for Stock Screening

Metasites are Web pages that function as guides, bibliographies (for those of you who remember brick-and-mortar libraries), and links to *other* Web sites. Metasites usually focus on a single topic—investing, company information, financial planning, and so on. Metasites used to be maintained as a labor of love by individuals who simply cared passionately about a specific topic and who had compiled their own lists of the best of the Web on that topic. Today, many metasites are maintained by a company in that field or are sponsored by advertising. While some people decry the commercialism, this usually means that a metasite will be maintained and updated regularly . . . something not always possible in a volunteer-only setting.

If you want to browse through a number of stock screening tools, a metasite is often the best place to go. These sites often include descriptions of each site or downloadable program, and can be the best way to find the newest and best resources.

About.com

About.com (www.about.com) consists of a number of subject categories and subcategories, each maintained by a live, human *guide.* In its Finance/Investment area is a list of some sites that offer stock-picking tools. From the main About.com site, click the [Finance/Investment] link, then the [Stocks] link, then the [Research Tools] link. Scroll down the page to the listing of Screening Tools—Financial. See Figure 5.2 for About.com's list of tools. One of the benefits of this site is the accessibility of its guides; if you have a question about the site or content, there is a link to contact the guide directly. In addition, this is one of the few metasites that includes active discussion areas as well as links to Web-based resources.

InvestorGuide

The InvestorGuide (www.investorguide.com) is a general metasite of investment information. Within its site is a list of stock screening tools and a one-page write-up of how to use the screening process to select compa-

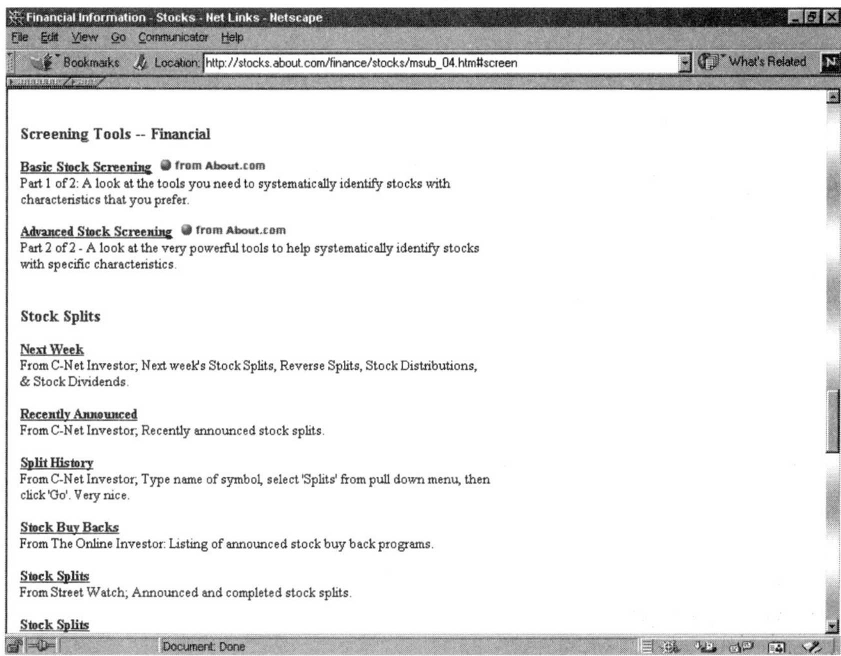

Figure 5.2. About.com's Stock guide maintains a two-part list of stock-picking tools.

nies to research further. At the main InvestorGuide page, click the [Stocks] link, then the [Stock Screening] link. It provides some discussion of screening techniques and links to several stock screening sites.

CyberInvest.com

Unlike most metasites, CyberInvest.com (www.cyberinvest.com) provides not only links to what it considers the best investment sites but also has a useful chart comparing the various features of each site. Click [Investing SuperSites] at the main Web page to get to the CyberInvest chart. Note that this site also has comparison charts for other investment-related topics such as online banking, electronic magazines on investment and finance, and mutual funds. See Figure 5.3 for a portion of Cyberinvest.com's "Investing Supersites" comparison chart.

CyberInvest also sends out an email newsletter titled "CoolTool Alert," that alerts readers to investment tools on the Net. Its publishing frequency varies from weekly to monthly, so be prepared to wait if an update doesn't come as frequently as you expect. To subscribe, fill in your email address at the box labeled [CoolTools Newsletter].

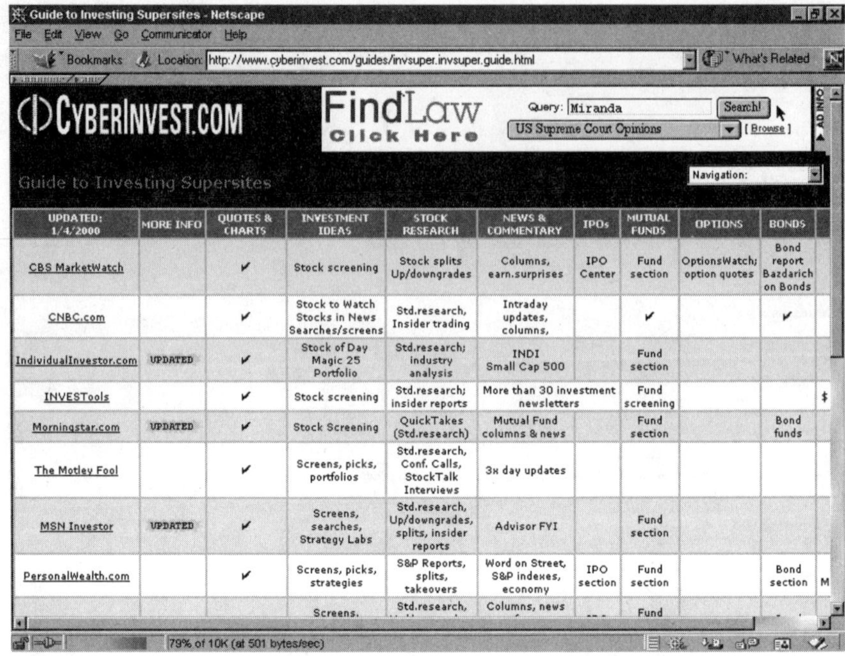

UPDATED: 1/4/2000	MORE INFO	QUOTES & CHARTS	INVESTMENT IDEAS	STOCK RESEARCH	NEWS & COMMENTARY	IPOs	MUTUAL FUNDS	OPTIONS	BONDS	
CBS MarketWatch		✔	Stock screening	Stock splits Up/downgrades	Columns, earn.surprises	IPO Center	Fund section	OptionsWatch; option quotes	Bond report Bazdarich on Bonds	
CNBC.com		✔	Stock to Watch Stocks in News Searches/screens	Std.research, Insider trading	Intraday updates, columns,		✔		✔	
IndividualInvestor.com	UPDATED	✔	Stock of Day Magic 25 Portfolio	Std.research; industry analysis	INDI Small Cap 500		Fund section			
INVESTools		✔	Stock screening	Std.research; insider reports	More than 30 investment newsletters		Fund screening			$
Morningstar.com	UPDATED	✔	Stock Screening	QuickTakes (Std.research)	Mutual Fund columns & news		Fund section		Bond funds	
The Motley Fool		✔	Screens, picks, portfolios	Std.research, Conf. Calls, StockTalk Interviews	3x day updates					
MSN Investor	UPDATED	✔	Screens, searches, Strategy Labs	Std.research, Up/downgrades, splits, insider reports	Advisor FYI		Fund section			
PersonalWealth.com		✔	Screens, picks, strategies	S&P Reports, splits, takeovers	Word on Street, S&P indexes, economy	IPO section	Fund section		Bond section	M
			Screens,	Std.research,	Columns, news		Fund			

Figure 5.3. CyberInvest.com's site provides a unique comparison chart of recommended sites.

Stock Screening Sites—Basic, Advanced, and Everything in Between

This section includes descriptions of some of the many stock screening tools available on the Web. Some require registration, but none charge a fee or otherwise restrict availability. Keep in mind as you review these tools that the one you prefer today may not meet your needs in a year. Your priorities may change; your need for sophisticated screening tools may increase; or you may decide that you prefer a PC-based software package rather than a Web site. Remember, too, that this is far from a comprehensive list of available Web sites; rather, it is a sampling of the kinds of resources available.

Virtually every online stock brokerage offers some form of stock screening, either accessible to all visitors or restricted to account holders. See Chapter 16 for further discussion of e-brokerages; if you have already set up an account with an online broker, compare the stock screening tool that it offers with those described here.

Quicken

Intuit, the producer of the popular personal financial software package Quicken, maintains a well-designed financial information portal at www.quicken.com. The stock screening tool on Quicken is one that can meet the needs of both beginning investors and those who have more sophisticated screening requirements. From the main Quicken screen, click [Investing], then [Screen Stocks]. Your three choices for screening are: [Popular Searches], which provides preset screens for popular investment strategies such as small cap growth stocks, high yield stocks, and fastest-growing stocks; [EasyStep Search], which walks you through six filters, including industry, market cap, valuation, yield, growth rate and price; and [Full Search], which includes the same six categories of filters as EasyStep Search but allows for more specificity. The EasyStep Search also includes two or three paragraphs at each step, explaining what the filters mean and how they are used, not included in the single-Web-page Full Search. The EasyStep and Full Searches allow you to type in specific minimum and/or maximum values as well as preformatted options. For example, the five-year revenue growth filter lets you enter any value or select among four choices—10 percent or less, at least 15 percent, at least 25 percent, or at least 50 percent. This makes screening more useful for investors who may not be familiar with average or typical values for some of these filters, since it spells out possible values.

See Figure 5.4 for the results of a stock screen search. Note that the Results screen can be customized; you can sort the companies by various criteria and select what information is displayed on each company.

Hoover's

Hoover's (www.hoovers.com) is known for its profiles of publicly and privately held companies. It also provides a stock screening tool, in recognition of the fact that many of its subscribers are using Hoover's to research companies for investment purposes. You can get to Hoover's stock screening tool by drilling down from the main Web page—click the [Money] link, then [Stocks], and finally [Stock Screener]. The stock screening page can also be accessed directly, at www.stockscreener.com.

All the search criteria are conveniently displayed on a single screen; you type in the minimum and/or maximum values you want for any of the criteria. One disadvantage of this tool is that you must fill in the specific values; an option allowing users to choose among typical ranges ("market cap of $1 to $5 billion," "yields of at least 7 percent") would make this a

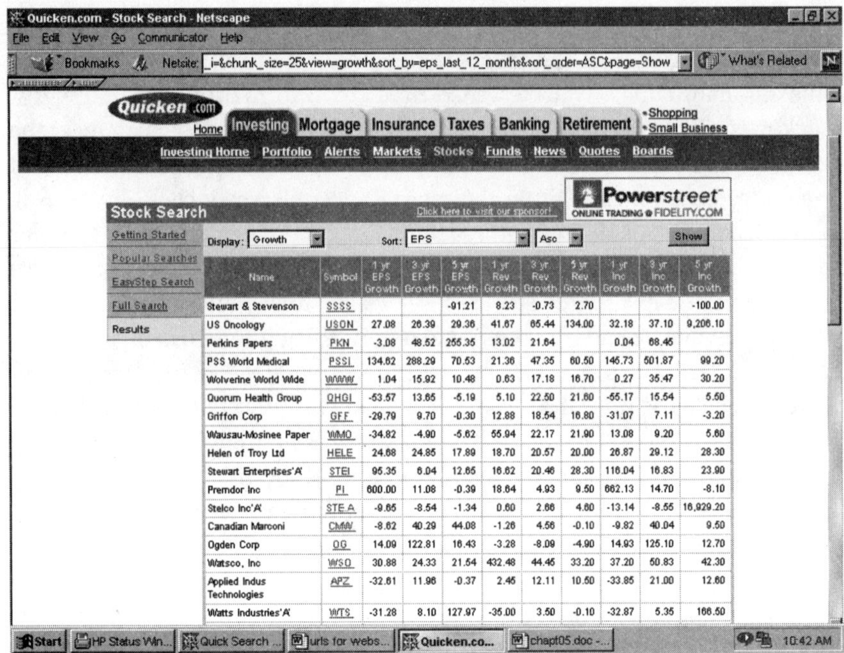

Figure 5.4. Quicken.com lets you customize the search results screen.

more valuable screening tool. As such, stockscreener.com is perhaps best suited for an investor who is past the novice stage. One nice feature is the ability to jump from the stock screen results page to the company profiles for which Hoover's is known. See Figure 5.5 for the Hoover's stock screening search page.

Wall Street City

Some areas of the Wall Street City (www.wallstreetcity.com) site are restricted to subscribers only; however, some of its useful stock screening tools are available without paying a fee. At the main screen, click the [Search for an investment] link. At the next screen, called ProSearch, use the [Quick Search] box, which lets you screen by a series of categories—small-cap stocks, high-growth stocks, *unheralded* stocks, and so on. The screen results screen is well-designed; a very useful feature is a chart titled "How well has this search been working?," which shows how well the stocks selected in your selected screen would have performed each month over the past year.

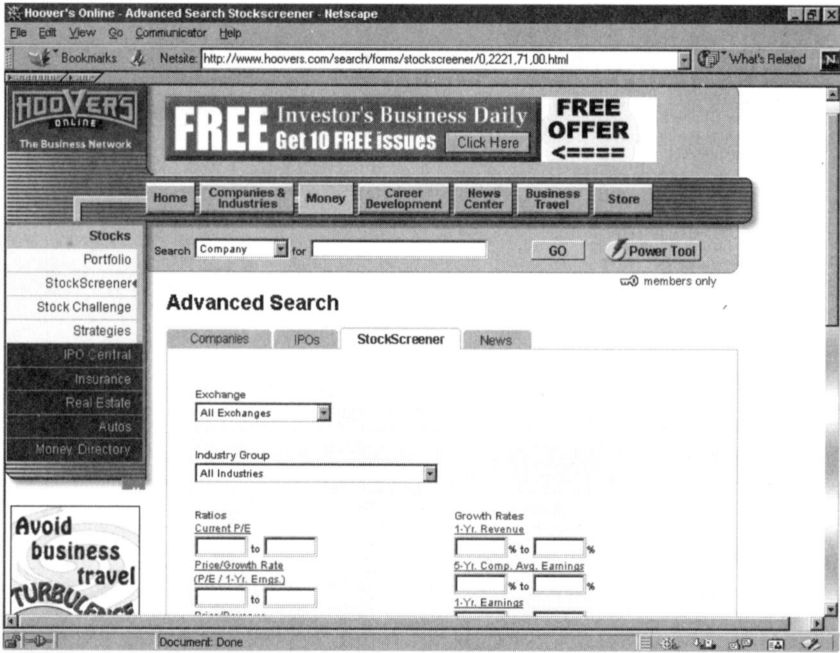

Figure 5.5. The Hoover's stock screening tool is best suited for more advanced investors.

Wall Street City also has several useful collections of prebuilt stock screens based on a wide variety of criteria: weak stocks showing signs of recovery, low or high price/book ratio, stocks held by the fewest institutions, stocks showing an increase in insider trading, and so on. You have a limited ability to fine-tune these prebuilt screens by specifying the type of stock to search. From the ProSearch screen, click the [Backtested] link for the list of prebuilt screens. You can also review the site's preformatted advanced screens for such criteria as momentum, *stochastics* (the position of a stock relative to its most recent trading range), or moving average. Click the [Technical Breakouts] link for these screens. And finally, you can screen for *breakouts*—stocks that have been trading within a flat or narrow range for a period of time and have just broken out of that range to a new high or low.

This is a useful site to visit if you want some ideas on how to best fine-tune your stock screening or to get ideas on ways to filter stock selections. See Figure 5.6 for the search results screen of a Quick Search.

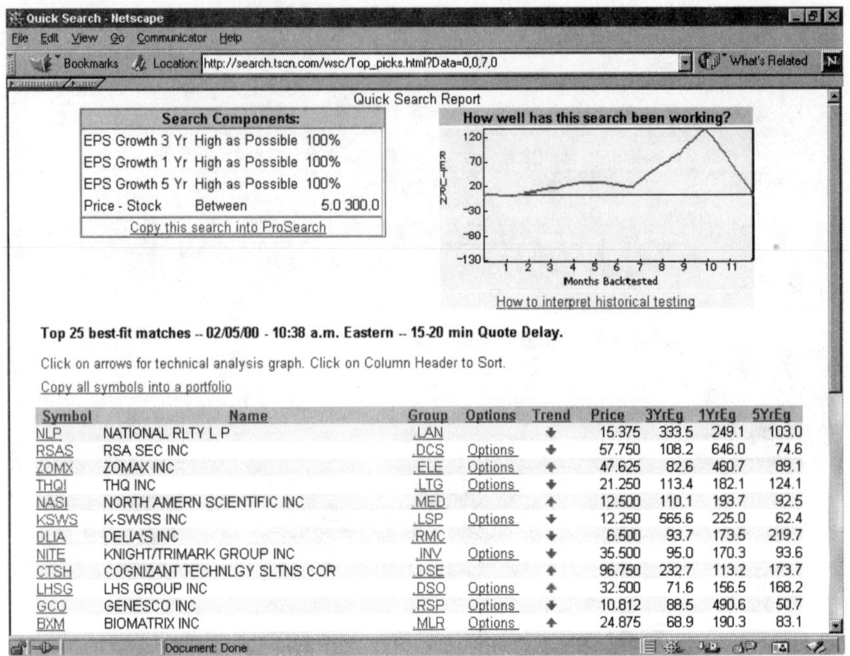

Figure 5.6. Wall Street City provides a historical perspective on the results of a stock screen.

SmartMoney

SmartMoney is a magazine published by Dow Jones, the same folks that bring you *The Wall Street Journal.* The Web site, www.smartmoney.com, includes articles from the magazine, investment tools, daily news, and a collection of tutorials under the heading "SmartMoney University." Smartmoney.com doesn't offer a traditional stock screening tool; however, it develops its own daily screen of the market and publishes both the results of its screen and the *recipe* used to filter stocks. You may find its screens useful as preformatted tools. Alternatively, these are good resources for learning *how* a stock screen is constructed. Each screen has a particular focus—e-commerce software companies, balance sheet, earnings revisions, biotech industry. The Daily Screen includes an extensive discussion of the top-rated company, why it came out on top, and how the screen was constructed.

You may want to look through the screen recipe and then take those criteria and use one of the stock screening tools described in the section to construct a new filter with updated data. See Figure 5.7 for the *SmartMoney* retail screen.

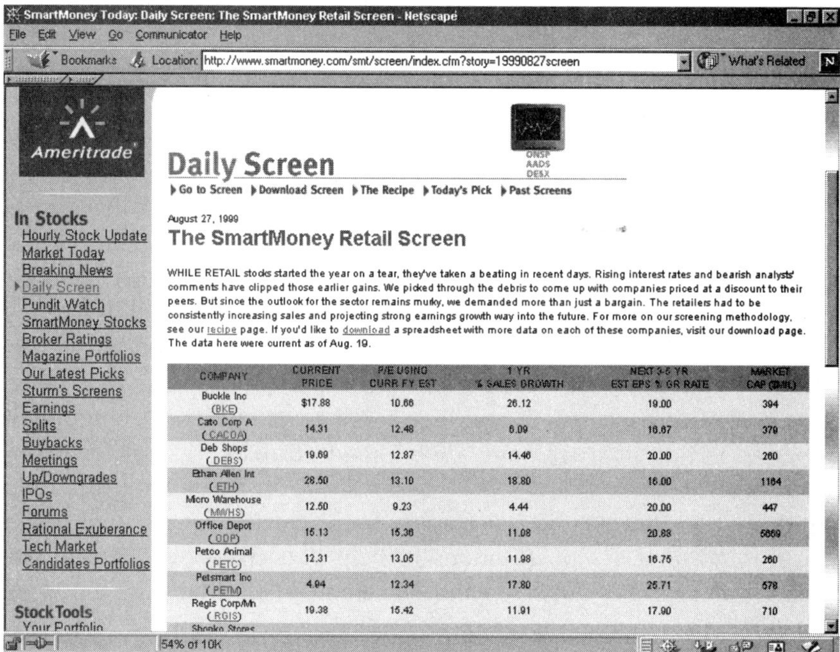

COMPANY	CURRENT PRICE	P/E USING CURR FY EST	1 YR % SALES GROWTH	NEXT 3-5 YR EST EPS % GR RATE	MARKET CAP ($MIL)
Buckle Inc (BKE)	$17.88	10.66	26.12	19.00	394
Cato Corp A (CACOA)	14.31	12.48	6.09	16.67	379
Deb Shops (DEBS)	19.69	12.87	14.46	20.00	260
Ethan Allen Int (ETH)	28.50	13.10	18.80	16.00	1164
Micro Warehouse (MWHS)	12.50	9.23	4.44	20.00	447
Office Depot (ODP)	15.13	15.36	11.08	20.83	5669
Petco Animal (PETC)	12.31	13.05	11.98	16.75	260
Petsmart Inc (PETM)	4.94	12.34	17.80	25.71	578
Regis Corp/Mn (RGIS)	19.38	15.42	11.91	17.90	710

Figure 5.7. *SmartMoney* provides a preformatted daily stock screen on a specific criterion, complete with description of how the screen was built.

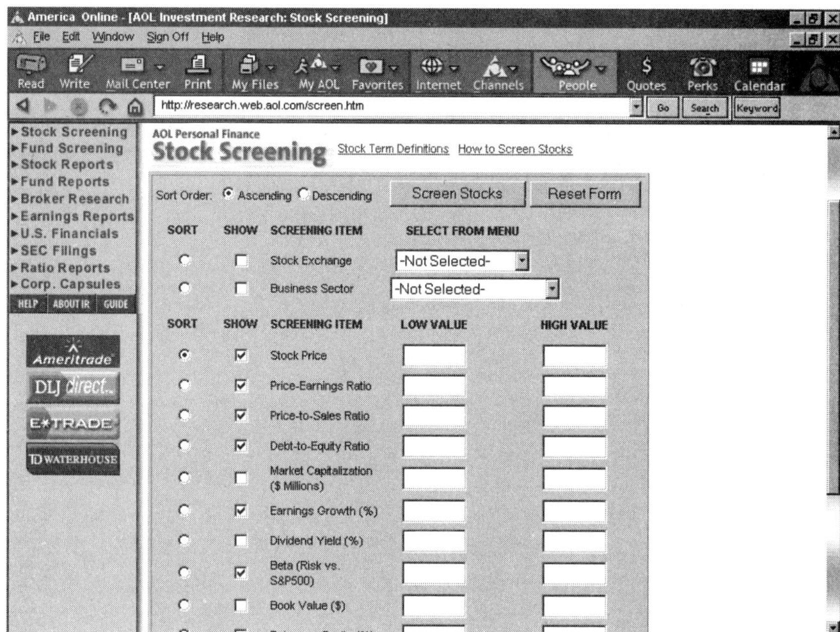

Figure 5.8. America Online subscribers have access to a proprietary stock screener.

AOL Screens

In addition to what is available on the public Web, America Online subscribers also have access to stock screening tools on AOL's proprietary site. Use Keyword: Stock Screening (don't you love it when it's that easy?), which takes you to the Investment Research area of the Personal Finance channel. This tool lets you screen by 12 numeric values such as book value, dividend yield, and price-to-sales ratio; you indicate a high and low value and whether you want the results sorted in ascending or descending order. One disadvantage of this product is that it assumes you know appropriate range values to use. Investors new to stock screening might prefer an option that has, say, "High Growth of Earnings per Share" or "Moderate Return on Equity %." Curiously, AOL offers a mutual fund screening tool that has both a Step-By-Step Screening guide that walks you through a series of questions to help you choose an appropriate mutual fund, and a Custom Fund Screening guide that, like the stock screening tool, assumes more experience. See Figure 5.8 for the AOL stock screening tool.

6
Bonds on the Net

Investing in bonds may not be as sexy as that other Bond, but they're an option to consider, particularly when you want a reliable stream of income or a tax-free investment. This chapter looks at how to find basic information on investing in bonds, both corporate- and government-issued; how to get ratings of bonds; the difference between bonds and bond funds; and how to decide whether stocks or bonds are a better choice for you.

Bonds 101

What's confusing to many investors is that good economic news is bad news for bonds. A stock purchase is an investment in a company, with all the attendant risks of ownership. Bonds, on the other hand, are loans to a company, for which the company promises to pay the bond holder back the principal plus interest at a fixed rate over a fixed period of time.

Bonds are an attractive option for retirees who want a predictable source of income; for young investors saving for a purchase of a house who need a predictable return on their investment; or for parents investing to pay for a child's college expenses. Having a steady income is attractive, particularly if you aren't in a position to sit out a downswing in the stock market. (You can't just tell your kid to put off college for a few years because the stock market is going through an adjustment, can you?)

General Guides to Bond Investments

There are two general kinds of bonds—those that are issued by a company and those issued by a federal, state, or local government. Interest from the

latter are exempt from either state or federal income tax. The trade-off is that tax-free bonds usually offer a lower interest rate.

There are a number of Web sites that help you figure out which kinds of bonds are best for you. One starting point for information can be a relevant trade association. Sure enough, the Bond Market Association's Web site (www.investinginbonds.com) features a selection of online publications written for the beginning bond investor. Figure 6.1 shows the first of the Bond Market Association's "seven steps to educate yourself about investing in bonds."

The Investor's Checklist, available through a link on the left side of the Bond Market Association's Web page, is particularly useful in determining whether investing in bonds is a smart move for you. It walks you through a series of questions about your investment goals, and it includes an explanation of why each question is being asked. Be sure to check out the Investor's Guide to Bond Basics, also available via a link on the left side of the Web page. This guide introduces you to basic terminology, gives pointers on how to read credit ratings, and discusses how the economy and interest rates affect bond prices. Although it goes into a fair amount of detail, it's clearly written and easy to understand.

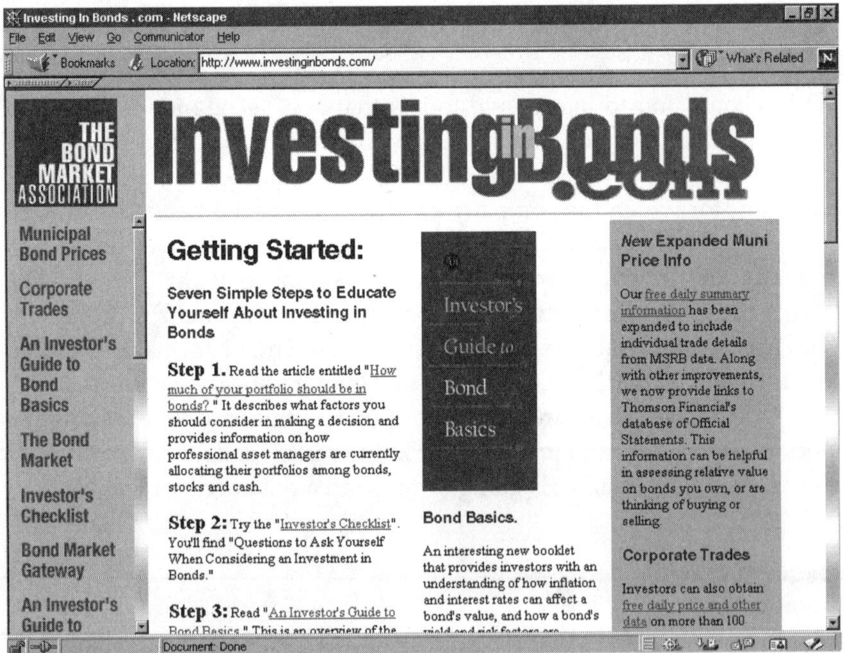

Figure 6.1. InvestinginBonds.com has a number of tutorials on bonds.

Another good source for basic information on bonds is at *SmartMoney* magazine's Web site (www.smartmoney.com). At the main Web page, click [Bonds], then [Bond Investing] for a well-organized collection of resources for the beginning bond investor, shown in Figure 6.2.

The drop-down menu directs you to a collection of bond basics, including investing for income or for profit, 10 things your broker won't tell you about bonds, and bond allocation strategies. Take advantage of the bond calculator, available on this page, to calculate the value of a bond. Figuring out the yield of a bond is complicated, since you have to factor in the interest rate (*coupon*), the percentage of face value at which you purchased the bond, and the date the bond matures. Don't try this at home, kids—use one of the handy calculators on the Web, like the bond calculator on the *SmartMoney* site.

A third source for basic information on bonds is *Money* magazine's Money 101 course. Head over to www.money.com, then click the [Investing in Bonds] link listed under the Money 101 logo. You'll learn how bonds work and how to buy bonds, read a glossary of bond-related terms, and even take a test at the end to see how much you really learned. This lesson also includes a tax-equivalent yield calculator to compare the yield

Figure 6.2. *SmartMoney* features James Bond in its bond investing area.

on taxed and tax-exempt bonds by converting the yield of tax-exempt bonds to their taxable equivalent. Is a federal-tax-exempt bond with a 6 percent yield better than a taxable bond with an 8 percent yield? Plug in your federal income tax rate and find out.

About.com, a site that features expert guides who develop collections of links to relevant Web sites, has a strong selection of information on bonds. Start at bonds.about.com, which will give you a collection of links to bond-related sites, as well as discussion forums on bond investing, articles on the bond market, and an electronic newsletter written by the site guide. See Figure 6.3 for the home page for the bonds guide at About.com.

For a one-stop collection of bond value and yield calculators, your best bet may be FinanCenter (www.financenter.com), known for its wide variety of finance calculation tools. At the main site, click [Investing], then use the "ClickCalc Bonds" pull-down menu to select the specific calculator you need, as shown in Figure 6.4. These range from helping you decide whether to invest in taxed or tax-free bonds, to figuring out when to sell a bond, to determining what your return would be if you sold a bond today.

Figure 6.3. About.com has a well-designed guide to bond information on the Web.

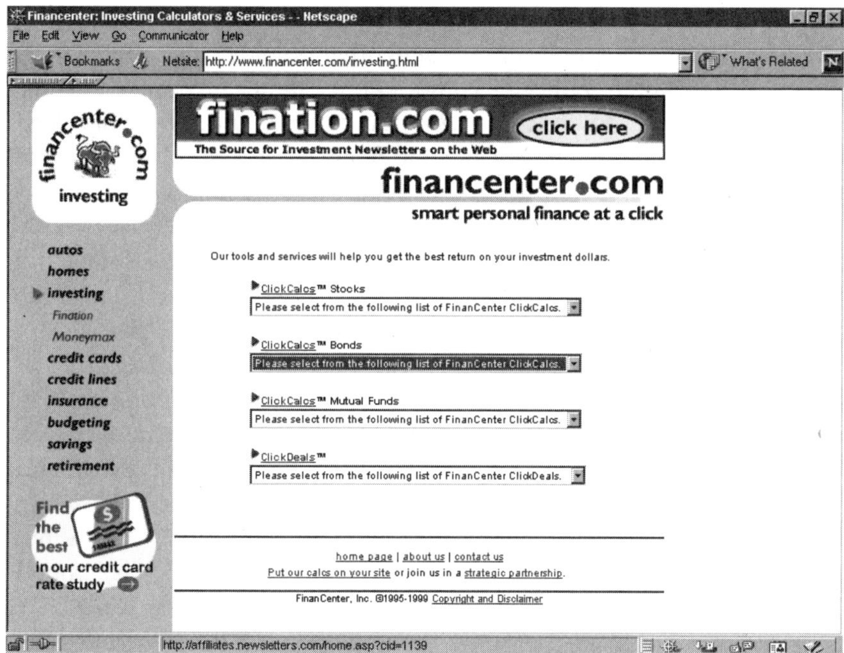

Figure 6.4. FinanCenter has a wide variety of online financial calculators.

Government Bonds: Lending Money to the Government

Even if you weren't alive during World War II, you've probably seen the vintage posters of Uncle Sam exhorting you to "Buy Bonds." At that time, people were encouraged to lend money to—invest in—the U.S. government to fund the war effort. While there is no longer a need for war bonds, the U.S. Treasury, as well as state, county, and city governments, still issue bonds to raise money. Other quasigovernmental organizations, such as municipal water companies, public hospitals, and public transit authorities also issue bonds, usually to fund construction or other capital improvements.

Unlike corporate bonds, federal, state, county, and city bonds are always at least partially tax-free. The interest income from U.S. Treasury bonds is not taxed by states, counties, or cities; the interest income from state or local bonds is exempt from federal income taxes. Since Treasury bonds are backed by the "full faith and credit" of the U.S. government (and its ability to impose taxes to raise money), they are seen as one of the safest forms of bonds—and this is why they often carry relatively low interest rates. Some municipal bonds can be seen as slightly more risky; bonds issued by local public utilities and other public entities (public hospitals, transportation authorities, and so on) are not guaranteed by the local government's ability to generate tax revenue, but are guaranteed only by the revenue of the project being financed. As a result, the yield is usually higher than for those bonds issued by state, county, or city governments themselves.

Assuming that the U.S. Department of Treasury would have something helpful, I headed over to www.publicdebt.treas.gov, the Web site of the department's Bureau of the Public Debt. How did I know the URL? I started with the Library of Congress' catalog of government agencies at lcweb.loc.gov/global/executive/fed.html, and browsed through the listings under U.S. Department of Treasury for a likely-sounding department. Sure enough, the Bureau of the Public Debt has a link to [T-Bills, Notes and Bonds]. Click that link and you'll get a straightforward list of resources about Treasury securities, as shown in Figure 6.5. The text is a bit dense, but the "Frequently Asked Questions About T-Bills, Notes & Bonds," found under the [General Information] link, are useful and straightforward.

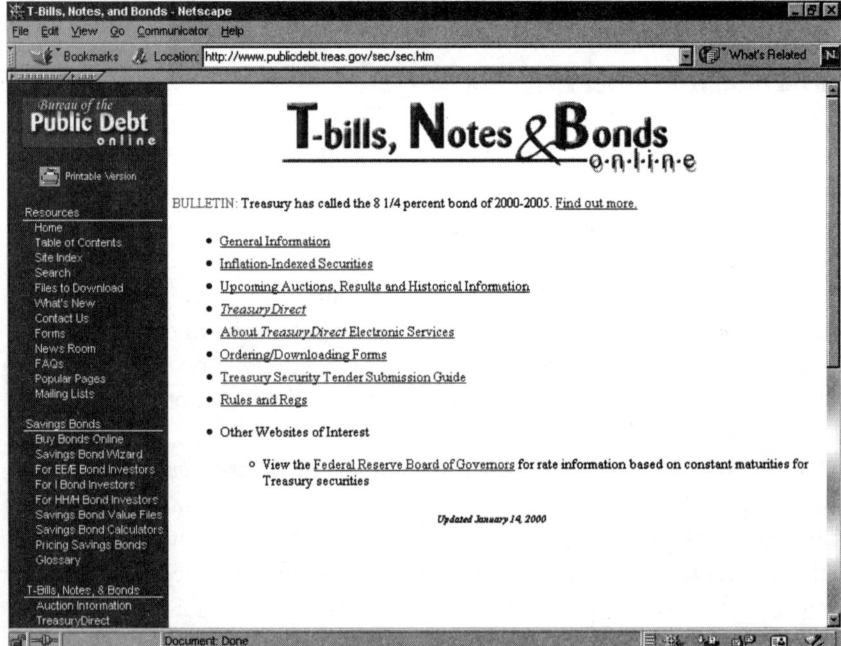

Figure 6.5. The U.S. Treasury is a wealth of information on government bonds.

Another source of basic information on government bonds, particularly Treasury bills, is Women's Wire—and no, you don't have to be a woman to find the information at this Web site (www.womenswire.com) useful. At the main Web page, click [Money], then [Bonds]. You have a couple of resources available here. Start with *Basics: Treasury Bills, Notes & Bonds.* Be sure to click the [continue] link at the bottom of the first page; this will take you through a nontechnical discussion of what T-bills and other government bonds are, how to buy and sell them, and how to find the current rates. Other useful resources are *I-Bonds Information* (which describes the relatively new savings bonds that are indexed to the inflation rate) and *How to Buy Treasury Bills, Notes & Bonds.*

Bond Ratings: How Risky Is This?

Finding information on a stock, tracking its performance, and evaluating its relative strength is reasonably easy to do, once you find the tools and understand the lingo. Evaluating bonds can be a bit more difficult, because they aren't as frequently traded by individual investors and because they just don't have the same sex appeal as stocks. Fortunately, several companies provide ratings of corporations' creditworthiness (remember, a bond is a form of debt owed by the company to its bondholders) and assessments of the creditworthiness of debt issued by state and local governments, public utilities, and other public agencies. The rating system usually consists of a series of letters ranging from AAA (highest) to C (lowest). Within this range, a three-letter AAA rating is higher than AA, which is higher than a single A. Keep in mind that credit rating companies do not conduct their own audit of the company or agency issuing a bond; they base their rating on their estimation of the institution's ability to meet its payment obligation and their evaluation of the relative likelihood of payment should the organization go into bankruptcy.

What bond rating is most appropriate for you? It depends on your tolerance for risk and how long you intend to invest. As you would expect, higher-risk bonds pay a higher rate of interest and carry a higher chance that the issuing institution may not be able to make its payment obligations. If you choose to invest in bonds because they are a more secure investment than stocks, you will probably want to look at the higher-rated bonds.

Standard & Poor's

One of the better-known of the credit ratings companies is Standard & Poor's, or S&P. S&P's main ratings Web page (www.standardandpoors.com/ratings/index.html) provides information on a number of its services, including:

- How to read its ratings (what exactly *does* a rating of "A-1+" mean, anyway?)
- Commentary on the credit quality of various industry groups such as department stores, North American airlines, and chemical companies
- In-depth analyses of selected companies and discussions of why each company was assigned its credit rating

See Figure 6.6 for an example of a corporate rating on a company, available through the S&P Web site by clicking the [Commentary] link.

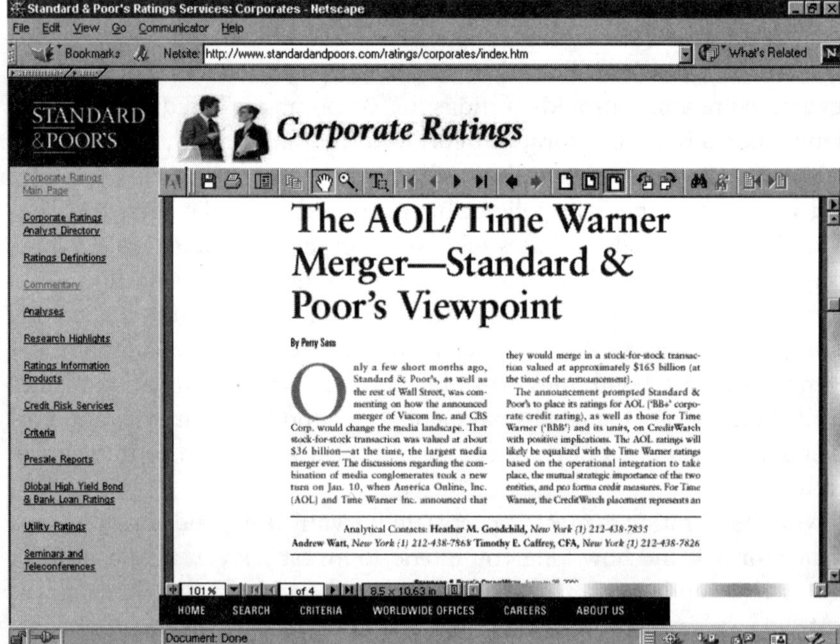

Figure 6.6. Standard & Poor's provides detailed information on the creditworthiness of companies.

Note that Standard & Poor's rates insurance companies on their ability to pay claims, as well as the viability of money market funds, banks, thrifts, credit unions, and other financial institutions. S&P even rates the stability of the currency of sovereign countries; Australia and Canada have very positive ratings, for example, while perhaps not surprisingly, Russia is currently listed as vulnerable.

This site also has a form through which you can request the credit ratings for individual bonds. While S&P is in the business of selling information about companies, it also provides this information to individuals at no charge, on a limited basis. You can request up to five ratings by clicking [Ratings Inquiries] at the main Web page.

Other Options for Bond Ratings

Moody's Investors Service is the other major player in the credit ratings market. Like Standard & Poor's, Moody's uses the Aaa-through-C scale to rate the creditworthiness of a bond, insurance company, financial institution, or country's currency. Moody's doesn't provide as much information on its public Web site as Standard & Poor's does, but you can scan through recent changes in ratings by going to www.moodys.com, clicking the [Ratings] link, then browsing through the "rating actions."

Note that many public and university libraries subscribe to the print or online versions of Standard & Poor's and Moody's ratings services. The material may not be as easy to read as what's available on the rating companies' Web sites, but the subscriber versions usually provide more depth. Ask a business librarian for help in using the resources the library has.

While you may not be able to search all bond ratings services directly on the Web, there are Net resources that enable you to search for municipal bonds by Standard & Poor's or Moody's rating, maturity date, coupon, or other criteria. Bondtrac (www.bondtrac.com) is one such resource. Note that Bondtrac is geared more for the broker community than individual investors; although it has a great database of information on bonds, it doesn't make the information directly available to us little guys. Instead, Bondtrac's Web site has pointers to a number of bond dealers who make use of Bondtrac's database. Start at the main Bondtrac Web page, click [Information], then click [Advisors]. You'll see a collection of links to individual brokers' Web sites; click any of them to search the Bondtrac data. See Figure 6.7.

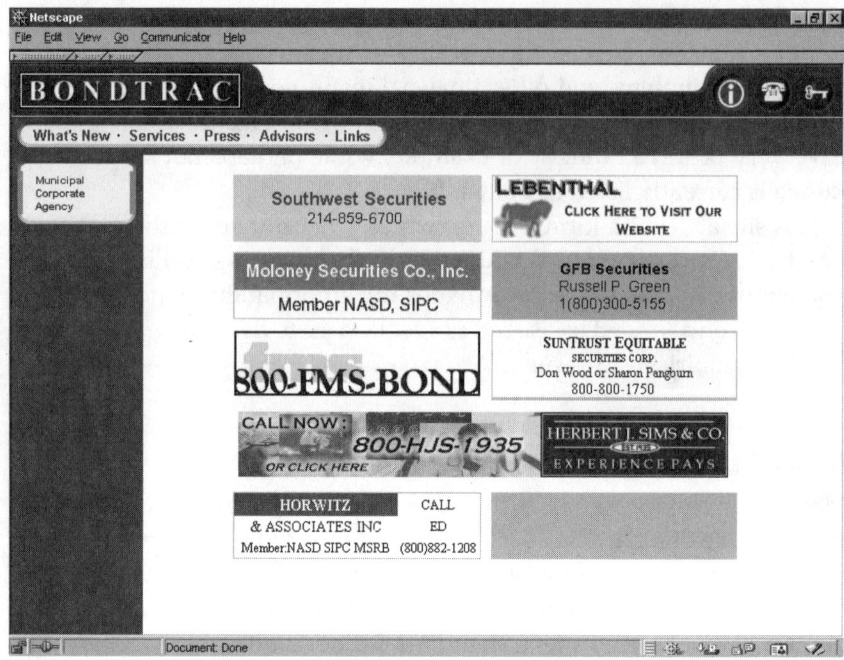

Figure 6.7. Bondtrac has links to a number of bond dealers who provide access to the Bondtrac database.

Bonds or Bond Funds: How Do You Decide?

Investing in individual bonds is not as simple as investing in a stock, if for no other reason than selling a bond before its maturity date can significantly impact its value. And figuring out the best price for a bond, at least one that will probably be sold before maturity, is tricky. On the other hand, income from a single bond is predictable, and if the bond is held to maturity, the yield is guaranteed.

Income from a bond fund is less predictable, and its per-share value will change over time, just like stocks and unlike a single bond. Also similar to a stock or stock fund, a bond fund can't offer a guaranteed value at the end of a set period of time. On the plus side, bond funds relieve the investor of the need to calculate the current value of a bond compared to its value at maturity; they offer greater liquidity and flexibility; and they permit regular investment in smaller quantities than is often possible when purchasing individual bonds. You also are freed from the worry of the bond holder calling in (i.e., repaying) the bond before its maturity date, thus requiring you to reinvest your money before you had expected to, and perhaps at a less favorable rate.

So, how do you decide which is a better choice for you? The MSN MoneyCentral site has a good discussion of bond funds and their benefits and drawbacks as compared to investing in individual bonds. Start at moneycentral.msn.com/investor, and click [Quick Reference]. At the next screen, select the [Q&A] button, and click [Bonds] in the Topic list. At the next screen, shown in Figure 6.8, click [Bond Funds]. This will bring up a discussion of the various types of bond funds and whether or not you should invest in bond funds.

SmartMoney magazine's site (www.smartmoney.com) also has an article on "Bonds vs. Bond Funds," complete with a graphic of two James Bond-like characters engaged in a tug of war. To get to it, click the [Bonds] tab at the main screen, then click the [Bond Investing] link. The next screen shows a number of useful articles on bonds, including the "Bonds vs. Bond Funds" item. And in case you're feeling comfortable investing in bonds through a broker, see "10 Things Your Broker Won't Tell You About Bonds" for a somewhat contrarian view of the bond market, including the

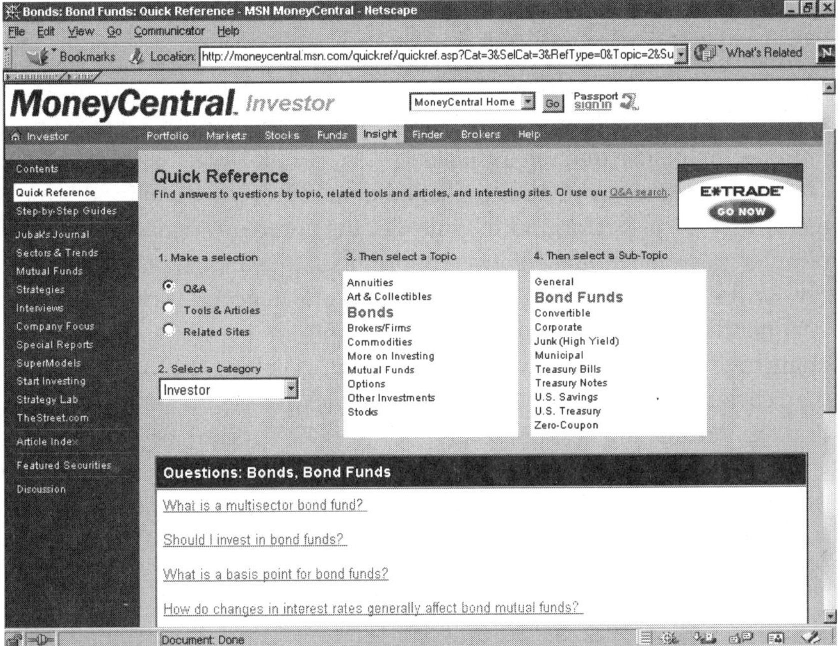

Figure 6.8. MoneyCentral has a number of Q&As on investing in bond funds.

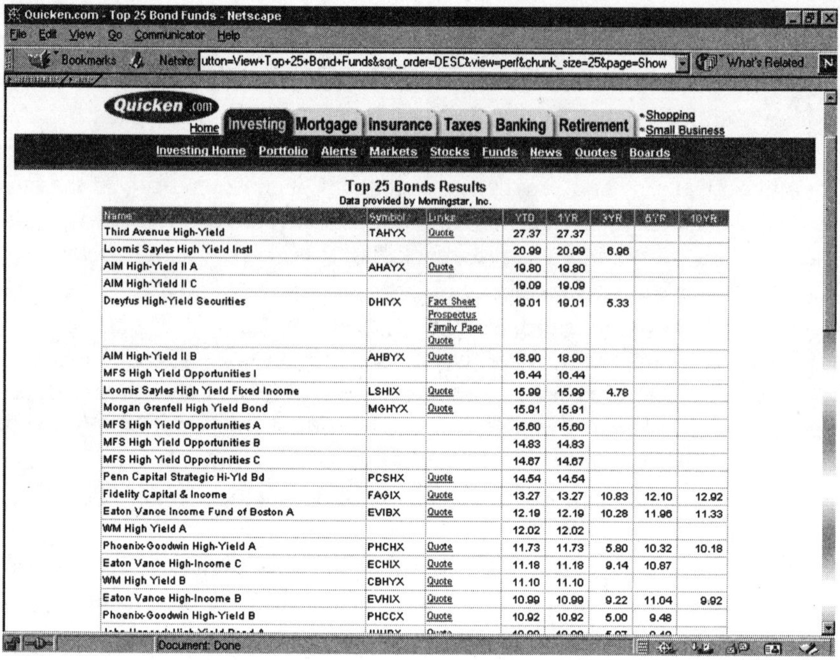

Quicken.com - Top 25 Bond Funds - Netscape

Top 25 Bonds Results
Data provided by Morningstar, Inc.

Name	Symbol	Links	YTD	1YR	3YR	5YR	10YR
Third Avenue High-Yield	TAHYX	Quote	27.37	27.37			
Loomis Sayles High Yield Instl			20.99	20.99	6.96		
AIM High-Yield II A	AHAYX	Quote	19.80	19.80			
AIM High-Yield II C			19.09	19.09			
Dreyfus High-Yield Securities	DHIYX	Fact Sheet Prospectus Family Page Quote	19.01	19.01	5.33		
AIM High-Yield II B	AHBYX	Quote	18.90	18.90			
MFS High Yield Opportunities I			16.44	16.44			
Loomis Sayles High Yield Fixed Income	LSHIX	Quote	15.99	15.99	4.78		
Morgan Grenfell High Yield Bond	MGHYX	Quote	15.91	15.91			
MFS High Yield Opportunities A			15.60	15.60			
MFS High Yield Opportunities B			14.83	14.83			
MFS High Yield Opportunities C			14.67	14.67			
Penn Capital Strategic Hi-Yld Bd	PCSHX	Quote	14.54	14.54			
Fidelity Capital & Income	FAGIX	Quote	13.27	13.27	10.83	12.10	12.92
Eaton Vance Income Fund of Boston A	EVIBX	Quote	12.19	12.19	10.28	11.96	11.33
WM High Yield A			12.02	12.02			
Phoenix-Goodwin High-Yield A	PHCHX	Quote	11.73	11.73	5.80	10.32	10.18
Eaton Vance High-Income C	ECHIX	Quote	11.18	11.18	9.14	10.87	
WM High Yield B	CBHYX	Quote	11.10	11.10			
Eaton Vance High-Income B	EVHIX	Quote	10.99	10.99	9.22	11.04	9.92
Phoenix-Goodwin High-Yield B	PHCCX	Quote	10.92	10.92	5.00	9.48	

Figure 6.9. Quicken.com helps you identify the top bond funds in a number of categories.

opinion that "low-risk" bond funds may not be as safe as they appear. As always, read all of these with a careful eye, and be sure to get more than one opinion before making a choice.

Of course, one way of deciding whether to invest in a bond fund is looking at its typical performance. Quicken, the company that publishes the popular personal finance software, provides a search screen to let you review the top 25 bond funds in a number of categories—emerging markets bonds, long-term municipal bonds, and so on. Get to this tool by going to the Quicken site (www.quicken.com), clicking the [Investing] tab, then clicking the [Bonds] link, and finally clicking the link at [*Click here* to find top performing bond mutual funds in 16 categories], or go directly to www.quicken.com/investments/bonds/top25/. At this point, you select the type of bond fund you're interested in, and the return period, from 1 to 10 years. See Figure 6.9 for an example of the results from this screening tool.

Chapter 7 focuses on mutual funds; be sure to use the resources described there in deciding whether to invest in a mutual fund or to roll your own.

7

Finding and Evaluating Mutual Funds Online

Years before the Internet made individual investing both feasible and attractive, mutual funds offered a way to share the risks and rewards of investing in the stock market. I remember investing my college loans in a mutual fund way back in the mid-1970s, and being delighted that my return was far greater than the 3 percent interest I was charged for the loans. While I had neither the time nor inclination to track the stock market, I was still able to benefit from a relatively high return, at least compared to my options at the time as a financially challenged student.

While you may use the rest of this book to research and then invest in individual stocks, there's always a place in your portfolio for mutual funds. These investment vehicles offer diversification—by definition—and enable you to invest in higher-risk areas such as foreign companies or small companies, or an industry sector such as precious metals or biotechnology that you might not be familiar enough with to select individual stocks. While investing in a mutual fund may carry additional risk when compared to a blue-chip stock, you are benefiting from the expertise of professional fund managers who are presumably more familiar with the focus of the fund than you are.

This chapter looks at sources for basic information on mutual fund investing, resources for evaluating the relative merit of various mutual funds, tools for selecting the best mutual fund for you, and sources for news on mutual funds.

Mutual Fund Basics

Investing in a mutual fund takes as much care as investing in an individual stock. While the selection criteria may be different and the length of your investment will probably be longer with a mutual fund, you still need to read the fine print. Where do you start? The sites listed in this section help you understand how mutual funds work and the types of mutual funds—socially responsible funds, closed-end versus open-end funds, index funds, and so on—as well as providing advice on investment strategies.

Once you've selected a fund that looks appropriate for you, be sure to read its prospectus, which describes the fund's objectives, management, fees, and features such as check writing privileges, investment options, and so on. Most large mutual fund companies maintain Web sites and have a link from the main page to the most current prospectus. (Note that these are often in PDF format, which means that you'll need to have a copy of Adobe's free Acrobat Reader software. If you don't have a copy, head over to www.adobe.com/prodindex/acrobat/readstep.html and follow the directions to download the software.) If the mutual fund does not maintain a Web site, you can find the prospectus at the U.S. Securities and Exchange Commission's EDGAR site at edgar.sec.gov. The default search tends not to retrieve these reports reliably, though. For best results, go to edgar.sec.gov/edaux/formlynx.htm, which lets you search by specific filing form, shown in Figure 7.1. Use the pull-down menu to select Form 485 (mutual fund prospectuses), type in the beginning of the fund name in the company name box, then click [Submit Choices.]

The company's annual report is also available through the EDGAR site. The discussion by the senior executives of the fund's performance over the past year is particularly useful. To find the company's annual report on the SEC's EDGAR site, use the "Form Pick" site previously described (edgar.sec.gov/edaux/formlynx.htm). Type *N-30D* in the search box labeled "If form is not listed, enter type:" and the beginning of the fund name in the company name box. The results of your search will be sorted by company name, then by date. Click the company name link of the annual report you want to read.

Dow Jones Primer

Dow Jones, the publisher of *The Wall Street Journal,* is a good source of information on mutual funds (not surprisingly, given its prominence in

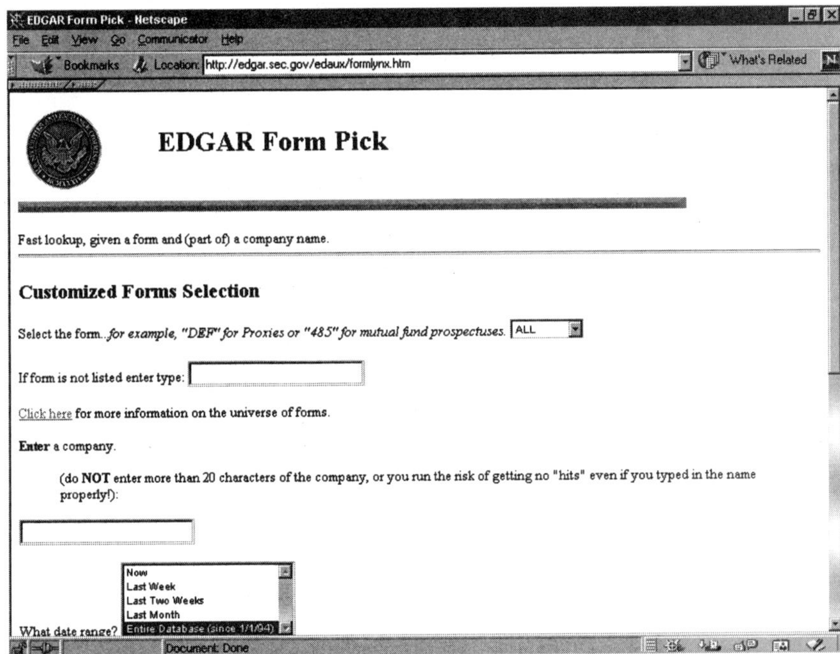

Figure 7.1. The best way to find a mutual fund's prospectus and annual report on the EDGAR site is through its Form Pick search.

the field of financial news and information). To get to its Mutual Funds 101 site, go to the main Dow Jones Web site (dowjones.wsj.com), click the [Personal Finance] link, then the [WSJ Guide] link, and finally [Mutual Funds]. This guide is broken down into five sections:

- *Mutual Funds Marketplace,* which describes the various types of mutual funds—stock, bond, and money market funds
- *Targeted Investments,* which examines the three goals of mutual funds—current income, income and growth, and future growth
- *Tracking Fund Performance,* which looks at ways to measure the performance of a fund by examining its share price, yield, or total return
- *The Prospectus,* which walks you through the sections of a fund's prospectus
- *Mutual Fund Quotes,* which deciphers *The Wall Street Journal*'s monthly review of mutual fund performance

Mutual Fund Investor's Center

The Mutual Fund Education Alliance is a trade association of the mutual fund industry. It maintains the Mutual Fund Investor's Center at www.mfea.com, a site designed to introduce mutual fund investing to the public. Not only does it have news items and general articles on mutual funds, but it also has an in-depth tutorial on mutual funds. Figure 7.2 shows the main Web page, along with the pull-down menu that enables you to select which part of the tutorial to read.

One of this site's more unusual features is its collection of pamphlets, booklets, reports, and other material produced by association member companies. Click the [Literature] link, then select a general topic—asset planning, investing for retirement, taxes, and so on—and you will get a listing of the publications available. Virtually all materials are free of charge; you check off the items you want and provide your mailing address, and the material is sent to you.

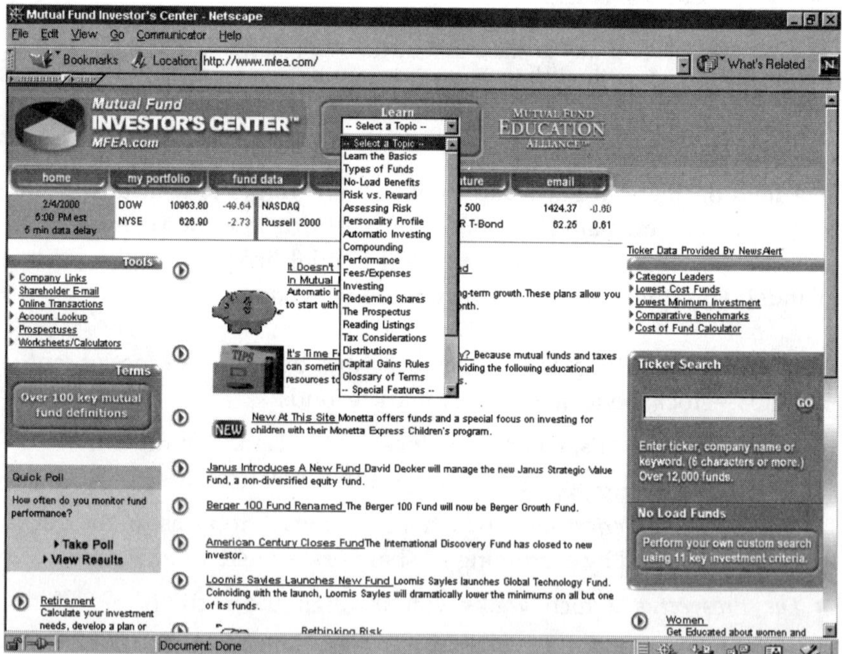

Figure 7.2. The Mutual Fund Investor's Center has a lengthy tutorial on mutual funds.

Vanguard University

The Vanguard Group, a mutual fund firm, maintains the *Vanguard University* on its Web site. This university is a collection of courses on mutual funds, complete with homework and quizzes at the end of each lesson. You can jump from section to section; in fact, many lessons contain links to related lessons in other courses. To get to the university, go to the main Vanguard site at www.vanguard.com, click the [Education, Planning and Advice] link, then click [University]. As shown in Figure 7.3, you can even see how long each lesson is expected to take.

Keep in mind that this material is written by a company that's in the business of managing mutual funds. The information is useful and clearly written, but it tends to downplay the disadvantages of mutual funds, such as a lack of control over your investments, high costs, and underperformance when compared to the market. Compare the Vanguard University lessons with those of the Fool School, described in the next section.

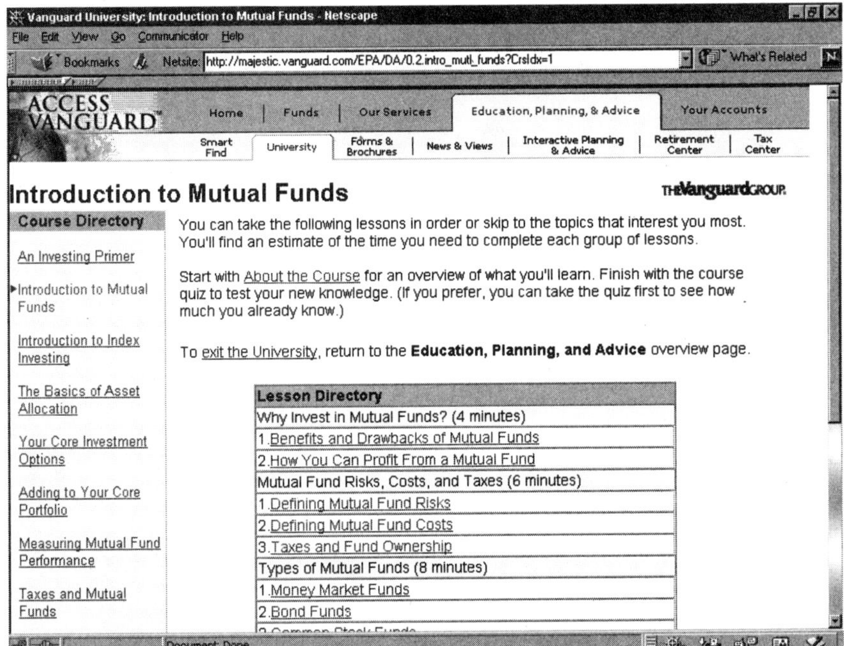

Figure 7.3. Vanguard Group has an online series of lessons on mutual fund investing.

Fool's Guide to Mutual Funds

The Motley Fool (www.fool.com) is not a big fan of most mutual funds, saying that most investors are better off investing in individual stocks, or, if they must invest in a mutual fund, an index fund. Even with this somewhat pessimistic perspective on mutual funds, The Motley Fool's tutorial on mutual funds is useful, if only to alert you to some of the drawbacks of mutual funds. From the main Fool Web page, click [School], then [Mutual Fund Fundamentals] to get to "The Truth about Mutual Funds" as shown in Figure 7.4. The section on Choosing a Mutual Fund is particularly useful, even if you don't subscribe to the Fool's aversion to mutual funds and their expense ratios.

The Motley Fool site also hosts discussion forums on mutual funds; click the [Mutual Funds Message boards] to read and participate in discussions about mutual fund investments. Note that you can read the Fool's School material and discussion forums without registering at the site; if you want to post a message on the board, you will have to register. There's no charge to register with the site.

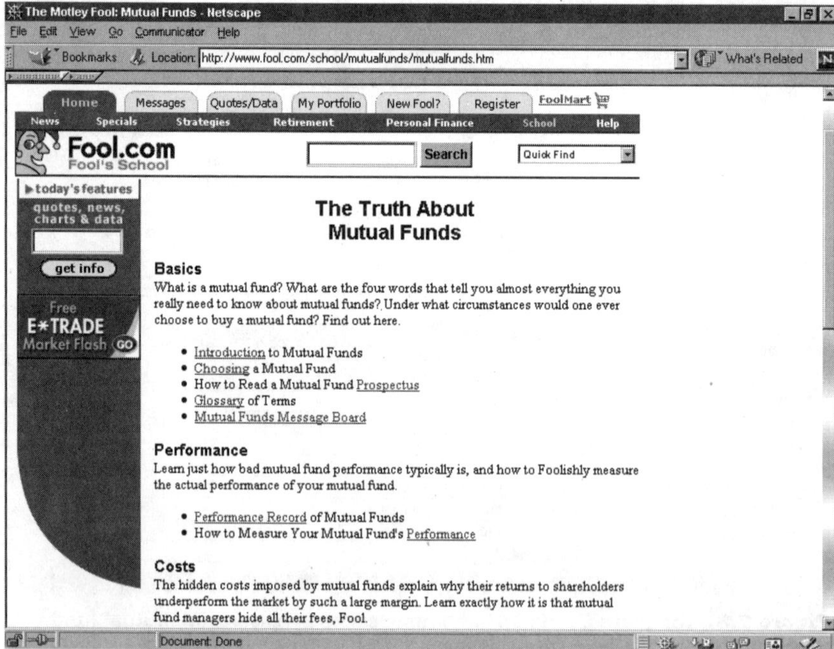

Figure 7.4. The Motley Fool's School has basic information on mutual funds.

Other Sources for Mutual Fund Basics

One megasite for information on mutual funds is About.com (www.about.com). Live guides maintain individual sections of this site; each section includes links to Web sites, commentary by the guide, news, discussion forums, and other Web-based resources. The About.com guide on mutual funds (mutualfunds.about.com) has a collection of Web sites that provide basic information on mutual funds. Click the [Mutual Funds 101] link to see an annotated list of sites, ranging from the "Young Investor's Guide to Accumulating Wealth" to "Test Your Mutual Fund IQ."

Chapter 13 describes Usenet newsgroups and other online discussion groups. The newsgroup that focuses on mutual funds, misc.invest.mutual-funds, maintains a well-written file of frequently asked questions at www.moneypages.com/syndicate/faq/toc.htm. To read current postings in this newsgroup, head over to RemarQ (www.remarq.com), type in *mutual funds* in the search box, and click [Find]. At the next screen, click the link to misc.invest.mutual-funds; this will take you to a list of recent postings, as shown in Figure 7.5. To read all the postings on a particular topic, just click the subject listing, such as "Listing of Sector Stocks." Remember to take all information gleaned from newsgroups with a grain of salt; the participants may be longtime investors, but it's also possible that they're just plain wrong.

Several periodicals that focus on personal investment maintain basic information on mutual funds on their Web sites:

- *Worth*—www.worth.com. Click [Search] at the main Web page, then type *mutual funds* in the search box. Select the article titled simply "Mutual Funds." Alternatively, you can go directly to this introductory article by pointing your browser to www.worth.com/articles/Q06.html.
- *Individual Investor*—www.individualinvestor.com. Click [Education] at the main Web site, then select [Mutual Funds], which takes you to a collection of articles on mutual funds, or [How to Read a Prospectus].
- *The Washington Post*—www.washingtonpost.com. The *Post* isn't a newspaper you would ordinarily think of for financial and investment information; I view it primarily as the newspaper of record on the federal government. But it maintains a good collection of columns on mutual fund investing. It takes some drilling down to find this collection, though. From the main Web page, click [Business/Tech], then [Mutual Funds], and finally [Resources].

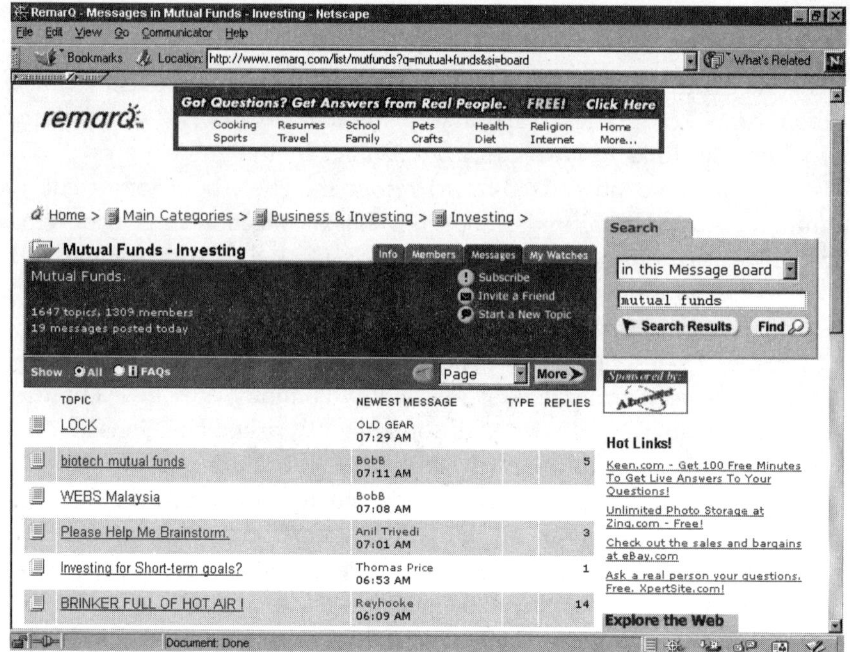

Figure 7.5. You can read the misc.invest.mutual-funds newsgroup at Remarq.com.

Mutual Fund Ratings: How'm I Doing?

Morningstar, Lipper, Value Line, and Standard & Poor's are the best-known sources for ratings of mutual funds. Each bases its rating on factors such as risk, performance, cost, and capitalization. Keep in mind that most ratings rely on *past* risk, performance, and so on, which means that an otherwise mediocre fund that has one good year may result in it getting a high rating due to a quirk in the market. There is no assurance that it will continue to perform well. Remember, too, that even a highly rated fund may not be right for you, if its objective or risk tolerance doesn't mesh with yours.

Not surprisingly, most of the mutual fund rating services choose not to make their information available to nonsubscribers on the Web. Fair enough. Fortunately, there is plenty of information at the Morningstar site to help you decide which mutual funds to invest in.

Morningstar

If you want direct access to Morningstar's complete ratings of mutual funds, you'll have to pay for it. Fortunately, you can use Morningstar's fund report feature without cost to see the rating on any individual mutual fund. To look up the rating for a fund, go to the Morningstar Web page (www.morningstar.com) and type in either the name or ticker symbol of the fund in the [Quotes & Reports] search box. Voilà! Figure 7.6 shows the fund report available, including the Morningstar rating, a brief description of the fund's focus, annual performance, and listing of some of its major holdings. Morningstar assigns from one to five stars to a fund, depending on its relative strength. The top 10 percent of funds in a category get the top, five-star rating.

If you want to see a list of some of the top-rated funds within a particular category, use the Morningstar fund screener, which will display the top-rated funds in the category you select. Click [Fund Selector] from the main Web page, then use either the Basic Screen or Preset Screens to

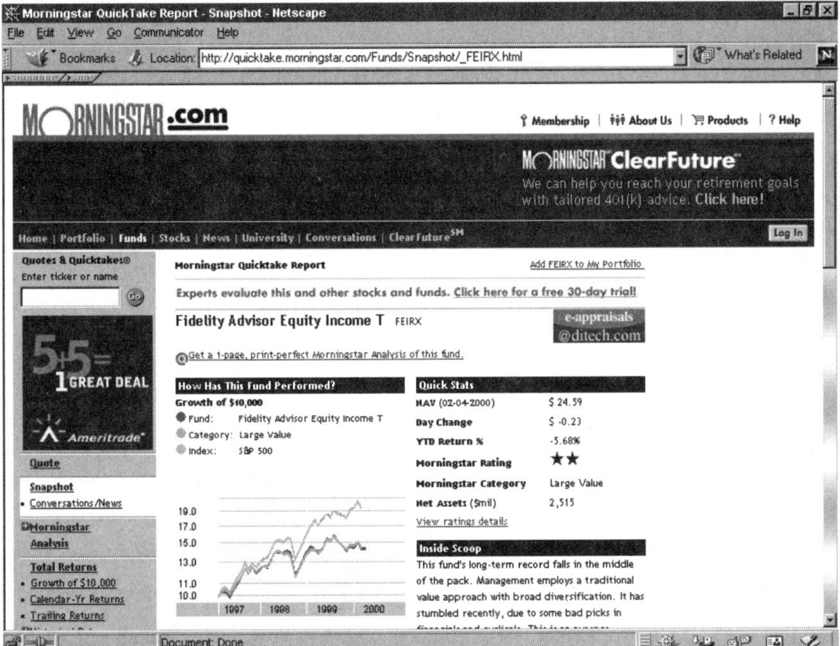

Figure 7.6. Morningstar.com provides information on and ratings of individual mutual funds.

choose a category of funds. The Basic Screen fund categories include U.S. stock funds, international stock funds, bond funds, or hybrid funds. Be sure to select Morningstar Rating from the [Select Screen Field] pull-down menu. The [Preset Screens] option lets you review the top-rated small and strong funds, "good 'n' grey" funds (those with managers who have been on the job for more than five years), "bargain bin" (those with low expense ratios), and so on.

Magazine Top Picks

Many investment-related magazines publish annual reviews of mutual funds, along with the editors' picks of the best funds, by category. Here are some of the better-known publications, along with pointers on how to find their mutual fund review issue.

- *Barron's* (www.barrons.com)—requires a subscription to the Wall Street Journal Interactive Edition (wsj.com). *Barron's* has an annual "Best of the Best" ranking of the top 100 mutual fund managers, which usually appears in a July issue.
- *Business Week* (www.businessweek.com)—Click [BW Investor] on the main Web page, then click [Interactive Scoreboard], which appears under the Mutual Funds column. The ratings are from Morningstar (described earlier in this chapter); the scoreboard shows the fund's rating and its performance, both short-term and prior 10 years. Funds can be sorted by total return, by rating, or by category. This scoreboard is updated monthly.
- *Money* (www.money.com)—Click [Mutual Fund Center] on the main Web page, which will take you to "The Money 100: The World's Best Mutual Funds." The table of the top 100 can be sorted by annual return, sales charge, annual expense, or minimum initial investment.
- *USA Today* (www.usatoday.com)—At the main Web page, click [Money], then click [Mutual Funds]. You can look up individual mutual funds, search for funds that meet your investment criteria, or read *USA Today*'s annual report on the best and worst mutual funds.
- *The Wall Street Journal* (www.wsj.com)—This site requires a subscription of $59 per year, a small price to pay for access to the newspaper of record for financial and investment news. At the main page, click [Money & Investing], then scroll down to the bottom of the page, where you'll see a listing for Mutual Fund Quarterly Reports. Click the link for U.S. (or

Europe or Asia, if that's what you're interested in). This will take you to a collection of recent articles on mutual funds as well as the *Journal*'s quarterly report on mutual funds.

Picking a Mutual Fund

You can use the ratings services described in the previous section to identify top performing mutual funds in a category, but you may need additional help in determining funds that will best meet your particular investment goals. Do you want a fund that invests in emerging markets? Will you only invest in highly rated funds? Is it important to invest in a fund that has been managed by the same person for at least three years? Do you want a fund that does not require a minimum investment of $1000 or more? And do you want to find the funds that meet *all* of these criteria? Don't panic—there are several Web sites that provide mutual fund screens that let you select by a number of variables. (Don't you wish you could search for a mate the same way? "Loyal, trustworthy, good sense of humor, willing to get up and make coffee before I wake up, and can cook a killer omelet.")

Quicken.com

Quicken and QuickBooks (for small businesses) are popular financial management software packages. Intuit, the publisher of Quicken and QuickBooks, maintains a well-stocked Web site at www.quicken.com, with investment information, portfolio management tools, and investment news. From the main Web page, click [Investing], then [Funds], and finally [Fund Finder] (try saying that fast five times!). As shown in Figure 7.7, the Fund Finder offers three search options:

- *Popular Searches*—which includes prebuilt searches for common criteria such as funds ranked highest for their 5- or 10-year performance, highly ranked small-cap funds, and best funds for beginning investors.
- *EasyStep Search*—which takes you through a five-step process of specifying the type of fund you are looking for.
- *Full Search*—which displays all the search options on a single page. If the Popular Searches page doesn't include the criteria you want, this is probably the best way to search the Quicken.com database of funds.

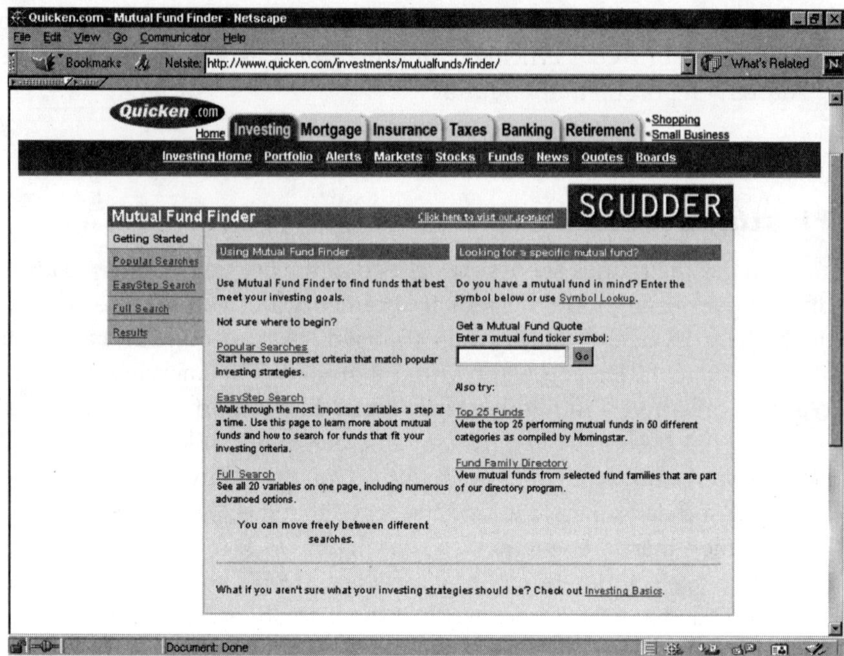

Figure 7.7. Quicken.com's Fund Finder offers three ways to screen mutual funds.

America Online's Screening Tool

All of the resources I've covered in this chapter are available on the Web, so they are also available to America Online subscribers. But AOL also offers a proprietary mutual fund screening guide available only to AOL members. From the Welcome screen, click the Personal Finance channel, then [Mutual Funds], then [Fund Screening]. You'll see two options at this point—a step-by-step screening tool for beginning investors, and a custom fund screening tool for investors who know what criteria they want to use in screening funds.

The step-by-step tool is particularly useful if you want an explanation of each aspect of a screening program. You're asked questions about your level of investment, what kinds of funds you want to invest in (e.g., socially responsible funds, index funds), the maximum amount of turnover you would accept in a fund, Morningstar rating, and so on. Each question comes with an explanation of what issues to consider before selecting an answer. The step-by-step tool also lets you set up a customized chart comparing selected funds—a nice touch.

E*Trade

Many of the online brokerages offer some type of mutual fund screener. One of the more powerful of these is the screening tool on E*Trade (www.etrade.com). From the main Web page, click [Mutual Funds], then [Power Search]. The advantages of the Power Search screen include the ability to:

- Make multiple selections within a single criterion, such as Growth OR Growth/Income OR Technology stocks
- Search by several risk measures
- Limit the search to mutual funds qualified in your state

See Figure 7.8 for the top portion of the Power Search mutual fund screening tool.

If you're confused by any of the choices, click [Help] at the top of the screen. This opens a separate browser window with an extensive collec-

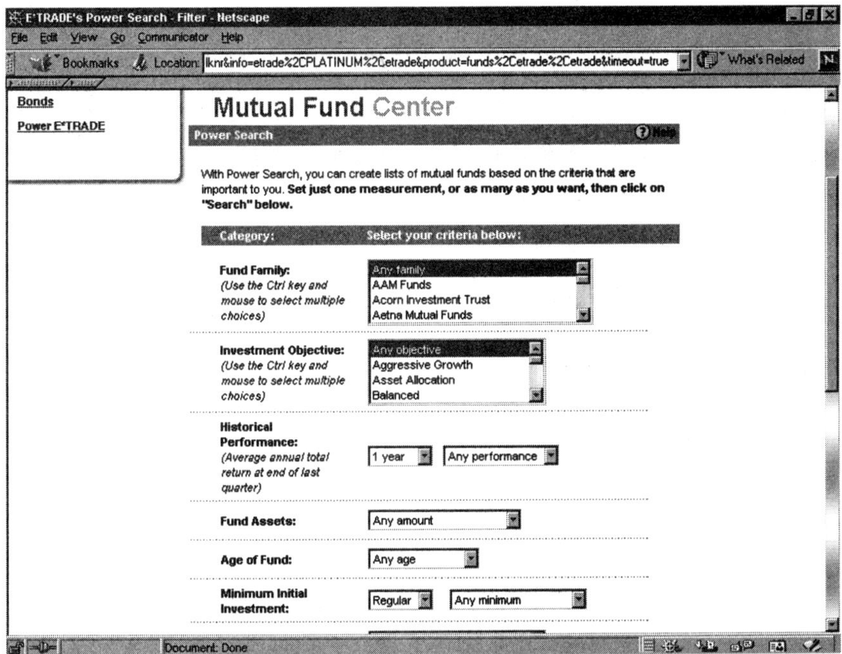

Figure 7.8. E*Trade has a mutual fund selection tool for experienced investors.

tion of search tips, definitions of mutual fund selection criteria terms, and advice on sorting, viewing, and comparing your search results.

CyberInvestor

What if you still haven't found a mutual fund screening site you like? Don't give up yet . . . CyberInvestor has a chart of almost 20 Web sites that provide information on mutual funds, including ratings, fund profiles, news, and screening tools. Start at www.CyberInvest.com; click on [Mutual Funds]; then select [Mutual Fund Research Guide]. You'll get a useful and detailed table of sites, as shown in Figure 7.9. You can click any of the links shown in the guide to go directly to the site listed.

Mutual Fund News

Now that you've identified likely mutual funds, you'll want to keep an eye on news of the funds and see what the industry analysts think. Start with *The Wall Street Journal*'s site, www.wsj.com. As noted earlier in this

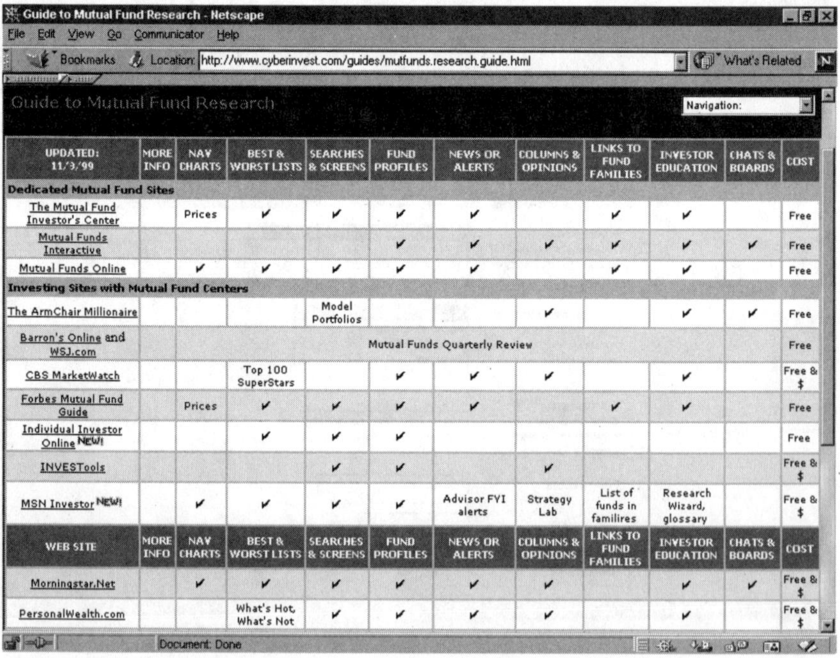

Guide to Mutual Fund Research

UPDATED: 11/3/99	MORE INFO	NAV CHARTS	BEST & WORST LISTS	SEARCHES & SCREENS	FUND PROFILES	NEWS OR ALERTS	COLUMNS & OPINIONS	LINKS TO FUND FAMILIES	INVESTOR EDUCATION	CHATS & BOARDS	COST
Dedicated Mutual Fund Sites											
The Mutual Fund Investor's Center		Prices	✔	✔	✔	✔		✔	✔		Free
Mutual Funds Interactive					✔	✔	✔	✔	✔	✔	Free
Mutual Funds Online		✔	✔	✔	✔	✔		✔	✔		Free
Investing Sites with Mutual Fund Centers											
The ArmChair Millionaire				Model Portfolios			✔		✔	✔	Free
Barron's Online and WSJ.com		Mutual Funds Quarterly Review									Free
CBS MarketWatch			Top 100 SuperStars		✔	✔	✔		✔		Free & $
Forbes Mutual Fund Guide		Prices	✔	✔	✔	✔		✔	✔		Free
Individual Investor Online NEW!			✔	✔	✔						Free
INVESTools				✔	✔		✔				Free & $
MSN Investor NEW!		✔	✔	✔	✔	Advisor FYI alerts	Strategy Lab	List of funds in familires	Research Wizard, glossary		Free & $
WEB SITE	MORE INFO	NAV CHARTS	BEST & WORST LISTS	SEARCHES & SCREENS	FUND PROFILES	NEWS OR ALERTS	COLUMNS & OPINIONS	LINKS TO FUND FAMILIES	INVESTOR EDUCATION	CHATS & BOARDS	COST
Morningstar.Net		✔	✔	✔	✔	✔	✔		✔	✔	Free & $
PersonalWealth.com			What's Hot, What's Not	✔	✔	✔	✔		✔		Free & $

Figure 7.9. CyberInvestor has a preformatted table of mutual fund Web sites.

chapter, it's a subscription-only site, so plan on paying $59 per year for access. Once you've signed on, click [Article Search], then type the fund name in the search box and click [Go]. The headlines of articles that mention the fund will be sorted by date, with the most current article appearing first. There is no charge for the full text of any of the articles.

If you want commentary on the performance of funds, head over to *Individual Investor*'s site at www.individualinvestor.com. At the main Web page, click [Funds]. This takes you to headlines of recent articles on mutual funds, including interviews with fund managers, discussions of the performance of various fund categories, and analyses of individual funds. One new article is posted each day, so visit the site once every week or so to keep updated.

For a different perspective on the mutual fund industry, try the Mutual Fund Café at www.mfcafe.com. This site is targeted to people who run and market mutual funds. Browsing the site is rather like being able to sit in on a group of fund managers talking shop, and is useful if you really want to know what drives the mutual fund industry. The whole site is very food-oriented, befitting its name. There's the Blue Plate Special (daily news item), Burgers 'n' Acquisitions (merger and acquisition activities), Legal Stew (regulatory news), and even Bean Counters (covering mutual fund accounting issues). Don't visit this site on an empty stomach! While the site sounds lighthearted, it's not light fare but substantial news and commentary on the mutual fund industry.

8
Advanced Investing

Most investors stick to the basics when it comes to risking their money—stocks, bonds and mutual funds, primarily. And most information on the Web focuses on these relatively traditional investment vehicles. But what about initial public offerings (IPOs), microcap stocks, real estate investment trusts (REITs), and day trading? While information on these investment opportunities is not as plentiful as is information on the more traditional avenues, some resources have emerged as useful investment tools. Keep in mind that these investments are inherently more risky than the lower-return, traditional options, so watch your footing as you make your way through the thicket of advanced investing.

Investing in IPOs

We've all heard the stories . . . get in on an IPO of a hot dot.com company, watch your investment triple before your very eyes, and make a killing. Back in the days before online investing, the big institutional investors were privately courted prior to an IPO and usually had first crack at the stock. Now, a number of electronic brokerages advertise that even we individual investors can participate in IPOs through their services. See the following section, "IPOs and E-Brokers," for information on some online brokerages that offer IPOs.

Before you jump onto the IPO bandwagon, you'll want to read up on what's involved, the special risks involved in IPO investment, and how to read the prospectus and decipher the fine print. CBS' MarketWatch has a useful four-part series on IPOs, covering the basics, the IPO process, and IPO investment strategies. Go to the MarketWatch site (cbs.marketwatch.com), scroll down to the bottom of the screen and click [More Tools & Data], then select [IPO Basics].

Hoover's IPO Central, described in the next section, also has a Beginner's Guide to IPO Investing. Head over to ipocentral.hoovers.com and click [Beginner's Guide]. A useful guide to understanding Securities and Exchange Commission filings related to IPOs is available by clicking [Meet the S-1]. (The S-1 is the SEC form filed for most initial public offerings.)

A good collection of IPO-related sites, maintained by a University of California, Los Angeles faculty member, is IPO Resources (www.iporesources.org). This site includes summaries of what IPOs are, articles on how to invest in them, online sources for upcoming IPOs, and pointers to IPO services and advisors. The site is low on graphics (see Figure 8.1) but high on content.

Watching for IPOs

If you're not a relative or close personal friend of the CEO of a company about to go public, how do you find out about the next hot IPO in time to

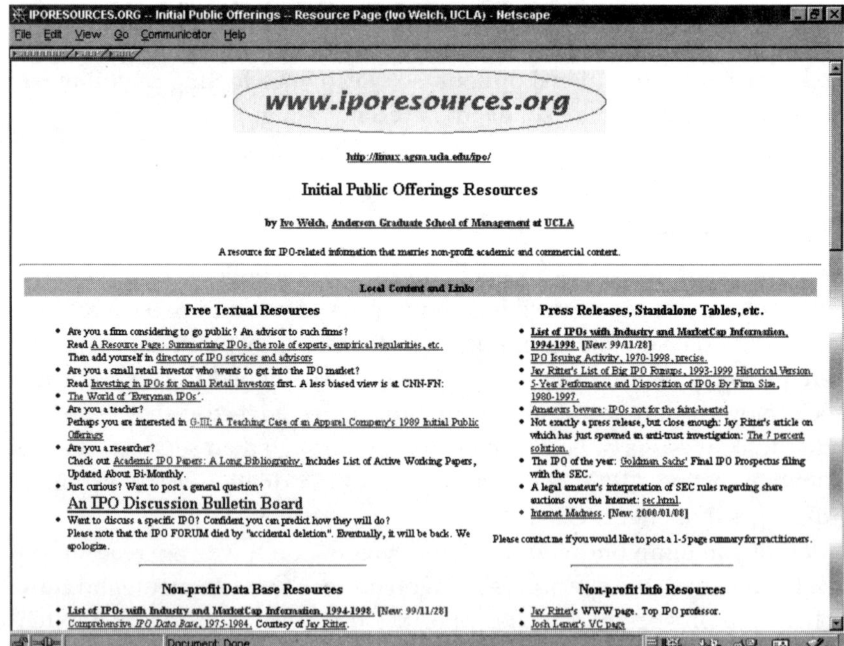

Figure 8.1. IPO Resources is a good collection of information on the world of initial public offerings.

get in on the ground floor? Your best bet may be one of the Web sites that track SEC filings and list upcoming IPOs.

Hoover's IPO Central (ipocentral.hoovers.com) is useful in that it not only lists the IPOs due out during the current week, but also links you to the company profiles in the Hoover's database. You must be a subscriber to read detailed information (and subscription is a reasonably modest $14.95 per month), but even the free company capsule gives a good overview. Subscribers can sign up for a weekly email update of upcoming IPOs. Another reason to subscribe is the ability to search for IPOs, using a number of criteria such as company location, underwriter, price range, or industry. Go to www.hoovers.com/search/forms/ipo/ to use the Advanced Search feature, once you've sign up as a subscriber. See Figure 8.2 for the top half of the search screen.

If you don't want to pay a subscription fee and you're looking for just the facts, ma'am, IPO-Home may meet your needs. This site, maintained by an investment firm, provides well-designed lists of upcoming IPOs and historical tables showing performance of prior IPOs. From the main page at www.ipo-fund.com, click one of the three IPO Calendar links—

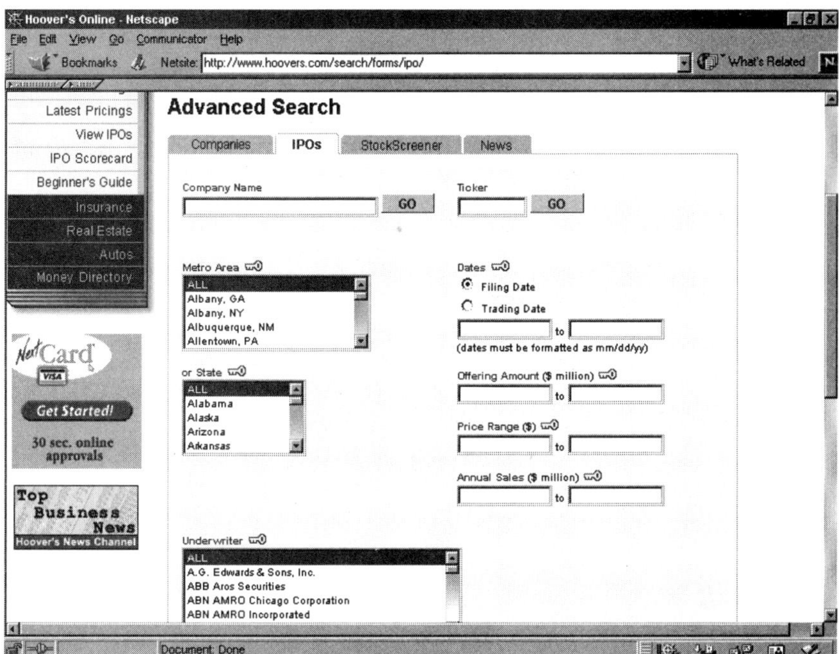

Figure 8.2. IPO Central on Hoover's lets you search using a number of criteria.

[This Week], [Next Week], or [Coming Attractions]—to see what's coming up. To review a list of past IPOs to see how well they performed, click [This Year's] IPO Pricings, or for more dramatic views of the IPO market, click the [Best] or [Worst] rankings links.

A third option for tracking upcoming IPOs is the IPO Express, available on Edgar Online (www.edgar-online.com). While most of the high-value information on Edgar Online requires a subscription, there's a lot in here that you can read before you're asked for an ID and password. From the main Web page, click [IPO Express]. At this point, you can scan upcoming offerings or search for IPOs of a certain size or in a specific region or industry; you can even limit your search to IPOs that are for "Internet-related" companies (click [IPO SuperSearch] to take advantage of all the search criteria options).

IPOs and E-Brokers

Not all online brokers offer IPOs, and those that do typically limit participation to investors who demonstrate that they are knowledgeable about the risks involved in this kind of more speculative investment. The following is a list of some e-brokerages that provide access to IPOs to online investors:

- *DLJ Direct.* Go to www.dljdirect.com and click [IPO Center] for information on who is eligible to participate in IPOs through DLJ Direct.
- *E*trade.* Go to www.etrade.com, click [IPOs], then [How to Participate] for details.
- *Fidelity Investments.* Go to www.fidelity.com, click [Brokerage], then click [Stocks, Bonds and Options], and finally click [IPOs and Fixed Income Offerings] for information on who is eligible to participate in IPOs.
- *Charles Schwab.* Schwab limits access to IPOs to its Signature Services accounts. To find out if you quality for Signature Service, start at the main Web page at www.schwab.com, click [Accounts & Services], then click [Go] under the "Schwab Signature Services" description.

Investing in REITs

Real Estate Investment Trusts, or REITs, are trusts that invest in various types of real estate—mortgages as well as actual property such as shopping centers, office buildings, warehouses, and so on. Mortgage REITs invest in mortgages and lend money to real estate owners; equity REITs limit their holdings to real estate property and receive most of their income from rent; and hybrid REITs include a combination of the two. REITs' shares are traded on exchanges and pay dividends just like common stock; there are even mutual funds that specialize in REIT investments. REITs are regulated by the U.S. Securities and Exchange Commission, so, just as with common stock, be sure to read the 10-K (annual financial statement) and proxy statement before considering investing in a REIT.

REITs have come into favor in the past five years or so with some investors, with the upswing in real estate markets. For background on how REITs work, check out the National Association of Real Estate Investment Trusts at www.nareit.com. At the main Web page, move your mouse over any of the topics and you'll see a drop-down menu appear for selections within that topic, as shown in Figure 8.3. The [About REITs] subject provides a glossary and Frequently Asked Questions file, along

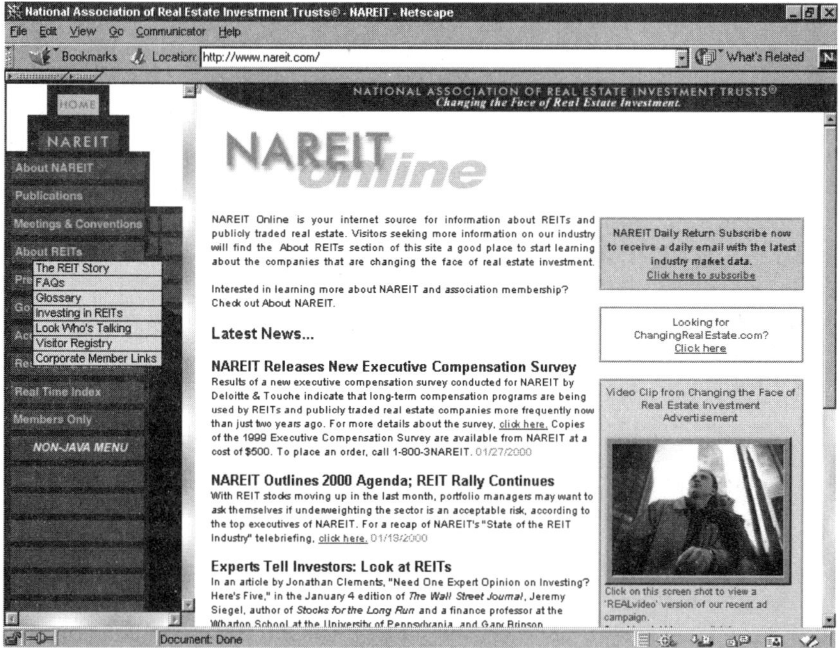

Figure 8.3. The National Association of Real Estate Investment Trusts provides information on REITs.

with recent news about the REIT industry. Keep in mind that since this is an association of and for REITs, it's likely to present a fairly optimistic picture of the benefits of investing in REITs.

And how do you identify REITs? They're not as closely covered in the usual investment news sources, and they don't have the same buzz-factor as initial public offerings or other more glamorous investment vehicles. REITNet Online, a Web-based service developed by a financial information service company, has a REIT Locator service that lets you search for trusts meeting several broad search criteria such as type of REIT, type of real estate investments, and whether the REIT focuses more on investment or property. Click on the link to the REIT Locator from the main Web page at www.reitnet.com. If you want more detailed information or want to conduct more sophisticated research, REITSearch—a premium search service—is available for a monthly fee.

Microcap Stocks

Some investors have nerves of steel; others hesitate to invest in anything that doesn't guarantee them a modest but steady return year after year. Only those on the far end of the steel-nerve spectrum invest in microcap stocks—stocks with microcapitalization, meaning the total value of the company's stock is under $100 million or so. In fact, the average market cap of microcap stocks is more like $25 million. Usually, these stocks have very low prices, and the price can fluctuate wildly. Since companies with assets of less than $10 million don't have to file reports with the Securities and Exchange Commission, it can be difficult to get reliable information on companies offering microcap stock. If you don't find any information in the SEC's EDGAR database (edgar.sec.gov) on a stock you're considering, contact the company directly and ask for information from its investor relations department. Keep in mind that even if a company doesn't have to file with the SEC, it may have to submit financial reports to state regulatory agencies. See Chapter 9 for guidance on tracking down state securities regulatory offices.

There often tends to be only a spotty market for a microcap stock, which means that it's a prime target for fraud. Some of the common techniques of scam artists include issuing press releases that include inflated promises of new products or services or exaggerated sales figures; paid promoters hyping the stock in newsletters, on investment forums on the Net, or in Usenet newsgroups; and boiler rooms of sales people paid to hype the stock through cold-calling.

The U.S. Securities and Exchange Commission has a guide for investors interested in microcap stocks, which takes a somewhat cautionary tone—after all, it's the SEC that has to go after microcap companies that defraud or mislead their investors. At the main SEC page (www.sec.gov), click [Investor Education], then [Search Key Topics], and scroll down the list of topics until you find *Microcap Stock.* While you're at it, you can scroll through the rest of the titles to see if any of the other consumer-oriented papers interest you. The SEC's Investor Education division produces clearly-written guides on a number of investment-related topics.

You can read a slightly more optimistic perspective on microcap investing and get tips on researching microcap stocks from the *Smallcap Investor News,* an email newsletter and electronic forum for smallcap/microcap investors. This newsletter is produced by the folks at FinancialWeb, and their site provides a good collection of resources for anyone interested in microcap investing. Start at the main FinancialWeb site at, yes, www.financialweb.com, then click [Smallcap Investor], listed under the "Editorial" heading. See Figure 8.4 for the SmallCap Investor page.

Figure 8.4. The Smallcap Investor newsletter and Web site has information on small/microcap investing.

Day Trading

Anyone who's read a newspaper in the last year has heard of both the splendor and the horror of day trading: either it's the way to make a quick killing or it's a way to sustain serious losses. Actually, it's both, but the odds are against you. Betting on the fluctuations of a stock's price during the course of the day can result in profit, but that can easily be eaten up by commissions and by downturns in the price of a stock. Several industry observers have compared day trading to gambling, with the chances of winning big about as slim as winning the lottery.

For starters, read the SEC's cautionary publication "Day Trading: Your Dollars at Risk," at www.sec.gov/consumer/daytips.htm. It notes that "day traders typically suffer severe financial losses in their first months of trading, and many never graduate to profit-making status."

The North American Securities Administrators Association, an organization of the administrators in state securities regulatory agencies, produced a report in August 1999 on day trading firms and the day trading industry. Their conclusion? Most investors will lose money day trading. For the full text of the report, start at the NASAA's Web site (www.nasaa.org), and click [Report: Findings & Recommendations, 8/9/99].

For a different perspective on day trading, see the 10-part series of articles, titled "Becoming a Trader," which focuses on what's involved in getting into day trading full time. This series was written by the expert guide who maintains the day trading section of About.com, the collection of human-built guides to the Net. Start at daytrading.about.com and click [So You Wanna Be a Trader], shown in Figure 8.5.

Want to Play?

Once you've fastened your seatbelt and prepared for the wild ride, you can join online discussions with other day traders (although one wonders how they have time for participation in online forums when they should be monitoring the market). In any event, #DayTraders maintains a site for day traders that contains a number of links to current financial news as well as a live chat room. Head over to www.daytraders.org and click [Live] to monitor chat, and [Join] for instructions on participating.

Most electronic brokers are not geared toward day trading. About.com has a list of some e-brokers who focus on day traders. Start at

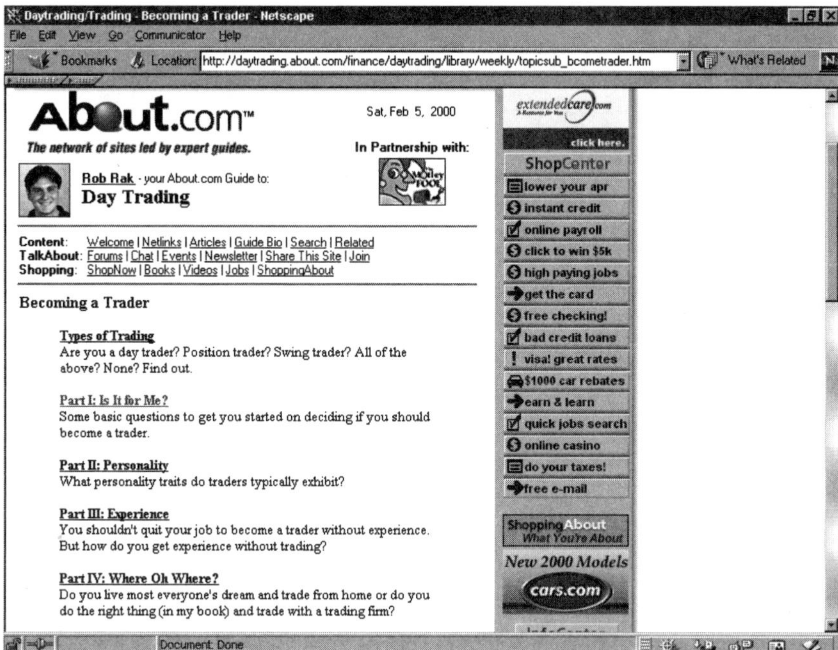

Figure 8.5. About.com has a useful 10-part series on day trading.

daytrading.about.com and click [Brokers], then [Day Trading Brokers]. Yahoo! also has a category for day trading firms; start at the main Web page (www.yahoo.com), click [Business and Economy], then [Companies], then [Financial Services], then [Investment Services], then [Brokerages], and finally [Daytrading]. Whew!

9

Uncle Sam and Financial Information

When most of us think of the federal government in the context of financial information, the Internal Revenue Service comes to mind. Fortunately, not only does the IRS provide useful information for investors, but other branches of the federal government have well-stocked Web sites as well. The Securities and Exchange Commission has a tremendous amount of information filed *by* publicly traded companies; state governments often provide similar information on a local level. This chapter will examine the various sources for government information and will try to put to a test the old saying, "We're from the government and we're here to help."

As with finding anything on the Web, the first thing to ask yourself is, "Who would care about this information?" Answering this will guide you to the most likely sources—this is even more the case with government agencies than it is with the Web in general.

U.S. Securities and Exchange Commission

The SEC was established in 1933 following the enactment of laws requiring companies to disclose detailed financial information to potential investors. There is an alphabet soup of forms that are filed by publicly held companies, companies about to go public, investment companies, and related organizations. (The list of the forms required to be filed electronically on the SEC's Web site is 11 pages long!) Some of the reports that must be filed with the SEC are of particular use to investor and financial researchers. They include:

- *10-K*—the annual report of how the company fared. A 10-K form is not to be confused with a company's Annual Report, that glossy public relations piece designed to convince clients, investors, and employees that the company is doing well. Rather, the 10-K must disclose the financial status of the company, describe the competitive and regulatory environment the company is in and the products or services it provides, disclose the risks that an investor is taking when investing in this company's stock, any significant legal proceedings in which the company is involved, and so on.
- *10-Q*—the quarterly equivalent to a 10-K form, disclosing unaudited quarterly financial statements and providing a continuing report on the company's financial status during the year.
- *8-K*—a current report form that discloses any significant event that would have an effect on investors. This form is filed as the event occurs, so it is more current than a 10-K or 10-Q. Examples of events disclosed in a Form 8-K include a merger with another company, a buyback of stock, or a major lawsuit against the company.
- *Prospectus* or *S-1 Form*—the forms used when an issue of securities is going to be sold to the public. These forms describe the company, its anticipated growth in the market, the risks involved in investing in the company (including such factors as net losses in prior years), the company's current financial status, and related information. Most SEC filings are written by lawyers, and tend to be somewhat dense. However, the SEC now requires that registration statements be written in "definite, concrete everyday language" free of legal jargon. As companies (and their lawyers) become accustomed to these rules, we should start to see more clearly written filings.
- *Proxy Statement*—also known as a Schedule 14A. This form is sent out to all shareholders before an annual meeting. Its official purpose is to enable shareholders to vote on any pending matters if they cannot appear in person. Its use for investors is in the background information provided on the candidates for the board of directors and on the executive officers of the company, including their ages, the number of shares they hold in the company, how long they have worked for the company and where they were previously employed, and their annual compensation.

Note that you can request any of these forms directly from the company's investor relations office. However, let me introduce you to EDGAR.

Who's EDGAR?

For years, the SEC filings were a hidden treasure trove of information, available only to researchers who were within driving distance of one of the SEC's regional offices or to those willing to pay $10 or $15 to obtain the material from a professional online service. However, as of May 1996, all companies are required to file certain forms electronically. The SEC's Electronic Data Gathering, Analysis, and Retrieval system, known as EDGAR, makes these forms available at edgar.sec.gov.

Which forms are on EDGAR? Fortunately, all of the ones just listed, 10-Ks, 10-Qs, 8-Ks, registration statements, and proxy statements, are available 24 hours after they have been filed with the SEC. They are hardly an example of good desktop publishing—the filings are in plain text, with some additional formatting codes thrown in to the mix. See Figure 9.1 for an example of what an EDGAR filing looks like.

While they may not be easy on the eyes, these EDGAR filings are great sources of inside information on a company—how it is doing financially, what challenges it faces in the industry, and background information on the major executives.

So, how do you find these documents? You have a few options at the SEC site itself. The principal way of searching is to click [Search EDGAR Archives] at the main Web page. The next screen will explain the basics of how to search the site and give you the option to [Search the EDGAR Archives] or to conduct a [Quick Forms Lookup]. (There are also specialized search options at the bottom of the page.) The search of the EDGAR archives is a bit misleading—the search actually only looks in the *header* area, which includes the company name, address, SIC code, and so on. If you know what you are looking for—the latest filings from Amazon.com, for example—use the [Quick Forms Lookup] option. This search screen enables you to limit your search to a particular form and by date, or you can search for all filings by a company. See Figure 9.2 for an example of an EDGAR search.

Commercial Versions of EDGAR

While the SEC EDGAR database is a great resource—and you can't beat the price—there are times when it simply cannot provide you with all of

U.S. Car Market Shares*					
	Years Ended December 31,				
	1998	1997	1996	1995	1994
U.S. Manufacturers (Including Imports)					
Ford	19.2%	19.7%	20.6%	20.9%	21.8%
General Motors	29.8	32.2	32.3	33.9	34.0
Chrysler**	9.1	8.9	9.8	9.1	9.0
Total U.S. Manufacturers	58.1	60.8	62.7	63.9	64.8
Foreign-Based Manufacturers***					
Japanese	31.8	30.9	30.0	29.7	29.6
All Other	10.1	8.3	7.3	6.4	5.6
Total Foreign-Based Manufacturers	41.9	39.2	37.3	36.1	35.2
Total U.S. Car Retail Deliveries	100.0%	100.0%	100.0%	100.0%	100.0%

Figure 9.1. EDGAR filings from the SEC are functional but not presentation quality.

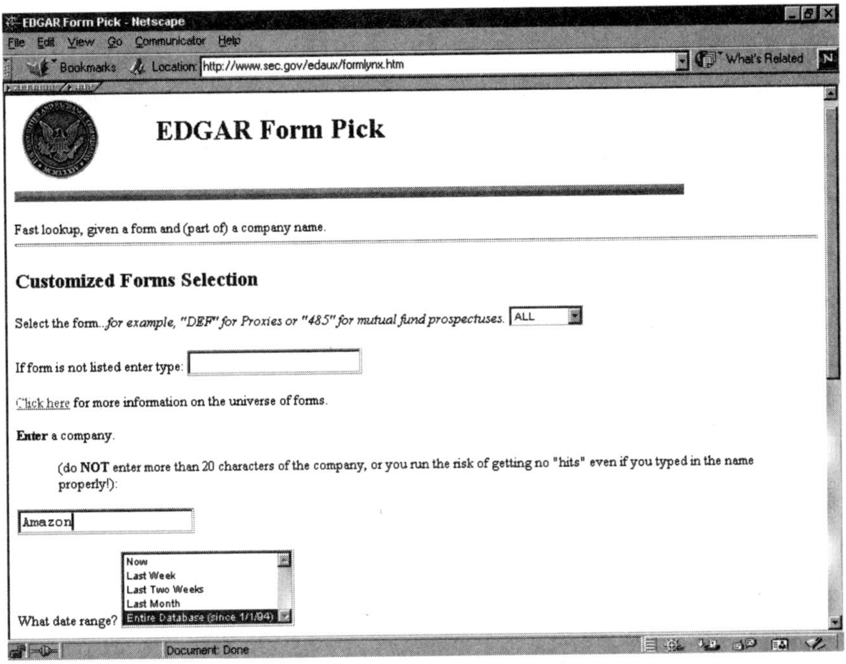

Figure 9.2. The Quick Forms Lookup lets you search for proxy statements filed by Amazon.com.

the search tools you need. Say you are looking for information on all the companies where a certain person serves on the board of directors, or any initial public offerings filed within the last month by companies that manufacture medical diagnostic equipment. You cannot run these kinds of searches at the SEC's site. You cannot search by ticker symbol, nor can you set up an automatic alerting service that notifies you when a company you are monitoring has submitted a form to the SEC. Note, too, that the SEC EDGAR site delays the release of filings for 24 hours. If you need to get a copy of a prospectus that was filed today, you will not be able to find it on the SEC's EDGAR database.

For any of these types of searches, you will need to go to one of the commercial versions of EDGAR that offer live or real-time access to EDGAR filings and power search tools to dig out the information you need from the EDGAR database. Many of these commercial sites offer a subset of the EDGAR database for free. You can often run your search and display the results at no charge; you will only be asked for your credit card number when you want to see a current day's filing, when you want to download a filing in a presentation-quality format, or when you want to set up a customized alerting service. Shop around for the best fee-based EDGAR service for you, based on your needs for timeliness, formatting, and other value-added features.

Some of the commercial EDGAR services include:

- Disclosure's EDGAR Access (edgar.disclosure.com/ea/)—$4.95 per month for 25 reports, additional reports $2 each
- EDGAR Online (www.edgar-online.com)—$9.95 to $99.95 per month, depending on the amount of information needed
- LIVEDGAR (www.livedgar.com)—$10 per search session (no limit to the number of searches) plus $1 per minute

See Figure 9.3 for an example of searching the EDGAR Access site for the prospectuses filed within the last month by any apparel companies (Standard Industrial Classification code 2300).

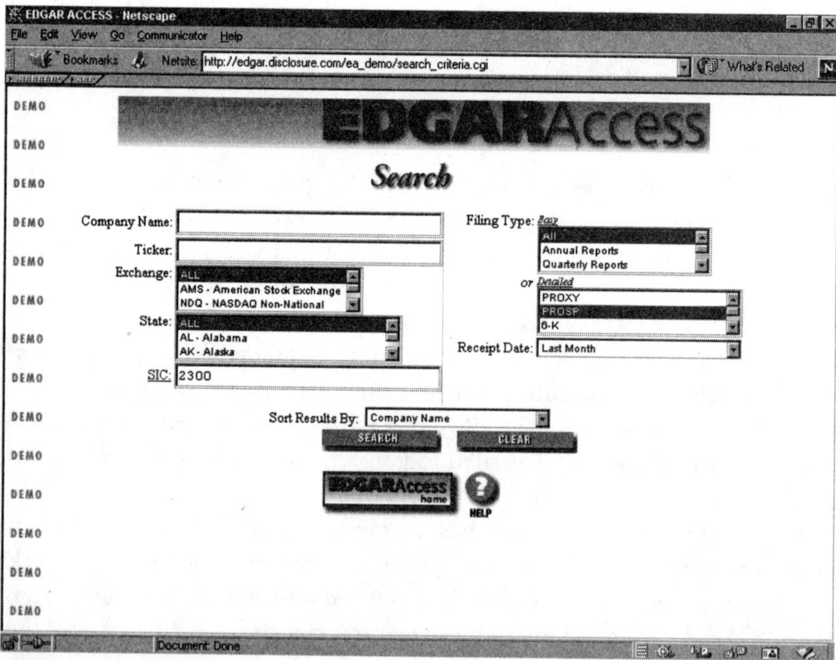

Figure 9.3. EDGAR Access lets you construct a more complex search than is possible on the SEC's site.

What About the States?

Every state regulates companies incorporated within that state, although there is no equivalent of the EDGAR database on the state level. You can at least confirm basic information, though, for companies that are incorporated but not publicly traded, and hence not regulated by the SEC. The Library of Congress has a good directory of state government Web sites, broken out by state. Start at lcweb.loc.gov and click [Using the Library]. At the next screen, click [Explore the Internet], then [State and Local Governments]. This will take you to a set of links for each of the 50 states, which in turn will let you explore a particular state government's Web page. Some states maintain thorough telephone directories; at the least, you should be able to find the office that regulates companies. Look for a Corporations Commission, Department of Commerce, Secretary of State, or Business Services Division (there isn't much consistency in what the regulatory body is called from one state to another).

The information available on states' Web sites varies considerably. To take one example, Washington State allows searches by company name and includes basic information on the company. See Figure 9.4 for

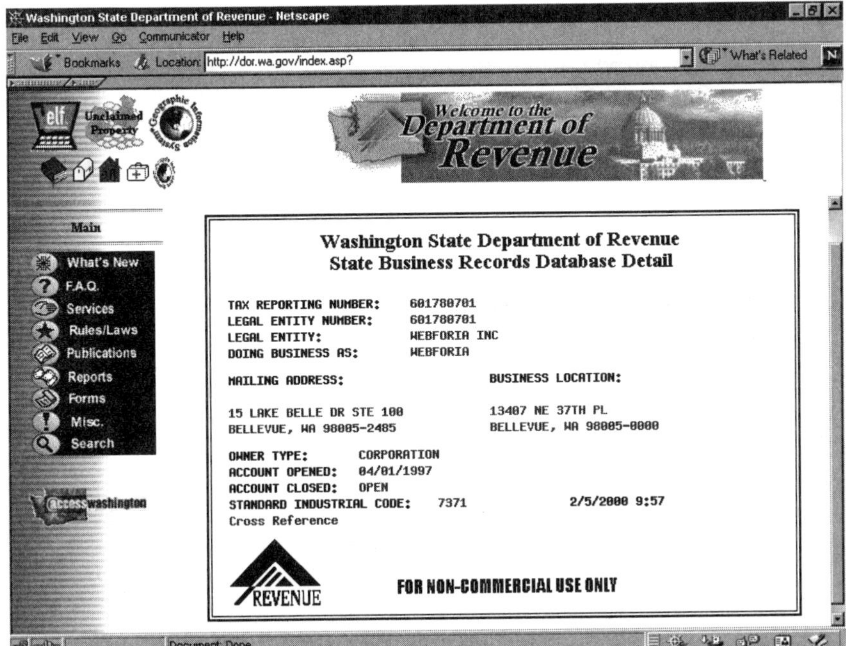

Figure 9.4. Washington State lets you look up basic information on companies incorporated in the state.

the results of a search for companies with the word "Webforia" in their names.

U.S. Internal Revenue Service

The IRS has an unexpectedly whimsical Web site (www.irs.ustreas.gov), updated frequently, with news items describing new features of tax laws, information on how to file your return electronically, and how the IRS's Taxpayer Advocate can help you resolve problems with the IRS. See Figure 9.5 for an example of the main IRS Web page.

This site is useful if you need copies of IRS forms or publications, information on the impact of new tax laws on your personal or business taxes, or help with electronic filing. It even has a What's Hot section, that begins "Here's one cool place to check out the hottest things going on at the Internal Revenue Service." Forget the stereotypes of green eyeshades and humor-impaired IRS agents. So, for example, if it's the day before taxes are due and you realize that you need an extension of time to get those taxes done, you

Figure 9.5. The front page of the IRS's Web site is designed as a tabloid newspaper.

can download IRS form 4868 (Application for Automatic Extension of Time to File U.S. Individual Income Tax Return) in Adobe Acrobat (PDF) or PostScript format, print it off, mail it in, and breathe a sigh of relief.

To navigate the IRS site, select the option you want at the bottom of the Digital Daily page. If you are looking for a tax form and do not know the form number, your best option will be to click [Forms & Pubs], then select [Search For a Form or Publication]. Type in only as much of a key word as you need (to find the right form for an extension of time, I just typed in *exten,* in order find the mention of *extension of time* or *extend the time* to file). You will see a list of the forms and publications that contain that word; click on the link to the appropriate publication, and the form will be downloaded to your PC.

Social Security Administration

Remember that mysterious "FICA" deduction in your paycheck? It looks like just another tax, along with the withholding for your federal and state taxes, for example. But at least in theory, you're earning credits that count toward eligibility for Social Security benefits. The most obvious one, of course, is the check you get every month if you retire after reaching the age of 65 (you receive a reduced amount if you retire at ages 62 through 64). Social Security also pays benefits if you become seriously disabled or, under certain circumstances, to your survivors when you die.

When planning for your retirement, you will want to know how much income you can expect from Social Security. Head over to www.ssa.gov for general information about the Social Security Administration, an overview of the benefits available, and information on the Social Security Statement—the report that tells you what you will receive in Social Security retirement and disability benefits, based on your earnings to date. It is a smart idea to order this, even if you are not thinking of retiring soon. It's a good way to check the SSA's records and make sure that it has credited your earnings properly.

You can request a copy of your Social Security Statement via the Social Security Web site, or you can download the PDF file to fill out the material and mail the request in. (See Chapter 1 for a description of PDF files.) Click the [Social Security Statement] at the main SSA Web page for both options. The report will be sent to you via snail mail within a couple of weeks; unfortunately, you cannot receive the information electronically. Figure 9.6 shows the first screen of the request form.

Social Security Statement - Netscape

File Edit View Go Communicator Help

Bookmarks Location: https://s3abaca.ssa.gov/pro/batch-pebes/npping.cgi What's Related

SOCIAL SECURITY statement

Form Approved:
OMB No. 0960

Warning!
If you are in a public place or are otherwise concerned about others viewing your information, we strongly advise exiting your Web browser upon completion of your Social Security Statement request.

Complete the following web form to submit your Social Security Statement request over the Internet.
Please do NOT mail us paper copies of this web form.

PLEASE DO NOT USE PUNCTUATION IN ANY BOX BELOW

Do you wish to receive your Social Security Statement in English or Spanish? MANDATORY	English Spanish	Please select one.

Please type your name and Social Security Number as shown on your Social Security Card.
We cannot process your request without a valid Social Security Number.

First Name: MANDATORY		(1-15 alphabetic characters)
Middle Initial: OPTIONAL		(None or 1 alphabetic character)
		(1-20 alphabetic characters)

Document: Done

Figure 9.6. You can request an estimate of your Social Security retirement benefits online.

U.S. Department of Commerce

Not surprisingly, the Commerce Department is a rich repository of business-related information, supported by your tax dollars. One of the best-known bureaus within Commerce is the Bureau of the Census (www.census.gov). While you may be most familiar with its once-a-decade questionnaire that asks for your age, sex, race, and how long you have lived at your present address, the Census Bureau collects information on a wide variety of finance-related topics as well.

Census Bureau

Every five years, the Census Bureau conducts its Economic Census, collecting information on all aspects of the U.S. economy. This information often takes several years to analyze, collate, and publish, so do not expect to find up-to-the-minute statistics. On the other hand, where else can you find such a comprehensive collection of data on the U.S. economy, at no charge?

While it sounds like Census results would be pretty dry reading, there is valuable business intelligence there if you know to look for it. Examples of what you can do with the information in the Economic Census include:

- Compare a company's operating expenses to the industry average, to see if the company's expenses are out of line.
- Calculate market share by dividing a company's sales by the state totals for similar businesses.
- Evaluate growth of a company's revenue by examining the growth of the industry over the past five years.

See Figure 9.7 for a sample of the statistics available through the Census Bureau.

Bureau of Economic Analysis

Based on the agency's name, you might think that the Bureau of Economic Analysis (www.bea.doc.gov) is about as exciting as a certified public

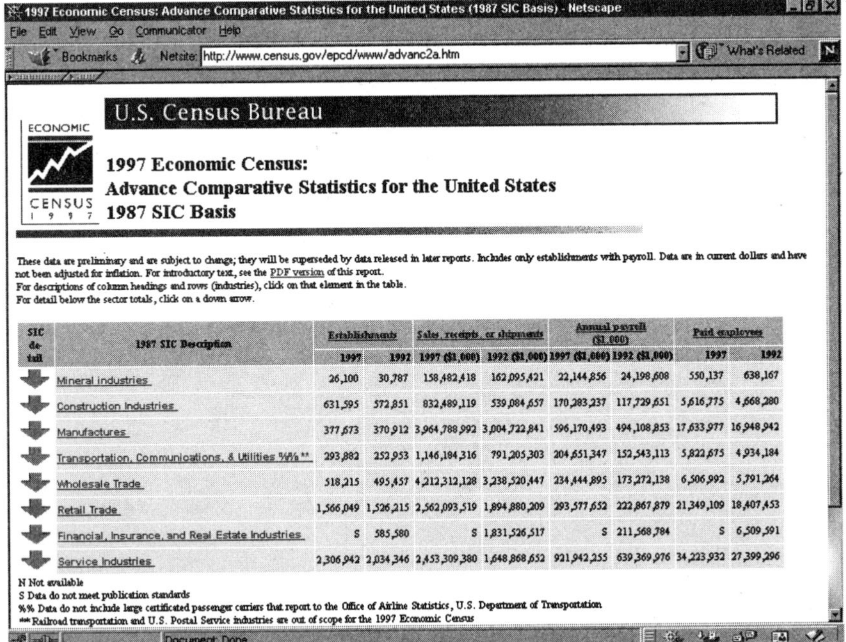

1997 Economic Census: Advance Comparative Statistics for the United States (1987 SIC Basis) - Netscape

http://www.census.gov/epcd/www/advanc2a.htm

U.S. Census Bureau

1997 Economic Census:
Advance Comparative Statistics for the United States
1987 SIC Basis

These data are preliminary and are subject to change; they will be superseded by data released in later reports. Includes only establishments with payroll. Data are in current dollars and have not been adjusted for inflation. For introductory text, see the PDF version of this report.
For descriptions of column headings and rows (industries), click on that element in the table.
For detail below the sector totals, click on a down arrow.

SIC detail	1987 SIC Description	Establishments		Sales, receipts, or shipments		Annual payroll ($1,000)		Paid employees	
		1997	1992	1997 ($1,000)	1992 ($1,000)	1997 ($1,000)	1992 ($1,000)	1997	1992
	Mineral industries	26,100	30,787	158,482,418	162,095,421	22,144,856	24,198,608	550,137	638,167
	Construction Industries	631,595	572,851	832,489,119	539,084,657	170,283,237	117,729,651	5,616,775	4,668,280
	Manufactures	377,673	370,912	3,964,788,992	3,004,722,841	596,170,493	494,108,853	17,633,977	16,948,942
	Transportation, Communications, & Utilities %% **	293,882	252,953	1,146,184,316	791,205,303	204,651,347	152,543,113	5,822,675	4,934,184
	Wholesale Trade	518,215	495,457	4,212,312,128	3,238,520,447	234,444,895	173,272,138	6,506,992	5,791,264
	Retail Trade	1,566,049	1,526,215	2,562,093,519	1,894,880,209	293,577,652	222,867,879	21,349,109	18,407,453
	Financial, Insurance, and Real Estate Industries	S	585,580	S	1,831,526,517	S	211,568,784	S	6,509,591
	Service Industries	2,306,942	2,034,346	2,453,309,380	1,648,868,652	921,942,255	639,369,976	34,223,932	27,399,296

N Not available
S Data do not meet publication standards
%% Data do not include large certificated passenger carriers that report to the Office of Airline Statistics, U.S. Department of Transportation
** Railroad transportation and U.S. Postal Service industries are out of scope for the 1997 Economic Census

Document: Done

Figure 9.7. Use the Census Bureau's Economic Census to find information on growth within industries.

accountant. And, indeed, the BEA does describe itself at its Web site as "the nation's economic accountant." An indication of its just-the-facts attitude is its main Web page—low on graphics, high on links to hard statistics—shown in Figure 9.8.

The BEA's best-known product is the calculation of the value of the GDP, or gross domestic product. But some of its other publications are also of use to investors or financial researchers. The *Survey of Current Business,* a monthly subscription-based publication, is a resource for current economic information. The table of contents to each issue is available through the BEA site, and selected articles are available in full text, even to nonsubscribers. Want information on what areas of the country have the fastest growing disposable personal income? Want to see the average change in revenue from quarter to quarter in the retail industry? Try looking through the recent issues of the *Survey of Current Business* for answers.

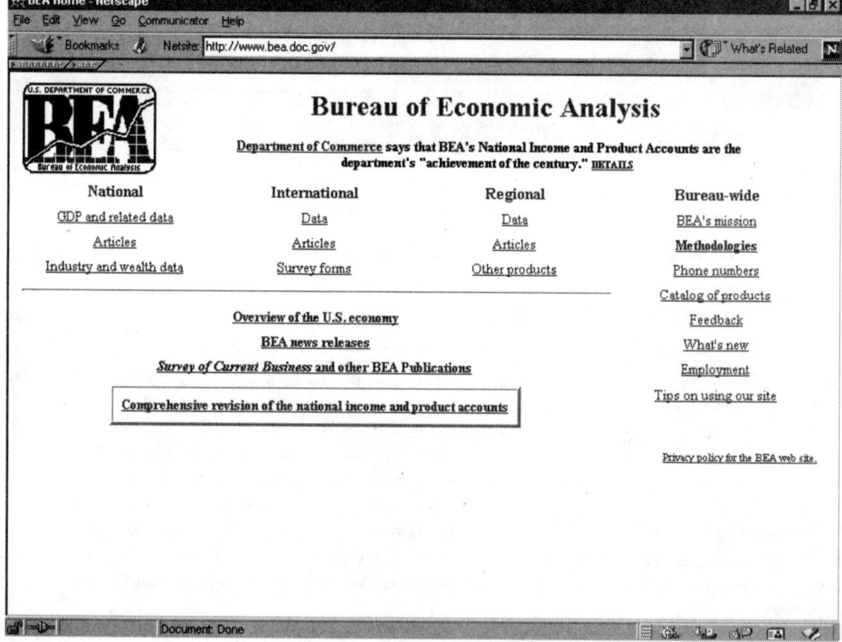

Figure 9.8. The Bureau of Economic Analysis provides statistics on business trends.

Stat-USA

Stat-USA is the fee-based service of the Department of Commerce, located at www.stat-usa.gov. The annual subscription price is $150 per year, or $50 per quarter. You can also purchase Stat-USA reports on an as-needed basis, although if you plan on buying more than a couple of reports the all-you-can-eat subscription plan is probably a better buy. Stat-USA contains a large collection of international market research reports, discussions of the best international market for a specific product, programs to encourage U.S. companies to develop import and export trade, and guides to doing business abroad.

The reports available in Stat-USA are usually written by U.S. government employees located in the countries being studied. Reports include information on local government contacts, trade magazines, industry associations, and upcoming expos and conferences. Whether you want information on the market for importing pet food in France or health foods to Thailand, Stat-USA probably has a report that addresses it. See Figure 9.9 for a summary of the information available on Stat-USA.

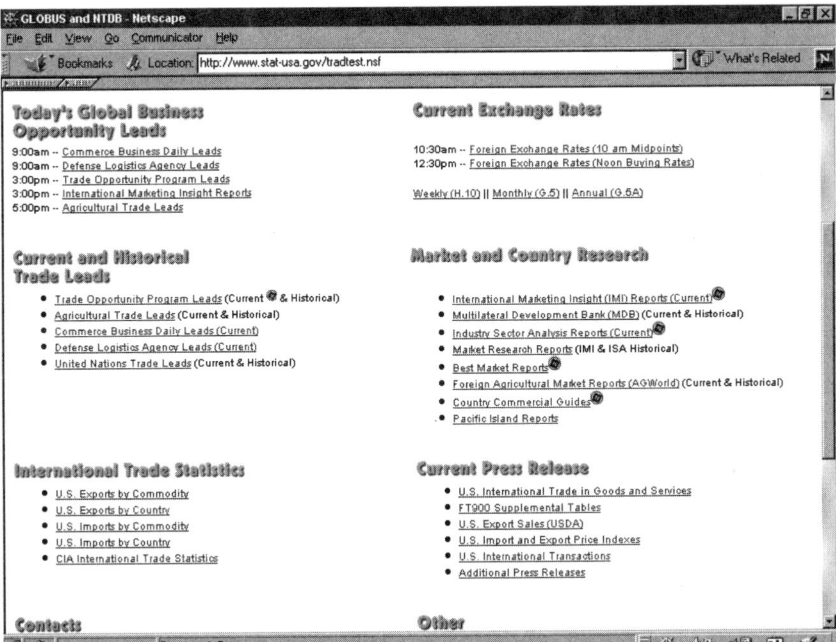

Figure 9.9. Stat-USA has reports on best overseas markets for a product, leads on business opportunities, and market research on international markets.

Other Sources for Economic Statistics and Forecasts

The federal government collects statistics on everything from the year's almond crop to the percentage of households with telephones. By thinking about which agency might need to collect information, you can often guess where to go for economic forecasts. For example, every year Congress has to approve a budget. In order to do so, the legislators need projections of sales and income tax payments and other sources of revenue. The Congressional Budget Office (www.cbo.gov) provides annual reports on the state of the U.S. economy, complete with 10-year projections of Treasury bill rates, unemployment rate, corporate profits, and so on. Figure 9.10 shows the CBO's main site, along with a listing of recent CBO publications.

Just as Yahoo! is one of the best catalogs of information on the Web, FedWorld (www.fedworld.gov) is a well-designed site for finding information from federal government sources. FedWorld is maintained by the

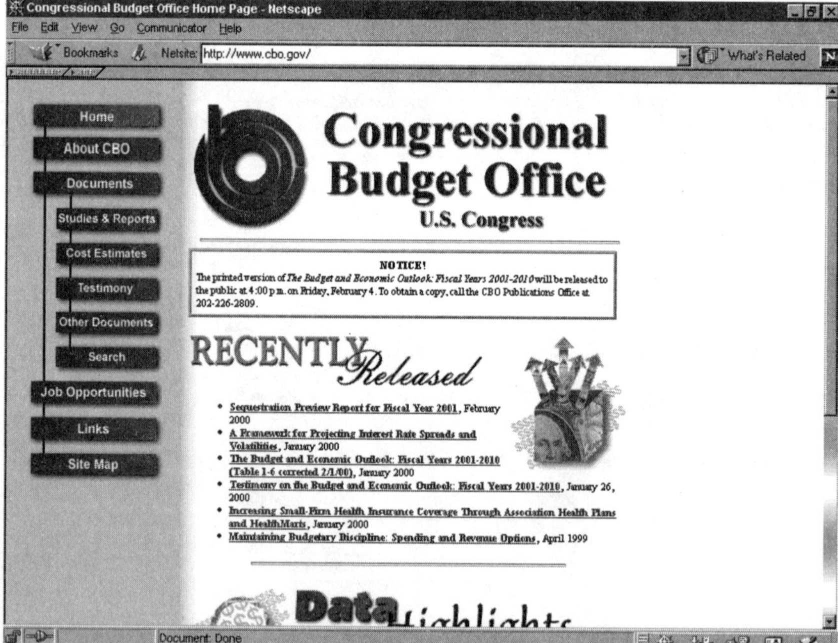

Figure 9.10. The Congressional Budget Office provides 10-year projections on the economy.

U.S. Department of Commerce but contains links to material provided by many federal, state, and local agencies. Note that not all the information in FedWorld is free; there also is information on printed reports that you can purchase, usually directly from the issuing agency.

A similar one-stop-shopping site, focused specifically on statistics generated by federal agencies, is FedStats (www.fedstats.gov). Whether you want information on the number of grade school students, broken down by state, or demographic information on recreational fishermen in South Carolina, you can find a pointer to the source at FedStats. This is a useful site if you want to determine the potential market for a company's product (just how many grade school kids are there in Missouri, who might buy that new cereal product?) or the economic impact of an industry to an area.

Many other countries have similar collections of statistical info. If you want projections of economic growth in a particular country, start with Yahoo!, drilling down either from the country category or from the

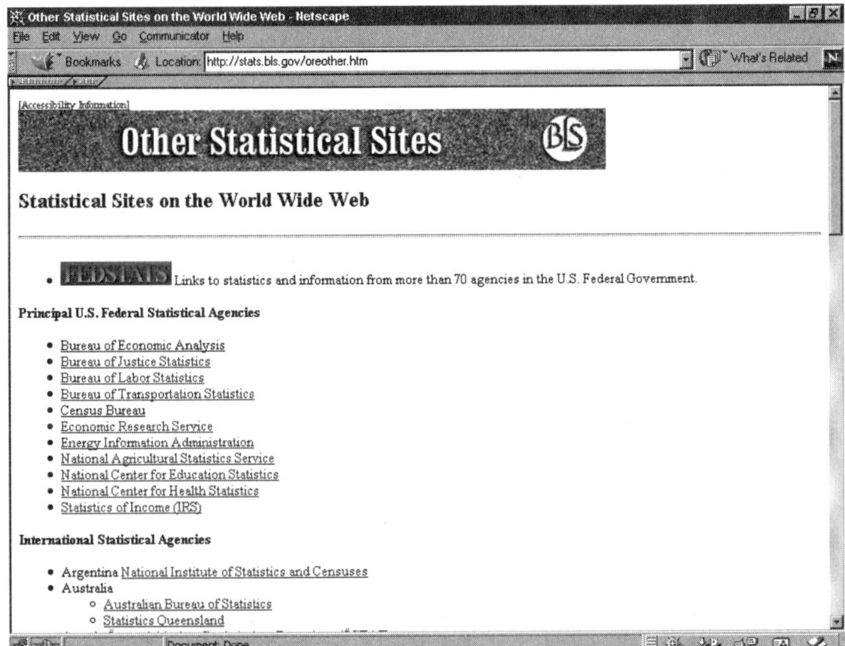

Figure 9.11. The Bureau of Labor Statistics maintains a comprehensive list of links to other countries' statistical agencies.

Government/Statistics category. (See Chapter 1 for a discussion of navigating Yahoo!) Also, the U.S. Department of Labor's Bureau of Labor Statistics has a very good collection of links to other countries' statistical pages, from Argentina to Yugoslavia (stats.bls.gov/oreother.htm). See Figure 9.11 for a sample list of the countries included in its list of statistical sites.

10
Covering the News

Finding background information on a company's strategic plans or on how to set up a Roth IRA is easy enough once you find the right places to go—see Chapters 12 and 3, respectively. But how do you keep track of changes in a company's upper management, or the emergence of a new competitor? How about changes in the tax laws pertaining to retirement savings?

Monitoring current news can be as simple as picking up today's paper or subscribing to a weekly business magazine. And virtually every major Web search engine offers current business and financial news at its site as an incentive for you to visit the site often. What sets a smart investor apart from the crowd is the ability to read between the lines, to recognize trends in the market before others do, to turn business information into market intelligence. This chapter looks at various sources for current news and electronic clipping services, so you can stay ahead of the market. American Online subscribers are reminded that, in addition to what is available on the Web, they can go to AOL's Personal Finance channel for access to Reuters news stories.

News from the Search Engines

It used to be that anyone who read the morning paper was considered to be on top of the day's news. The Web has changed all that; now you are expected to be watching the news on an hourly basis. Fortunately, all of the major Web search engines provide some form of a newswire feed, and they often offer a way to personalize the news so you see just those portions that interest you. Since every advertising-supported site wants to be as *sticky* as possible—that is, they want to attract you and encourage you to spend time at the site and, well, stick around—it is usually very easy to set up your own customized news profile that shows you only selected sections of the news. Table 10.1 shows how to find the business news for selected search engines.

Each search engine provides access to a different collection of news sources—some include press releases, some have the Reuters news feed, some have the AP or UPI wire, and most include stock quotes. You should check out several of these news portals to see which one offers you the best combination of news coverage and personalization. See Figure 10.1 for an example of Excite's business news page.

My Yahoo!

Yahoo! was one of the pioneers in customized Web pages. Its "My Yahoo!" service lets you create your own version of Yahoo!, complete with news on the industries you want, stock quotes, weather reports, and even your daily horoscope. You can also set up an electronic clipping file that watches for any recent newswire stories that mention whatever words or phrases you specify. If you want to see a daily tip for entrepreneurs, the latest industry buzz on high-technology companies, or an hourly report from *The Wall Street Journal*, you can add it to your personal Yahoo! page. You can also include specific Yahoo! categories you want one-click access to, if you find that you go to the same listings frequently. Note that this service requires that you set up a Yahoo ID, but the sign-up is free. See Figure 10.2 for an example of a customized My Yahoo! page.

Of the various major search engines, only Excite (www.excite.com) offers a comparable level of both customization and business news coverage.

Table 10.1. Finding Business News on Selected Search Engines

	Excite (www.excite.com)	HotBot (www.hotbot.com)	GO Network (mypage.go.com)	Yahoo! (www.yahoo.com)
Business newswires	Click [Business News]	Click [News Headlines], then [Business]	Click [Money]	Click [News], then [Business]
How to customize	Click [Create Your Start Page]	Not available	Click [Change my Page Layout]	Click [My Yahoo]

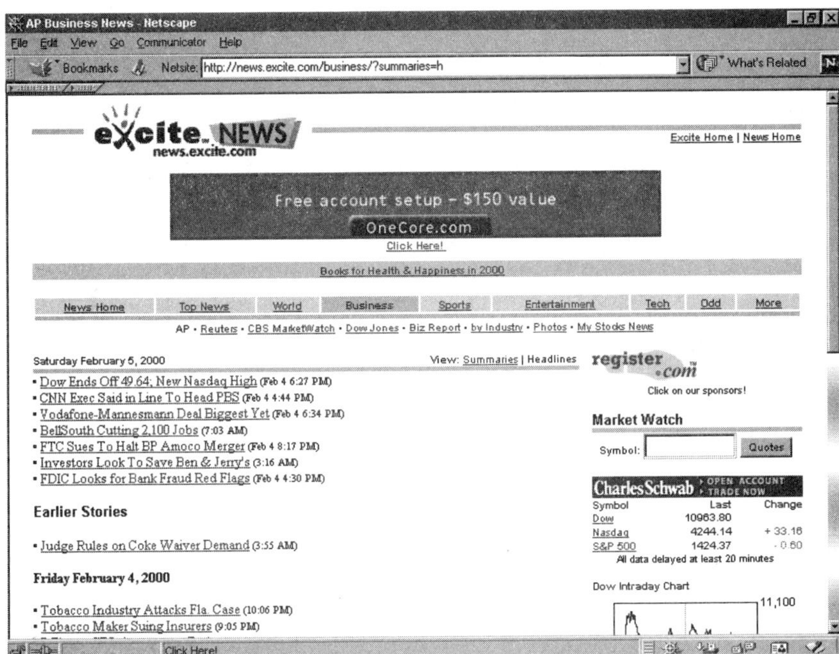

Figure 10.1. Excite offers a selection of business and press release newswires on its news page.

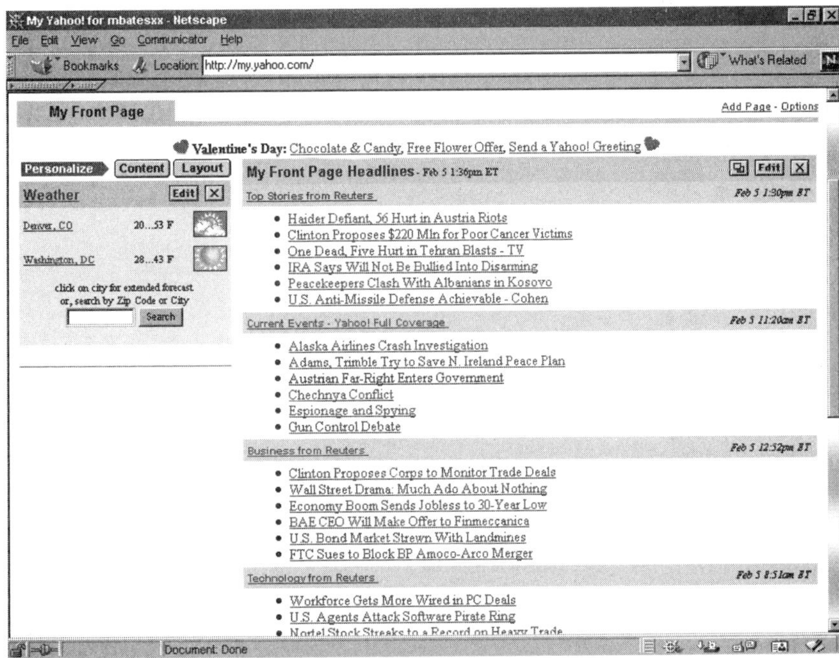

Figure 10.2. My Yahoo! lets you build a customized page of the news and information sources you want to monitor.

Making a News Page Your Starting Page

Once you have set up your My Yahoo!, you can make it your browser's default home page if you want. To do this, you will first need to store your Yahoo ID and password on your PC so that you are automatically logged on when you go to the My Yahoo! site. To do this, click the box marked [Remember my ID & Password] when you are prompted for your Yahoo! ID. The next step will depend on which browser you use.

For Netscape Navigator, pull down the Edit menu and select Preferences. Click the Navigator option, then select Navigator starts with Home Page. In the box labeled Location:, type in the full URL, http://my.yahoo.com, and then click [OK].

For Microsoft Explorer, pull down the View menu and select Internet Options. Under the General tab, there is a box labeled Address. Type the full URL, http://my.yahoo.com, in the box, and then click [OK].

Late-Breaking News

In addition to the search engines' and other portals' news offerings, there are a number of information providers specifically in the business of publishing news. The major television networks (ABC, CBS, and NBC) all have Web sites with current news, at www.abcnews.com, www.cbsnews.com, and www.nbc.com, respectively. For sites that focus on business and investment news, try the sources that are known for their coverage of the world of business.

Reuters

One of the oldest newswire services, Reuters has been following the global financial markets for close to 150 years. (A bit of trivia from Reuters' Web site—Paul Julius Reuter, the founder of Reuters, started his business by using pigeons to send stock prices between the German city of Aachen and Brussels, Belgium. And we complain about slow download times on the Web. . . .) In addition to its real-time news feeds provided to other news organizations, major corporations, and Web sites such as Yahoo! and Excite, Reuters maintains a site of current news at www.reuters.com/news/.

Reuters is known for its international outlook and focus—a refreshing change for those of us accustomed to the U.S.-centric approach of most news sources. The news site offers a category for top world news and one for business news, also viewable by subcategories of markets, economies, corporate news, commodities, and feature articles. The site is low on graphics, so it loads quickly and is easy to navigate. See Figure 10.3 for the main news page on Reuters.

CNNfn.com

CNN has made a name for itself as the cable broadcast station providing all news, all the time. One of the channels of news that CNN provides is CNNfn, focusing on financial news, at cnnfn.com. In addition to late-breaking news, this site has feature articles on personal finance (provided by Quicken.com), a *broker center* that provides links to online brokerage firms, even access to airline and hotel reservations. You can have a summary of recent news emailed to you at the end of every day; click on [fn to go] at the bottom of the screen, then select [Market Briefing]. That way, you don't even have to go to CNNfn; you can have it come to you instead.

One of CNNfn's best features is hidden behind a link labeled [Industry Watch]. Within this area you can view recent articles, newswire stories, and press releases from a wide variety of sources. The database of infor-

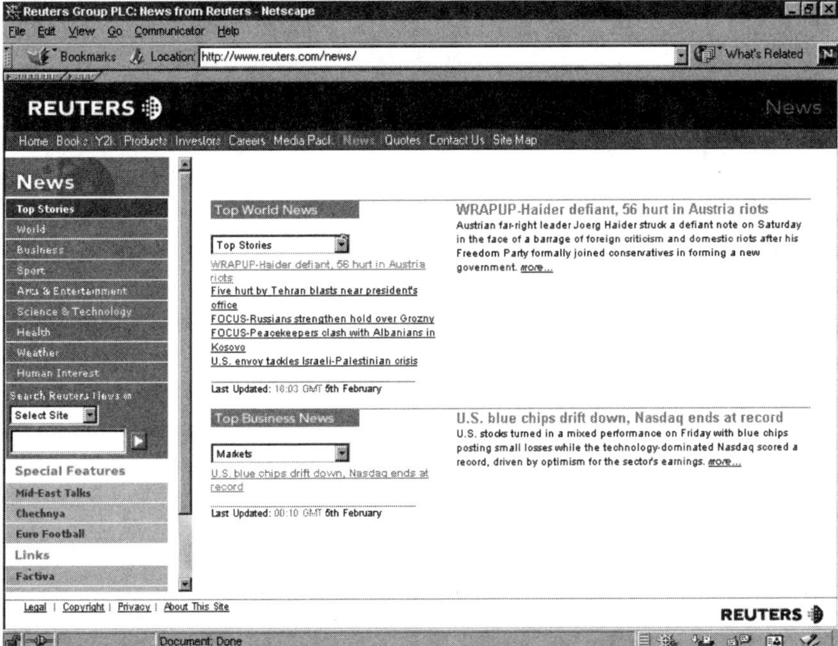

Figure 10.3. Reuters focuses on business news from around the world.

mation is broken out by general industry, so you can scan recent news on the food/drug industry, transportation, aerospace, Internet, or chemicals, to name a few. See Figure 10.4 for headlines from the Food category.

Online Versions of Newspapers and Magazines

It wasn't that long ago when industry pundits were predicting that we would be reading our newspapers from terminal screens at the breakfast table. No more newsprint on your fingers. No more fighting over who gets the sports pages. Well, my newspaper carrier seems as busy now as ever, so the day has not yet come that we can do away with newsprint. On the other hand, I value the fact that I can use the Web to browse my home town paper from 3000 miles away, read my favorite columns from business magazines, or monitor the business section of a local paper for coverage of a company.

Figure 10.4. CNNfn provides current news items on specific industries from a number of sources.

Many print publications offer Web access to their current issue—and sometimes an archive of back issues as well—at no charge. The benefit to the publisher is increased awareness of the publication and additional advertising revenue from the Web site. These sites usually require users to register, but with the notable exception of *The Wall Street Journal,* access to the electronic edition of publications is free.

The Wall Street Journal on the Web

The Wall Street Journal's Web site, known as the Wall Street Journal Interactive Edition (www.wsj.com), is one of the few daily papers that charge for access. WSJIE costs $59 per year, which includes a 30-day archive of the *Journal* and a two-week archive of *Barron's;* a collection of company profiles called Company Briefing Books; and the option to customize your online view of the *Journal.*

The Company Briefing Books are particularly useful when you need a quick compilation of news, investment house reports, and financials on a company, including material in *The Wall Street Journal* and Dow Jones newswire stories. See Figure 10.5 for the table of contents of the Briefing Book for Starbucks.

Local Newspapers

If your local paper has a Web site, you probably see it mentioned in the print version of the paper. Often, newspapers will provide supplemental information to articles on their Web site, links to additional resources, and archives of related stories. It pays to invest a bit of time familiarizing yourself with your local newspaper's site. Where is its search-this-site feature? Does it have profiles of major companies headquartered in the area? Does it offer convenient access to business newswires or stock quotes? Many newspapers provide updates to late-breaking stories during the day—if you are watching for news of a company's earnings, or suspect that a major announcement is coming up, see if your local paper provides news throughout the day on its site.

Remember that local papers are a great source of information on the major companies and industries in the area. That means that you may find yourself reading local papers from towns thousands of miles from where you live. If you are tracking the aerospace industry, you will be interested in *The Seattle Times* (www.seattletimes.com) and the *Seattle Post-Intelligencer*

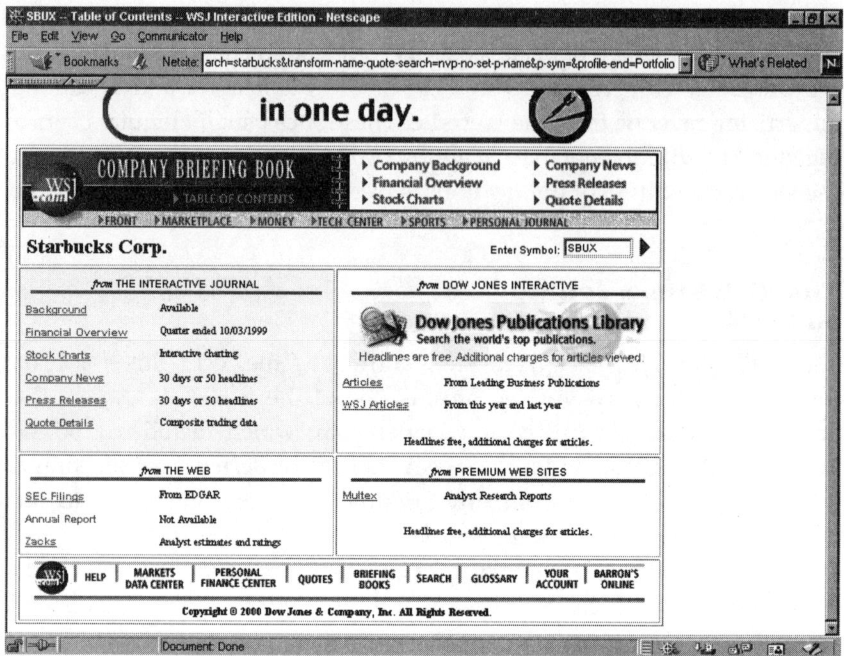

Figure 10.5. The Wall Street Journal Interactive Edition has useful Briefing Books on its site.

(www.seattle-pi.com), both of which cover the locally headquartered Boeing Co.

To find the Web address to a newspaper, you can look on Yahoo! to see if it is listed there. From the main screen, click [Newspapers] (which is listed under News & Media), then click [By Region], then click [U.S. States] (or [Countries] if you are looking for a non-U.S. paper), then select the state and city you want. Alternatively, you can use the *American Journalism Review*'s NewsLink site to look up the Web site for any local newspaper in the United States or around the world. Start at ajr.newslink.org and click [Newspapers]. Drill down by country, state, and city to find the appropriate newspaper's site.

Business Magazines and Weekly Publications

While daily newspapers' business sections often offer good coverage of local business news, for in-depth reporting on companies and industries you will usually need to look at the magazines that focus on financial and investment news. (Of course, the one daily that is required reading of many investment professionals is *The Wall Street Journal.* See the previous discussion about the Wall Street Journal Interactive Edition.)

Doing Business with *Business Week.* One of the leading business weeklies is *Business Week* (www.businessweek.com). Although it is a bit unclear from the site, selected articles from the current edition are available at no charge. You need to register for access; at the registration screen, select [Click for access to just the free areas of Business Week Online]. You will have to pay for copies of articles from prior issues, but some of the current issue's articles are available at no charge. The Web edition of *Business Week* even includes articles from the international edition of the print magazine—a nice feature for anyone watching the business world past the U.S. borders. You also have access to special sections devoted to small business, information technology, personal finance, and so on. See Figure 10.6 for the front page of www.businessweek.com.

Figure 10.6. *Business Week*'s site provides access to articles from the current issue as well as special features.

Forbes. This biweekly magazine, which facetiously bills itself as a "capitalist tool," has a Web site that perhaps predictably calls itself the "digital tool." Of all the Web equivalents of print publications, this is perhaps the most thoughtfully designed. Start at www.forbes.com/forbes/current, which takes you directly to the current edition of *Forbes*. Note that you are not asked to register before gaining access to the site—a surprising contrast to most print publications' sites. You can scan the table of contents just like in the print version (see Figure 10.7.)

Click on a headline of interest and you will see the full text of the article, along with the option to forward the article to someone else, display it in a more printer-friendly format, see other articles by the same writer, or see other articles from that section of the magazine. Clearly, this site was designed by someone who thought through how people actually read magazine articles and how they want to proceed after they've read the article. The *Forbes* site also offers transcripts and audio/video files of selected speeches from information-technology-related conferences sponsored by *Forbes*, as well as online discussion bulletin boards on topics of

Figure 10.7. *Forbes'* site offers full access to the current issue of the magazine, as well as audio and video conferences and supplemental information.

interest to *Forbes* readers. You even get a new quotation each time you move from screen to screen—"Memory presents to us not what we choose but what it pleases.—Montaigne"; "Killing time murders opportunities.—Anonymous," and so on.

Fortune. The other major biweekly business magazine is *Fortune.* Start at www.fortune.com; at this site you will see daily features, links to the *Fortune* 500 lists, and archives of back issues. If you are looking for the current issue, though, click the [Magazine] link to go straight to the most recent articles. You can scan the table of contents or search the current issue or the archives for articles on a topic. More than most, *Fortune*'s site also prominently displays other magazines of its publisher, Time, Inc.—*Money, Time,* and *Entertainment Weekly* are all featured on the *Fortune* Web page. See Figure 10.8 for the current issues page; it looks more cluttered than some Web sites, but recent issues are easy to access, and the full text of articles are easily retrieved.

Figure 10.8. You can scan the latest few issues of *Fortune* magazine on its Web site, as well as search for earlier articles.

Online Newsletters

So far, we have only looked at magazines and newspapers that eventually wind up in a printed format. One of the most striking effects of the Web has been the proliferation of newsletters that only exist in electronic format. Many of these e-journals could not have been published before the advent of the Net; the cost of printing and mailing alone would have made them prohibitively expensive. Interestingly, some electronic newsletters are using the same revenue models as their print counterparts. Instead of full-color display ads, emailed newsletters often have advertisements inserted between articles (clearly demarcated as commercial messages). While some e-journals charge for subscriptions, many do not. An electronic newsletter may be seen as a marketing vehicle for the sponsoring organization, or it may simply be a labor of love produced by people with the desire to write on a topic about which they care deeply.

Many of the Web sites that focus on investment topics offer a daily or weekly newsletter. TheStreet.com can be considered an electronic newsletter itself, since it contains a number of columns and features, none of which appear in a hard-copy format. But it also sends several updates to registered users during each business day, thus providing both *push* delivery of updates and *pull* delivery of the Web site. Similarly, Standard & Poor's site, www.personalwealth.com, delivers daily S&P Market Mail bulletins via email upon request.

There are many newsletters on the Net that focus on individual investors. As with any Internet site, be sure you understand the background and approach of the writer before relying on the source. Your best bet is to look for one that focuses on the type of investments you favor, shares your general investment philosophy, and is written by someone whose advice you respect. One of the first places to look for a list of newsletters is Yahoo!, the premier catalog of Web sites (www.yahoo.com). Start at the [Finance] link at the main Yahoo! page, then drill down the links through [Companies], then [Financial Services], then [Investment Services], then [Market Information and Research], and finally to [Newsletters].

Another good source of links to investment-related e-journals is Newsletter Access (www.newsletteraccess.com). It is based on a print publication called *Hudson's Newsletter Directory.* Many of the entries in this Web site require a subscription, but they usually offer the current issue's articles at no charge, as an incentive for you to subscribe. Click on the [Investment Center] link at the NewsletterAccess home page, and you will

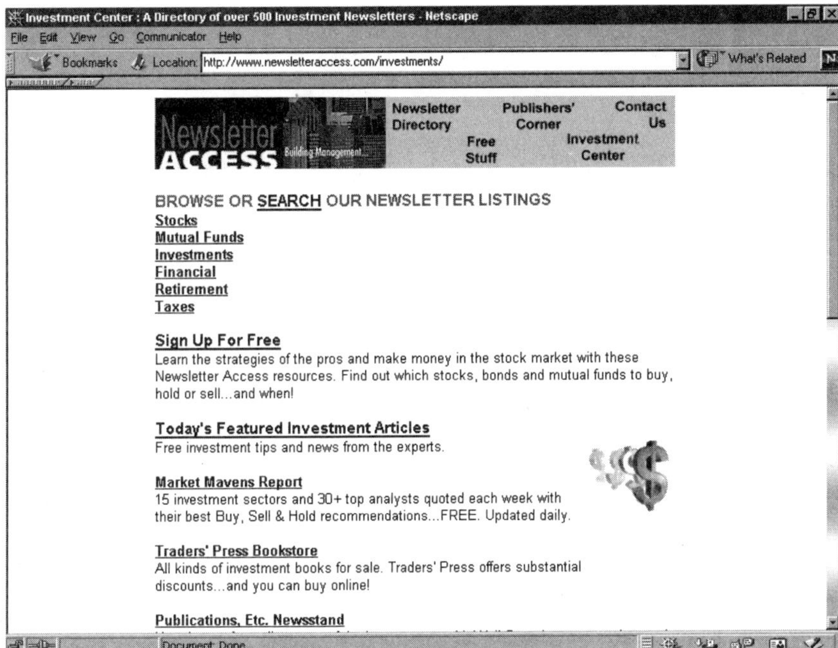

Figure 10.9. Newsletter Access is produced by the publishers of a well-respected print directory of newsletters.

be taken to its collection of links to newsletters that focus on finance and investment. See Figure 10.9 for a list of what's available at the site.

And keep in mind that with investment advice, as with most other parts of life, you get what you pay for. Evaluate every newsletter carefully before following its advice.

11
High-Powered Online Services

Most of this book focuses on information sources on the Web that are either free or that charge a minimal fee. There is, however, a whole other area of online information, if you are willing to pay for it. Often called *professional online services* or *value-added online services,* these are enormous collections of published material—articles from business and trade magazines, the full text of market research studies and analysts' reports, in-depth statistical data, companies' credit reports, and interviews with CEOs. This chapter covers the major business-oriented online services that offer high value and not-insignificant fees.

Why Not Just Use What's Free on the Web?

Professional online services provide high-powered research tools that you usually don't find in the free or almost-free services. Say you want to track down a rumor you saw on an electronic bulletin board. Rather than rely on investur3495@hotmail.com, you probably want to see if any of the more reliable investment news sources have picked up the news. One of the advantages of published news services such as the Dow Jones Wire or Bloomberg is that there are editors who (presumably) apply a skeptical eye to market rumors before putting them on the wire.

What about when you want to look through a number of news sources simultaneously to find any recent mention of a company or an industry? Sure, you can go to each newspaper's site, wade through the initial news screens until you find the [Search This Site] link, figure out how far back the paper's archives go, run your search, scan the results, download the ones you want, then repeat the process for each of the other sources you want to search. If that sounds like a lot of work, then you might consider using one of the value-added online services that lets you search hundreds of news sources at once. Not only do these services allow you to do all your searching at one time, but they also offer a standardized search screen, easy-to-read output formats, and access to material from three weeks, three months, even three years ago—something you are not likely to find on the free Web sites.

How would you go about determining the creditworthiness of a company? One of the standard sources for this information is the Dun & Bradstreet Business Information Report, which includes a history of how promptly the company pays creditors, background on the company and its principals, a listing of outstanding liens and significant litigation, and related information. You can establish an account with D&B directly, but this usually entails a significant up-front payment; most researchers find it much simpler to purchase D&B reports as needed from one of the professional online services.

And finally, there are times when you need to evaluate the size, growth potential, and key players of a market, whether it is automobile tires, airplane engines, or ATMs. There are consulting firms that charge thousands of dollars for market research reports, and naturally they don't give this information away on the Web. In fact, most consulting firms will not even *sell* their reports on their Web sites. However, there are several online services that have licensed the material from selected consulting firms and can sell you individual sections, chapters, or pages of a market report at a cost significantly lower than the sticker price for the entire report. Although even buying pages à la carte is not cheap, it beats paying for the full report when all you need are selected portions of it.

It Costs How Much?!?

A common question that arises when you start thinking about paying more than a couple of dollars for information on the Web is "Why shouldn't I just use all the information that's available for free? Why pay?" As just noted, sometimes the information you want is only available on the professional online services. Consultants' reports, professional and trade journals, and statistical data are the most notable examples of information that often is not available on the Web. In addition, some research projects are so much less time-consuming if the professional online services are used that it just doesn't make sense to try to rely on the Web. There are times when you have to factor in the value of your time when looking for information on the Web; if it takes four or five times longer to find what you're looking for on the free areas of the Web, it probably makes sense to spend the money to go to the fee-based services.

So how much money are we talking about here? Each of the major online services has a number of pricing plans, depending on whether you want to get an all-you-can-eat package or you want to pay per transaction. Even seasoned online researchers have trouble deciphering rate schedules and deciding which one is the most cost-effective. In general, it makes sense to pick one service you expect to use the most, and treat that as your home service. Given the steep cover charge that most online services require, you will probably find that one professional system is enough.

A convenient rule of thumb is that, regardless of the online service, searching the professional systems will cost about $100 to $150 an hour. (Note that when looking for market research reports, all bets are off. You can easily download a thousand dollars' worth of information within five minutes.) But very few online services actually have a pricing system as straightforward as $X per hour. Instead, you will usually see some combination of annual fee, per-article charge, and per-search or per-hour charges. The basic cost structures are described in the section on each online service.

When to Decide to Pay

Here's the big question—when do you look for information on the free Web and when do you take out your credit card and start paying? Table 11.1 shows some of the decision points that help you select the most appropriate source for information.

Research Tips

All of the services described here expect users to be familiar with Boolean logic—AND, OR, and NOT connectors that specify whether two words must, may, or cannot appear in the same record, respectively. Note that this is one significant difference between the professional online services and most of the search engines on the Web. In general, the latter look for any Web pages that contain any of the search words, and then rank the retrieved pages with the most relevant items at the top. A search will often

Table 11.1. Deciding When to Pay to Play

If you need:	Start with the free Web	Start with the fee-based online services
current stock quotes	✔	
historical stock quotes		✔
basic company information	✔	
in-depth company profile		✔
government data	✔	
current news	✔	
news from more than 2 weeks ago		✔
current articles from a newspaper	✔	
articles from 15 newspapers		✔
market research		✔
Dun & Bradstreet business credit reports		✔
articles from professional or trade press		✔

retrieve hundreds of thousands of pages, although of course you probably only skim through the first 40 or 50 before the relevance drops off precipitously. On the other hand, the professional online services use strict rules on retrieval—if you ask for articles with the words *Xerox* and *EDS* and *outsourcing,* you will only see articles that contain all three of those words. Needless to say, searching on the professional services requires a bit more thought and preparation to decide what the key concepts are and what synonyms to use.

Another secret to searching successfully is to think of what kinds of sources would have the information you need. Is this an issue covered in sufficient depth by local newspapers? Should you look in specialized newsletters on the subject? Are weekly or monthly trade magazines the best source? Do you need to get transcripts of television or radio broadcasts as well? And once you have decided what kinds of sources to search, take a minute to consider what words the source will use to describe the issue you are researching. It might be as simple as remembering that British publications talk about a company's *turnover* rather than its *revenue,* or that a beverage industry publication will use the term *isotonic* to refer to sports drinks.

The Major Players

There are three professional online services that dominate the market for business and investment information—Dow Jones Interactive, Lexis-Nexis, and Dialog. Each has exclusive rights to some sources that the others don't have, but for most research they offer pretty much the same selection of information. Your decision on which, if any, to subscribe to will depend on how much you expect to use professional online services, whether you need any of the additional features of one of the services, and which one offers you the best pricing options.

Each service has its own search commands, rules for indicating that words be searched as a phrase, and so on. Rather than go into a great deal of detail about how each online system works, I will provide a brief table at the end of each section showing how to construct typical searches. Use these tables as an indicator of how much training may be required before you become familiar with the service—one that uses intuitive search construction will probably be easier for you to learn than one that has more obscure conventions.

Dow Jones Interactive

Dow Jones Interactive, a Web-based professional online service (djinteractive.com) whose primary market is the business community, was originally developed by the publishers of *The Wall Street Journal.* Since then, it's been spun off as a separate venture, but DJI still retains some of the flavor of its parent. Although it helps if you have some familiarity with Boolean logic, DJI also has search screens that let you construct your search primarily with pull-down menus. For example, Figure 11.1 shows the Search By Industry window, in which you select the general industry you are interested in, specify the date range to search, select what publications you want to include, and then add any additional terms you want included in the search. In this example, the current and previous year of major news and industry sources are being searched for information on advertising in the industrial technology industry.

The results of this search will be displayed in a form similar to that of Web search engines—you will see the headline, date, length of the article, and first couple of sentences of the text. To see the full text of the article, you click on the headline. Note that unlike Web search engines, the default in DJI is to sort the retrieved articles by date, with the most current item appearing first. You can change that default, though, to have the results

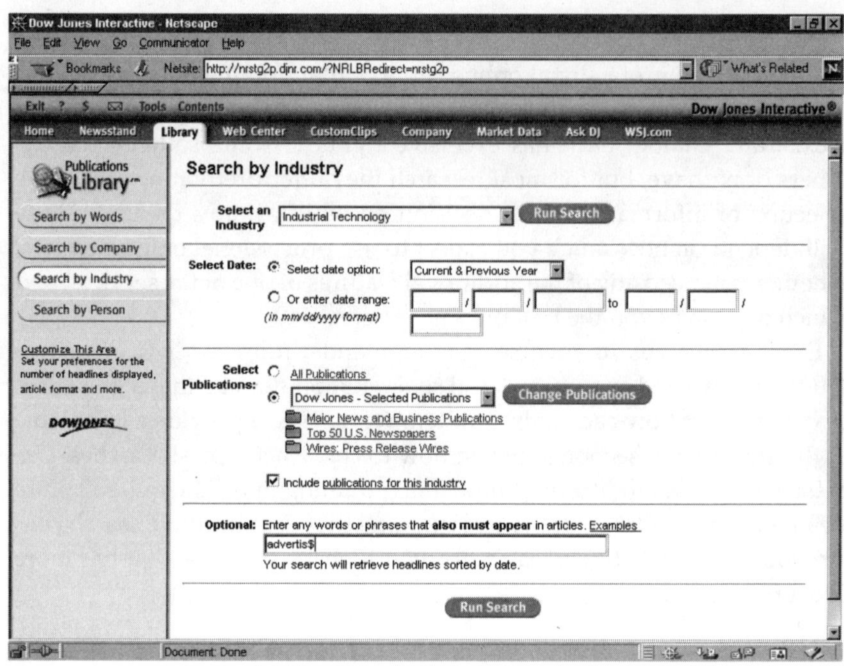

Figure 11.1. Dow Jones Interactive has an easy-to-use Industry Search screen.

sorted by relevance. And if you want to build a more complex search, you can click the [Search By Words] link on the left of the screen and you will be taken to a search window that lets you type in as complex a search as you need. Unlike most other professional online services, some of the articles in DJI's collection are available in PDF format, enabling you to see an image of the article, including any charts and photographs.

Table 11.2 shows the construction of several typical searches. Phrases can be typed as they are to appear in the article. Truncation—indicating that you want any word starting with a specified word stem—is done with a dollar sign ($) and, optionally, a number indicating the maximum number of letters that can follow the word stem. This is particularly useful for terms such as *hospital*, where you want to include *hospital*s but not *hospital*ity. Unlike Web search engines, DJI includes the ability to specify that you want a word to appear at least X times—a convenient way of ensuring that the article really *is* about that subject.

DJI is also known for its detailed statistical database. If you need stock prices going back 10 years, a report of the last 20 dividend payments a

Table 11.2. Basic Search Examples for Dow Jones Interactive

To Look For:	Type:
Articles on Glaxo and talks of mergers	glaxo and merg$3
Articles on Diet Pepsi or Pepsi One	diet pepsi or pepsi one
Articles with the phrase "mutual fund" in the title	hl=mutual fund
Articles that mention teaching hospitals	teaching hospital$1
Articles that mention Enron at least 5 times	atleast5 enron

company has made, exchange rates for the Polish zloty for the past year, or the last quarter's T-bill rates, DJI is your best source.

And what about pricing? DJI has one of the most straightforward pricing plans in the industry. You pay a yearly fee of $69, and then $2.95 per article (an additional $4 is charged for PDF images, available for selected articles). Statistical reports, D&B reports, and market research reports are priced per report or per page. There is no charge for searching DJI—only for the information retrieved. Subscription to DJI also gains you access to the Wall Street Journal Interactive Edition, which has a useful Company Briefing Books feature, described in Chapter 10.

Lexis-Nexis

Unlike Dow Jones Interactive, Lexis-Nexis (www.lexis-nexis.com) started out as an online service for the legal community with its Lexis service, which contains court decisions, statutes, and related legal material. The Nexis side of the service, though, consists of the full text of articles, company credit information, market research reports, and so on. In the past, Nexis has required that searchers use its proprietary software to access Nexis. Fortunately, it is migrating over to Lexis-Nexis Universe, a Web-based version of its search system.

Universe offers preformatted search screens that minimize the amount of typing and complex search strategizing required. See Figure 11.2 for the General News search screen, in which the past six months of major business sources are searched for significant stories on ecotourism. There are also search windows for specialized topics such as looking for information on people, on an industry, or for medical, government, or legal information. If you want to build a more complex search strategy, click the [Advanced Search] link on the left side of the screen.

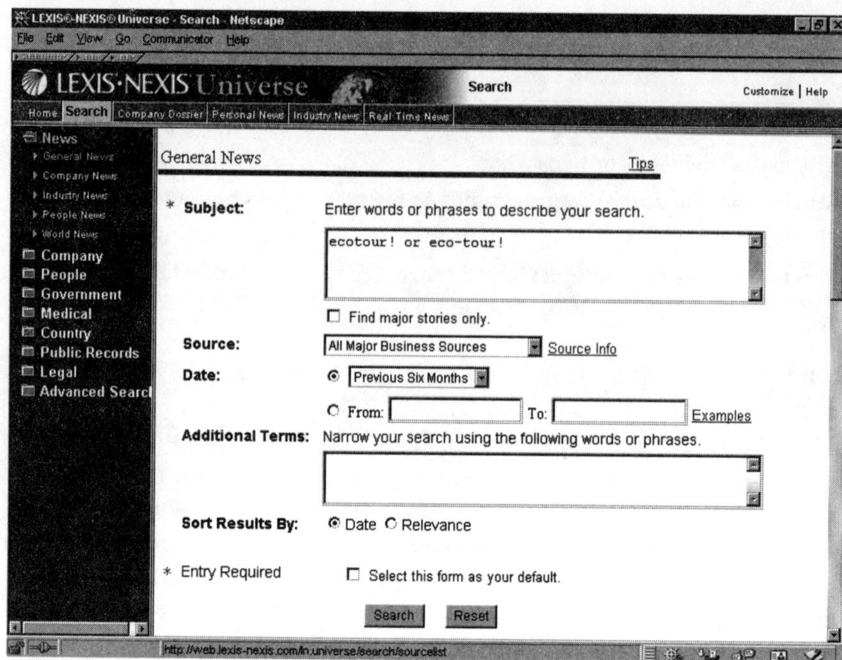

Figure 11.2. Lexis-Nexis Universe lets you search for specific industry phrases in its General News search screen.

The results of the search will list the headline, source, and date and length of the article; you can check off the articles you want to see in full text. The articles are normally displayed in reverse chronological order, with the most current article listed first. You can also have the results sorted by relevance. Universe offers an interesting feature called [More Like This]; if you see an article you like but that is somewhat tangential to your original search, you can click the [More Like This] link and Lexis-Nexis will look for similar articles.

Table 11.3 shows the basic commands for searching Lexis-Nexis. One of the unique features of L-N is that it automatically searches for both singular and plural forms of words, so that, for example, the search word *hospital* will retrieve articles that have either the word *hospital* or *hospitals* in them. L-N also automatically searches alternative spellings for words; this is particularly useful for Americans searching British publications and vice versa. It can be hard to remember to look for both *organization* and *organisation, labor* and *labour, aluminum* and *aluminium.* Like Dow Jones Interactive but unlike Web search engines, L-N provides the ability to

Table 11.3. Basic Search Examples for Lexis-Nexis

To Look For:	Type:
articles on Glaxo and talks of mergers	glaxo and merg***
articles on Diet Pepsi or Pepsi One	diet pepsi or pepsi one
articles with the phrase "mutual fund" in the title	headline (mutual fund)
articles that mention teaching hospitals	teaching hospital [Nexis automatically looks for both singular and plural forms of words]
articles that mention Enron at least 5 times	atleast5 (enron)

specify the minimum number of times a word must appear in an article—a useful way of limiting your search to only the most relevant articles.

Pricing on L-N is complex, and difficult to compare with other online services. For one thing, L-N has no published price list; it encourages subscribers to sign up for flat-fee all-you-can-eat contracts. While that might work well for large organizations with a staff of researchers, it is difficult to justify for the sole researcher. L-N offers several transaction-based pricing plans that include charges for some combination of the following:

- Each search you run
- The length of time you remain connected to L-N
- The number of lines of text you print
- The number of articles you download
- A yearly or monthly account-maintenance fee

Dialog

Designed originally for librarians and other professional researchers, Dialog (www.dialog.com) uses a fairly obscure set of search commands in its traditional, ASCII-based search service, known as *Dialog Classic.* Unlike Dow Jones or Lexis-Nexis, Dialog does not group its publications in categories such as Consumer Goods or Major News Sources. Instead, Dialog has *files,* which contain publications from whatever sources the database producer decided to include. Some files overlap significantly in content; some contain the full text of articles, and some only have summaries of articles. While the variety and depth of sources in Dialog is probably greater than either of its major competitors, it is also a somewhat confusing system to navigate. This is where the Guided Search option on DialogWeb comes in (www.dialogweb.com). Guided Search helps you select which databases you want to search by grouping them in broad categories—business news, medicine, electronics industry articles, and so on.

Dialog also offers a very user-friendly option called *DialogSelect* (www.dialogselect.com). The search screens offer fill-in-the-blank search composition and a simplified method for selecting what databases to search. One disadvantage of DialogSelect is that not every Dialog database is included in the service. For most business- or investment-related research, this should not be a limitation, though, since DialogSelect includes most major information sources.

See Figure 11.3 for the DialogSelect search screen, on which telecommunications industry databases are searched for articles written in 1999 or 2000 about Teledesic and the Federal Communications Commission. If

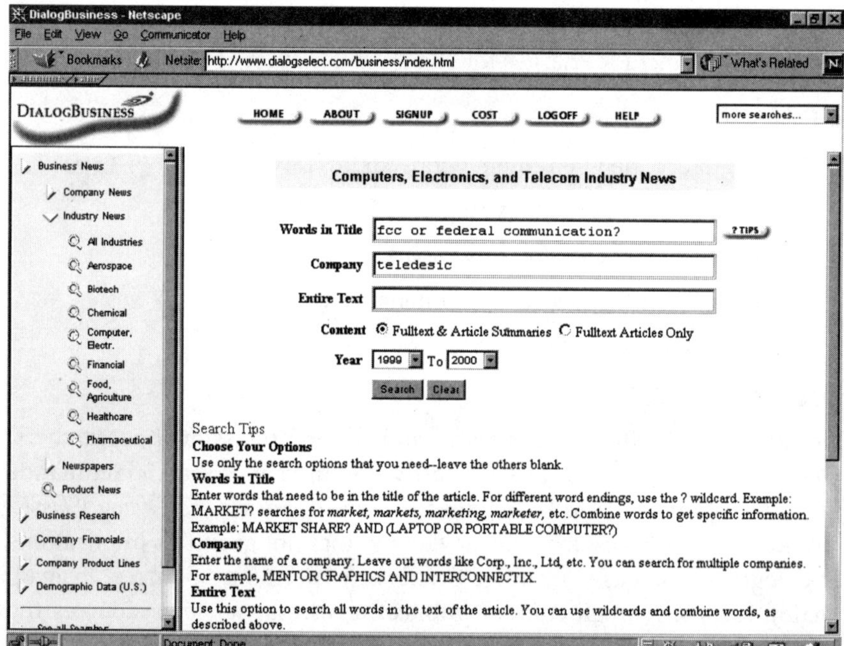

Figure 11.3. DialogSelect offers a streamlined format for searching industries.

you want to create a more complex search, you will have to log off of DialogSelect and run the search on DialogWeb (www.dialogweb.com) or Dialog Classic (telnet://dialog.com).

The articles that meet the search criteria are displayed in a brief format (title, date, and price of the article—no information on the publication source or the length of the article). To order the complete article, click the title. One distinction between DialogSelect and DialogWeb on the one hand and the ASCII-based Dialog Classic on the other is that the first two notify you ahead of time how much the article will cost. Since each file has different per-record prices, this is a convenient and necessary feature for cost-conscious searchers.

In addition to articles, market research reports, and company profiles, Dialog provides a gateway to Tradeline, the service that provides historical financial data also offered by Dow Jones Interactive. You must use an expert version of Dialog (Dialog Classic or the Command Search version of DialogWeb) to access Tradeline.

Unlike Dow Jones and Lexis-Nexis, you will use different search phrases depending on which version of Dialog you are using. Table 11.4 lists how to construct various searches using each of the three flavors of Dialog.

Table 11.4. Basic Search Examples for the Three Versions of Dialog

To Look For:	In DialogSelect, Type:	In DialogWeb Guided Search, Type:	In Dialog Classic, Type:
Articles on Glaxo and talks of mergers	glaxo and merger???	glaxo and merg???	glaxo and merg???
Articles on Diet Pepsi or Pepsi One	diet pepsi or pepsi one	diet pepsi or pepsi one	diet()pepsi or pepsi()one
Articles with the phrase"mutual fund" in the title	mutual fund [use the "Title" search bar]	mutual fund [use pull down menu to limit to Title]	mutual()fund/ti
Articles that mention teaching hospitals	teaching hospital? ?	teaching hospital? ?	teaching()hospital? ?
Articles that mention Enron at least 5 times	[this feature not available]	[this feature not available]	[this feature not available]

Dialog has gone through a number of iterations of pricing models, but in general search costs are based on a combination of per-record charges and either a per-minute or resource-usage charge. Dialog also charges a one-time fee of $295 to sign up with the service, a yearly fee of $144, and a monthly minimum charge of $75. One exception to these fees is a version of DialogSelect called OpenAccess (openaccess.dialog.com), which charges higher per-document costs but no monthly or yearly fees. Like Lexis-Nexis, Dialog strongly encourages its subscribers to sign up for flat-fee contracts; whether that makes sense for you will depend on how likely you are to use Dialog regularly.

Niche Information Providers

In addition to the big three contenders, there are a number of more specialized online vendors. Some, like InSite 2 and ProQuest, described in this section, are produced by the vendors who create the databases themselves, so they contain a subset of what you would find in one of the supermarket services such as Dow Jones or Dialog. Most of these services offer additional search features designed specifically for the databases they maintain, such as hypertext links to similar articles, and they generally do not require familiarity with specialized search techniques. Keep in mind, though, that with the exception of Northern Light these all require substantial yearly contracts that assume that a number of researchers will be using the service. If you are not in a position to use the service enough to justify the expense, contact the business branch of your local library and see if library users have access to the service there.

InSite 2

Developed by The Gale Group, an information provider that produces a number of business-related databases, InSite 2 (www.insite2.gale.com) lets you search articles from trade and professional magazines, major business news sources, industry newsletters, newswires, and newspapers. In addition to incorporating both a Quick Search and Power Search option, InSite 2 offers preformatted screens for searching by company name, industry, or personal name. Unlike most online services, even the Power Search option is straightforward and requires little familiarity with specialized system commands.

As mentioned at the beginning of this section, InSite 2 does not offer a transaction-based pricing option. The only subscription option is to sign a year-long, flat-fee contract, which makes sense if you work for a large organization in which a number of researchers need access to business data.

ProQuest Direct

Like InSite 2, ProQuest (www.umi.com/proquest) is a product of a large database provider, in this case Bell & Howell Information and Learning. ProQuest contains articles from business and industry publications, newspapers, newswires, and newsletters. Unlike most other online services, ProQuest also has a large collection of article images in PDF format, which provides an electronic snapshot of the article, including any charts, graphs, or pictures. This can be an extremely useful feature, since the usual format of an online articles is plain text, and graphs are usually omitted from the online text of the article.

ProQuest has a Basic and an Advanced Search option; the Advanced Search does not require much familiarity with the system beyond the ability to read the Help file. As noted earlier, ProQuest Direct does not offer a pricing plan that favors individual searchers. Sign up for it if you have enough researchers in your organization to justify the cost, or see if a local library subscribes to the service.

Northern Light

Unlike most niche players in the professional online market, Northern Light (www.northernlight.com) is an interesting hybrid of a Web search engine and a value-added information provider. Northern Light has one of the largest search engine databases, so Web searchers often use it when they are looking for a needle in a haystack. But NL also provides access to a number of the same databases found on the professional online services, in what NL calls its *Special Collection.*

The Special Collection includes articles from the business and trade press, newswires, company profiles, and some basic reference sources. While it does not offer the same comprehensive coverage as Dow Jones, Lexis-Nexis, or Dialog, the fact that NL does not require a subscription makes it an attractive option for basic research. You pay only when you want the full text of an article; most articles cost between $1 and $4.

As with most niche information providers, your search options are somewhat limited. Fortunately, NL's Power Search option gives you a cer-

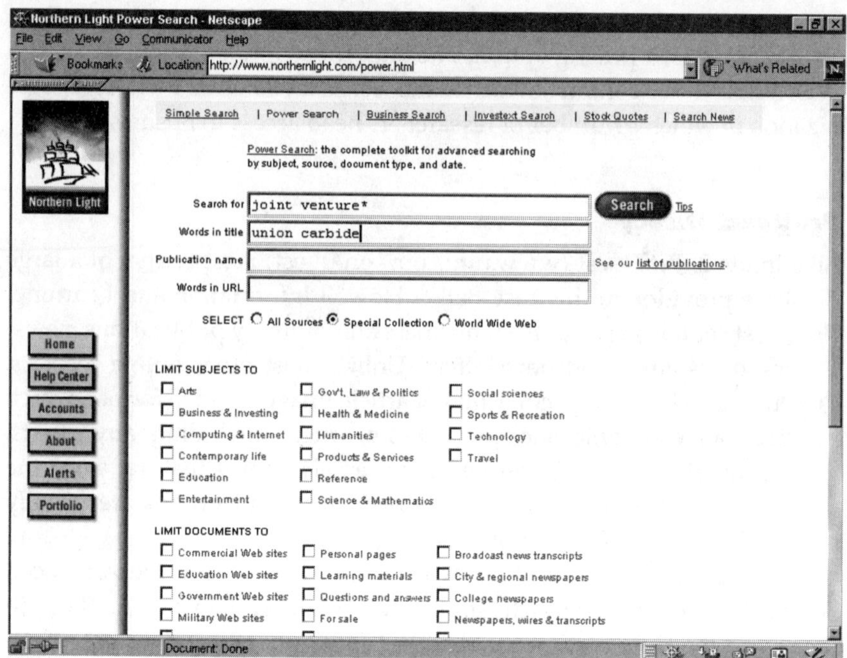

Figure 11.4. Northern Light's Special Collection lets you search the full text of articles as well as Web sites.

tain amount of flexibility in constructing your search. See Figure 11.4 for an example of a search of the Special Collection for articles on joint ventures that Union Carbide has entered into.

The search results screen displays only the title and source; you click on the headline and see the title, date, source, length of the article, and cost. At this point, you can purchase the article if it looks useful. Northern Light offers fewer search options than other information providers—you cannot easily limit your search to a subset of magazines, for example—but the fact that you do not have to pay for an annual contract makes NL an attractive option when you are considering which online service to use.

12
Scoping Out a Company on the Net

There are lots of reasons why you would want to dig up information on a company—as a possible investment, in order to compare a company to its competition, or even to consider it as a potential employer. While companies have always made at least some basic information available to the public, the amount of intelligence you can now glean from sources on the Net is truly extraordinary. This chapter will look at ways to find information on companies, both publicly held and private, and will show you how to efficiently work your way through a company's Web site.

Scouring a Company's Web Site

One of the reasons why the World Wide Web took off in the mid-1990s was the ability of companies to make information widely available at the click of a mouse. Electronic commerce (i.e., *e-commerce,* also sometimes called *e-retail* or even *e-tail*) has created such a buzz that an electronic book store like Amazon.com can consistently show a loss at the end of the year and still have its stock traded at up to $200 per share. What that means for you as you try to find substantial information on a company's Web site is that you will probably have to wade through several initial screens of marketing glitz before you get to the information you are looking for.

Where's That Road Map?

Let's take Dell Computers as a case study on how to dig through a company's Web site to find corporate and financial information. As already noted in Chapter 1, my first attempt to find a company's (in this case Dell's) Web site is to go with the obvious address—www.dell.com—and, sure enough, that is indeed Dell's address. This site (see Figure 12.1) is a good example of the need to look past the e-commerce material and home in on the corporate information.

Note a link at the top of the page [About Dell]. By clicking that link, you will get to a page with information on jobs at Dell, facts about the company and its history, and, more important for our purposes, links to the following resources:

- Press releases dating back to 1994
- Annual and quarterly reports, including the 10-K and 10Q
- A seven-page description of the company, its corporate strategy, and its core products

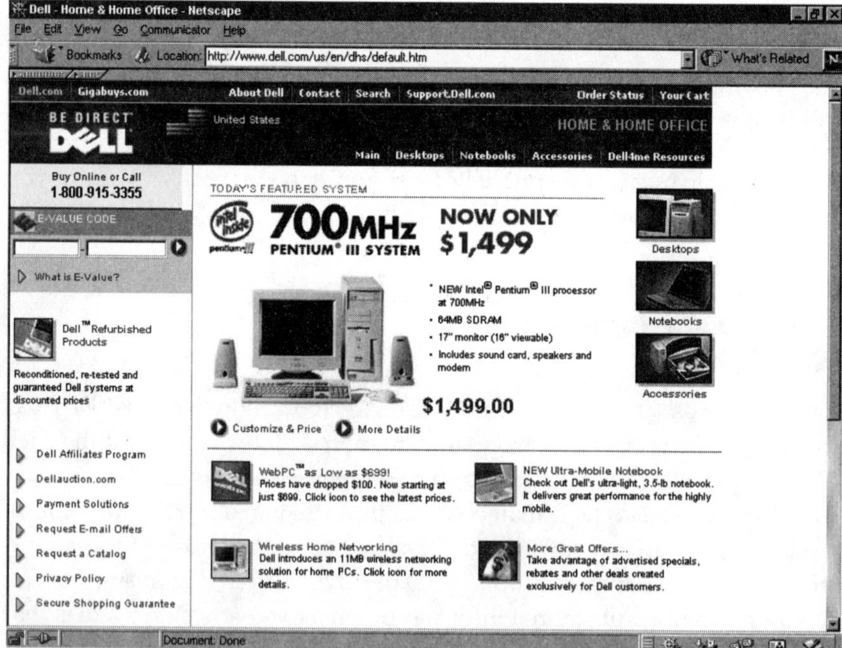

Figure 12.1. Dell Computer's home page has clear links to both their site map and corporate information.

- A sign-up form for receiving updates from Dell's Investor Relations office
- A FAQ of commonly asked investor-related questions

Would that every company made its corporate information so accessible!

What to Look For in a Company's Site

One of the tips mentioned in Chapter 1 was to be persistent and to assume that the information you need is available, somewhere. On the other hand, it is important to manage your own expectations and not spend an inordinate amount of time looking for information on a company's Web page that isn't likely to be there. Table 12.1 provides you with a checklist of the types of information most likely to be found on a company's Web site.

What About Those SEC Filings?

10-Ks, 10-Qs, proxy statements . . . you will often find these listed in a company's Investor Relations Web page. As already discussed in Chapter 9, these are, respectively, the annual and quarterly reports, and the shareholder material sent out before an annual meeting that all publicly traded

Table 12.1. Where to Look for Company Information

Company information	Likely link label
Press releases	[News] [Press Room]
Annual and quarterly reports	[Financial Information]
10-K, 10-Q	[Investor Relations] [Shareholder Information]
Profiles of executives	[Our People]
Stock price	often listed on the home page [Investor Relations]
Strategic focus	[Who We Are] [About Us] [Corporate Overview] [Vision]
Career opportunities	[Employment] [Jobs] [Careers] [Our People]
Products or services	[Lines of Business] [What We Do] [Products]

companies have to file with the U.S. Securities and Exchange Commission (edgar.sec.gov). They are dull as dishwater to read, unless you know what to look for.

10-K, the annual financial report of the company, is not to be confused with the glossy Annual Report, full of pictures of smiling employees and glowing reports of the company's success. The portions of most interest will be:

- *Business.* This is the section, usually at the beginning of the 10-K, in which the company describes what it does, its lines of business, its major products or services, its major competitors and the industry in general, and so on. This section often includes a breakdown of revenue by product line. For example, see Table 12.2 for an excerpt from Item 1 in the Ford Motor Company's 10-K, which contains useful information on the market share of its vehicles.
- *Executive Officers.* This section lists and provides pertinent data about the major executives of the company, usually down to the executive vice president level, and includes age, length of time with the company, and a paragraph of biographical information. Read this to get a sense of how strong the executive team is and to see if there has been significant turnover among the executive officers.
- *Selected Financial Data.* This is fairly self-explanatory—you will find detailed financial information, usually dating back five years. Often the company will break out its revenue by major product line and/or geographic area as well.

Table 12.2. Excerpt from The Ford Motor Company's 10-K

	U.S. Car Market Shares, Years Ended December 31				
	1999	1998	1997	1996	1995
Ford**	19.9%	20.4%	20.8%	21.6%	21.9%
General Motors	29.3	29.8	32.2	32.3	33.9
DaimlerChrysler	10.3	10.7	10.2	10.9	10.0
Toyota	10.2	10.6	9.9	9.3	9.2
Honda	9.8	10.6	10.0	9.2	8.6
Nissan	4.6	5.0	5.7	5.9	6.0
All Other	15.9	12.9	11.2	10.8	10.4
Total U.S. Car Retail Deliveries	100.0%	100.0%	100.0%	100.0%	100.0%

- *Management's Discussion and Analysis of Financial Condition and Results of Operations.* Here is where the rubber hits the road. Unlike the glossy annual report, the tone in the Management's Discussion is often dour and pessimistic—keep in mind that one of the purposes of the 10-K is to alert potential investors to the risks in investing in the company. So the outlook may sound fairly gloomy here, even if the company expects to show a growth in revenue over the next year. See the section labeled "Outlook" for a conservative prediction of the next fiscal year. The Ford Motor Company's Outlook, for example, includes the following:

```
Industry Sales Volumes

  Our outlook for car and truck (including heavy trucks) in-
dustry sales in 2000 in our major markets is as follows:

United States—approximately 17 million units, compared with
  the 17.4 million units sold in 1999
Europe—approximately 18 million units, compared with the
  18.3 million units sold in 1999 (both figures based on 19
  markets)
Brazil—between 1.3 and 1.5 million units, compared with the
  1.3 million units sold in 1999
Australia—slightly lower than the 787,000 units sold in 1999
```

The proxy statement is the form sent to shareholders prior to the annual business meeting. It enables the shareholder to confer to a company representative the right to vote the stock owned by the shareholder. This form is usually listed as DEF 14A or PRE 14A in the EDGAR Web site (edgar.sec.gov). The proxy statement is where you can find out what the board of directors and executives are paid—in salary, bonuses, stock options, and other forms of compensation—and get a one- to two-paragraph biography of each director and executive. You will also find any other matters that will be brought to the shareholders for a vote. Usually these concern a change of accountants, executive compensation plans, issuance of stock options, and related issues.

While most companies make these documents available on their Web pages, and they are also available at the Securities and Exchange Commission site, remember that you can always request a copy from the company's Investor Relations office as well. Look for an [Investor Relations] link for contact information.

Company Profiles, or All the News in One Place

While finding information on a company directly from its Web site can be useful, sometimes all you really need is a thumbnail profile of what the company does, its basic financials from the past couple of years, and a list of recent articles about the company. Finding that on a company's Web site can take a lot of time and mouse-clicks; consider using one of the one-stop sources for company profiles instead.

Hoovering the Information

Hoover's (www.hoovers.com) is perhaps the best-known of the Web sites specializing in providing company profiles. The appeal of Hoover's information is that it is clear and concise, well-formatted, and contains just about all the basics you would need on most major companies, both public and private. Hoover's focuses primarily on U.S.-based companies but also includes profiles for major foreign companies as well. Hoover's offers 14,000 company capsules (brief company descriptions and financials) for free and 8000 company profiles (company histories, strategies, market positions, major events, and other information) via online subscription. Figure 12.2 gives an example of the company capsule for Monsanto; the material indicated by key icons is available only to subscribers. (And no, the name Hoover's wasn't inspired by either the Hoover vacuum cleaner or J. Edgar Hoover's fame at finding information—it's the name of the founder of the company.)

Portals of Information

Although the term *portal* might suggest merely a doorway through which you pass without a moment's thought, in fact Web portal sites are designed to encourage you to come and stay for a while. One of the best-known and longest-running of the portals is Excite (www.excite.com), which started out as a Web search engine but has added a number of features that help you find information faster. For example, if you type in the word *Xerox* in the search box, instead of simply displaying all the Web sites in which that word appears (as you would expect from a Web search engine), Excite first shows a preformatted report on Xerox Corporation. See Figure 12.3 for the Excite results screen.

In this example, Excite has pulled together links to Xerox's corporate site; current stock information; a link to Quicken.com's company profile;

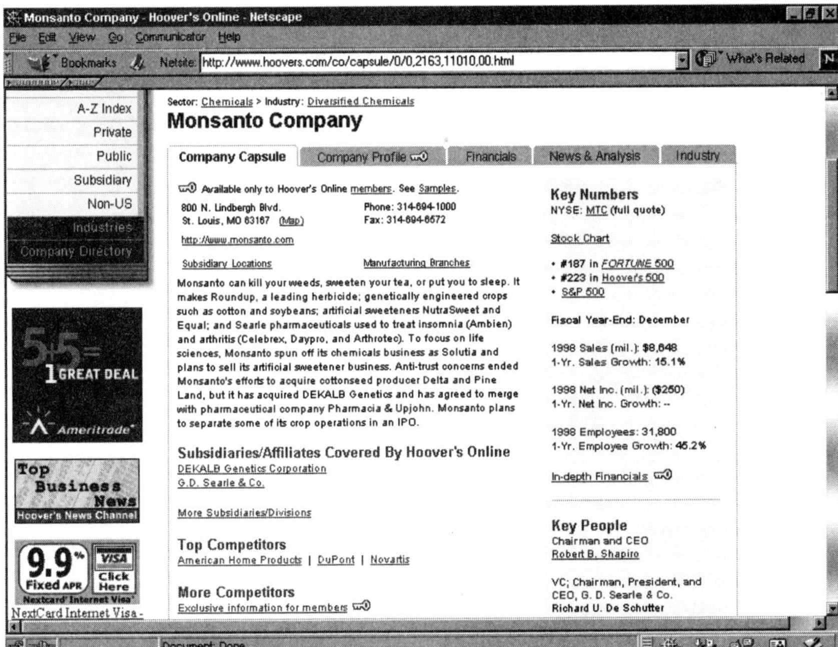

Figure 12.2. Hoover's provides well-written profiles for about 14,000 companies.

recent news items on Xerox; and then way down at the bottom of the screen, you see the typical Web search engine results for the term *Xerox.*

GO Network (infoseek.go.com) and AskJeeves (www.aj.com) offer similar services, although neither has as accessible a format as Excite.

Dow Jones Gives It Away

Dow Jones is known for several things, most notably its flagship production, *The Wall Street Journal,* and the fee-based online service, Dow Jones Interactive (djinteractive.com). (See Chapter 11 for a discussion of the Dow Jones Interactive service.) But Dow Jones also has a free Web-based information service at www.dowjones.com, which offers company news and press releases, current stock prices, and links to companies' Web sites. In addition, the site displays headlines for the five most current articles from *The Wall Street Journal,* although you have to subscribe to DJ Interactive or the Wall Street Journal Interactive Edition service in order to read the articles. See Figure 12.4 for an example of the result of a DowJones.com search for *Sony.*

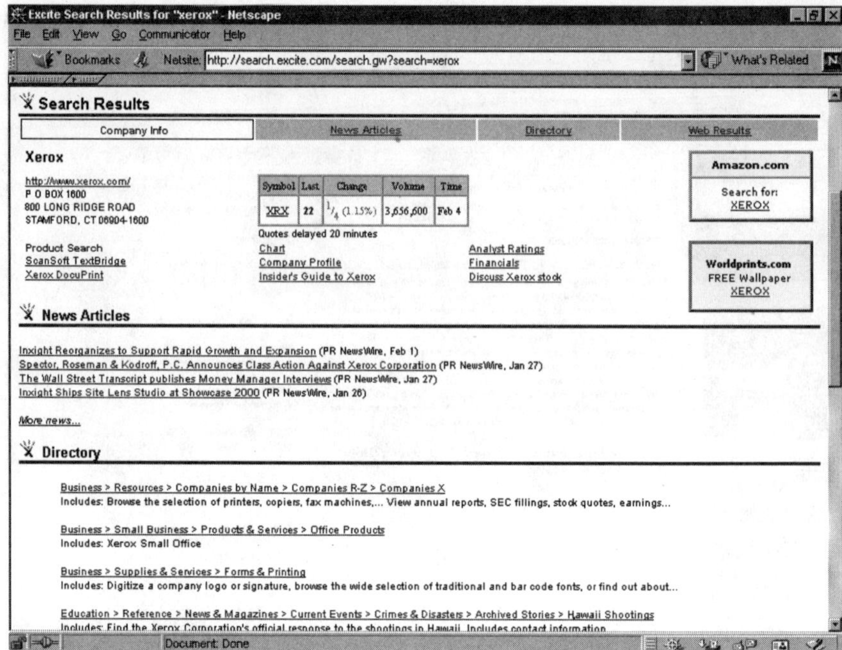

Figure 12.3. Excite.com's portal site assumes that if you search for the word *Xerox* you probably want information on Xerox Corporation.

Other Company Profile Metasites

There are plenty of other sources for company snapshots, and your selection may come down to what format and presentation style you prefer. The following two sites are more properly considered "metasites"; they compile links to other, primary sources, and their value lies is the fact that the Web site designers have done the legwork to identify the sources you will want to visit in order to get the company information you need.

The Wall Street Research Net (www.wsrn.com), described in Chapter 4, pulls together links to the financial filings, news, stock quotes, and analysts' reports of U.S. and Canadian companies in a single, somewhat dense format. Click [Research a Company] at the main screen to retrieve the company profiles. While WSRN compiles links to a number of sources, a disadvantage is that you must click separately on each link to dig down to the information on a company; you do not see all of the information displayed on a single screen.

Another company metasite, easier on the eyes, is CorporateInformation (www.corporateinformation.com). Unlike the other sites listed in this

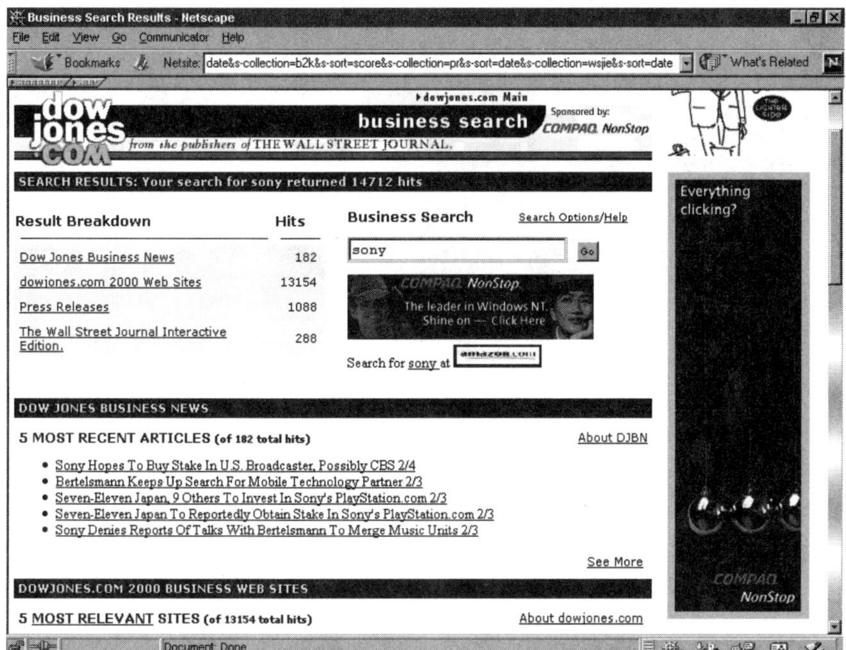

Figure 12.4. DowJones.com offers a quick overview of company news from its site at no charge.

chapter, this one began as a real labor of love by a researcher who was frustrated when trying to use Web search engines to find company information. (Click on [Why This Site?] for more background on the site.) Corporate-Information covers companies from around the world, although some countries do not offer much in the way of Web-based information on companies. Perhaps the most striking elements about this site are the specialized sources from which it draws. Figure 12.5, for example, shows the links for information on Moto Photo; the list even includes *Entrepreneur* magazine's Franchise 500.

Competitive Intelligence—You Mean Dumpster-Diving?

One of the uses of company information on the Web is for what is called *competitive intelligence.* In general, competitive intelligence (or CI) involves collecting information on the competitive environment that a company

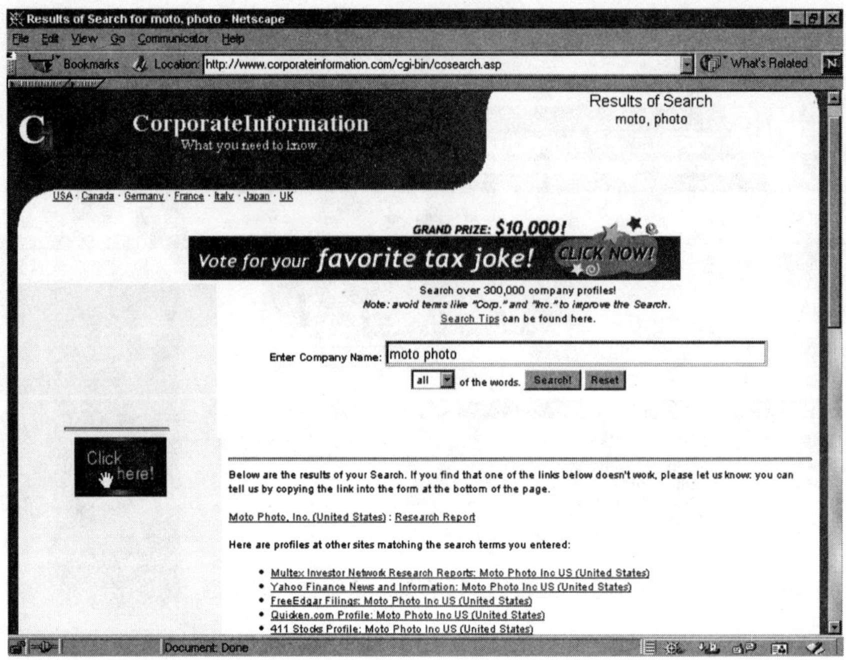

Figure 12.5. CorporateInformation.com draws from a wide variety of Web-based sources for its links.

faces, including information on actual and potential competitors. CI has suffered from a reputation in the past of involving "dumpster-diving"—digging through a competitor's trash to find confidential documents, discarded product prototypes, and other confidential information. However, CI is equally effective when done through legitimate (and clean) techniques, including scouring a company's Web site to see what information it is inadvertently giving away.

Snooping Through a Competitor's Web Site

If you are looking for information on a competitor, there are a number of things to look for on the Web. The following list only touches on some of the information likely to be found there:

- *The information technology used by the company.* Skim through the company's job listings and see what kinds of programmers and IT professionals the company is looking for. Go to the résumé data banks such as Monster Board (www.monsterboard.com) or Career Mosaic (www.careermosaic.com) and scan the job listings for the target company to see what types of skills they require. Likewise, look through résumés of current employees of the company and see what skills and experience they list. This can often indicate what technology is deployed in the company.

- *What area a company is expanding into.* Look for a concentration of job listings at the company's Web site in a certain geographic area or with a certain industry focus. Are they looking for lots of people with an expertise in a technology they have not ventured into before?
- *Who is talking about the company.* Use what is sometimes called a *reverse Web link look-up* to see what companies are linking *to* a site. Some of the major search engines offer this feature. For example, to look for any Web site that has linked to E.I. DuPont de Nemours, you can go to AltaVista (www.altavista.com), and type *link:www.dupont.com* in the search box. A similar technique works on HotBot (www.hotbot.com); type *www.dupont.com* in the search box, then pull down the menu under [Look For] and select [Links To This URL]. Google (www.google.com) is particularly strong in this area. Type *link:www.dupont.com* in the search box. Why would you care about this? Sometimes a small company will publicize the fact that it is a supplier to a large company and will provide a link to that company. While the larger company may not have publicized the relationship, the smaller company might describe on its Web site the products or services it has provided to the larger company. And the fastest way to find that relationship is by using the reverse link look-up.
- *What the local press is saying about the company.* Look up the local newspapers in Yahoo! (www.yahoo.com) by drilling down from the News & Media category. Sometimes a local newspaper or business journal will offer better coverage of a company than the major business magazines or trade press. See also Chapter 10 for more suggestions on how to track down news on a company.

For more information about techniques of competitive intelligence, check out the Web site of the Society of Competitive Intelligence Professionals (www.scip.org). The association has a good discussion of what is involved in CI at its [What is CI] link, which discusses ethical and legal considerations and provides a Frequently Asked Questions file about CI.

Letting Others Do Your Sleuthing for You

If it seems like too much work to monitor the competition yourself, there are Web sites that offer to do at least some of the work for you. Company Sleuth (company.sleuth.com) is a free service that monitors a number of sources on the Web for current information and discussions on whatever company you want to track. Obviously, it works best with larger companies; a small start-up that has not yet established a presence on the Net may not appear much in Company Sleuth's scanning. What does Company Sleuth look for?

- New patent filings
- SEC filings
- Job postings
- Mentions of the company on message boards
- Current business news
- Earnings estimates

Yes, you could find all this on your own: The advantage of Company Sleuth is that it sends the information automatically. Note that much of this information won't be found from a search in one of the search engines; you would have to go to each site individually and look up the company information. You can have this information delivered via email, or you can visit the Company Sleuth site to view it there. If you're tracking a large company, prepare for some large emails! Figure 12.6 shows the results of a "stake-out" of Amazon.com.

Should I Wear a Disguise?

What about the reverse angle of competitive intelligence research—what information are you giving away when you look through competitors' sites? A surprising number of company Web sites require that you register before you gain access to the site (surprising, because it would seem to deter visitors when most companies want to encourage traffic to their sites). Obviously, once you disclose your email address, your travels through the Web site can and may be recorded. And if you visit the site from your office, your company name is most likely going to appear in your email address.

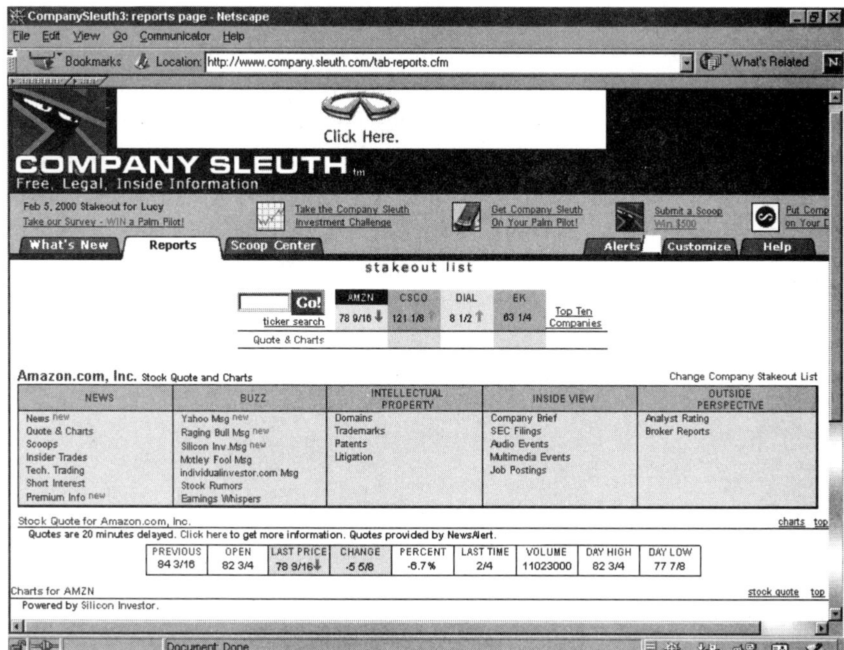

Figure 12.6. Company Sleuth tracks company information that can't be found on search engines.

In addition, many Web sites track the domain names of the visitors to their site regardless of whether you have registered or not, so they would have a record of the fact that someone at AcmeWidgets.com had been poking around in their Web site. Perhaps that would not be of particular note; it is also possible that you do not want to leave any footsteps behind when you visit a competitor's Web site.

If you are concerned about this, you have a few options for anonymizing your browser. The simplest and most foolproof solution is to use an outside telephone line (rather than your office's network) and connect to the Internet using a separate Internet service provider such as America Online. A Web site will see you as JoeSmith@aol.com, for example, rather than Joe_Smith@AcmeWidgets.com.

There are other ways of putting on a mask when browsing a competitor's Web site, most of which go beyond the scope of this book. You can check with your network administrator for help in turning off some of the information usually handed out by your browser. There are sites on the

Web that claim to strip all identifying information from your profile, enabling you to travel incognito. One of the best known is Anonymizer (www.anonymizer.com). If you are concerned about this, though, the best solution is to do your competitive intelligence surfing from home, using an Internet service provider that doesn't indicate your company name.

13
Let's Talk About It

You probably like making your own decisions regarding investments and financial planning; that is why you are reading this book instead of paying someone else to manage your money for you. But there are times when it is nice to hear what others have to say—such input provides you with useful perspectives; it can confirm a hunch; you might even learn something.

This chapter will cover electronic bulletin boards and discussion groups, forums on America Online and CompuServe, and other avenues for conversing with fellow investors.

Email Lists, Discussion Groups, and Message Boards

So, what's the difference between an email list and a message board? The major distinguishing factor is how the messages are delivered and what the interface looks like. The principal ways that people carry on electronic conversations with groups of others are:

- Electronic mail lists
- Usenet newsgroups
- Message boards, hosted on individual Web sites

Email lists are, as the name implies, discussions that appear as messages arriving in email. You don't have to do anything; the messages come to you (and depending on how active the discussion group is, they keep coming and coming and coming). Usenet newsgroups and message boards, on the other hand, require that you *go* somewhere to view messages and to post your own messages.

What's a Listserv?

One of the earliest uses of the Internet was email. We just can't resist talking with each other, and the development of Net-based electronic mail ensured that the Net was going to be a permanent fixture of the Information Age. In addition to using email to keep in touch with Aunt Flo and Uncle Pete, people started using email to broadcast a message to a group of recipients simultaneously. If someone wanted to respond, he or she would then send a reply to everyone on the distribution list. This became cumbersome, particularly as the number of participants in a discussion grew.

Enter the electronic mailing list manager. These are software products that simplify email discussion groups. Participants send their messages to a single address; the software automatically forwards each message on to everyone in the group. These electronic discussion groups are often called *listservs*. Note, though, that LISTSERV is a registered trademark of L-Soft. Since the name *listserv* often appears in the email address for a discussion group managed by the LISTSERV software, the name has stuck as a generic term. Other electronic mailing list management software packages include Listproc, Mailbase, Mailserv, and Majordomo.

One of the advantages of email discussion groups is that once you've joined you don't have to do anything to participate. You send one email message to start your subscription, then you automatically receive every message sent to the discussion group in your email. Obviously, this can also be one of the disadvantages of an email discussion group; a very talkative group could result in your receiving 100 or more messages a day. Most mailing list management systems offer the option of receiving the messages in a *digest*—a single email message sent out at the end of each day, with all the day's postings to the discussion group in a single, sometimes very long file. See Figure 13.1 for an example of a day's email from one investment discussion group.

You can subscribe to discussion groups on everything from day trading to offshore small-cap investors to the Ukrainian stock market. Remember that as a rule no one is reviewing each message for accuracy. Some of the postings may be self-serving, misleading, or down-

```
21 Dec 1999 20:45:56  -0000  From: oaktree150    Subj: VILN
21 Dec 1999 14:21:51  -0000  From: crowmom33     Subj: DATEK
21 Dec 1999 12:41:00  EST  From: Allyrip       Subj: Is This for Real????
21 Dec 1999 12:10:04  EST  From: OAKTREE150   Subj: Did you see this one?
21 Dec 1999 07:39:22  EST  From: Singh1997     Subj: FANTASY turned REALITY!!!!
20 Dec 1999 08:09:06  EST  From: raskaln_01     Subj: Re: Best Online Broker?
20 Dec 1999 07:19:06  EST  From: ldepasquale  Subj: 10 Free Shares of Stock
```

Figure 13.1. Electronic discussion groups deliver subscribers' messages directly to your email box.

right fraudulent. They may be advertising pyramid schemes or worthless investments. On the other hand, you can pick up some useful information from fellow investors, provided you keep your skepticism meter set on high. See Chapter 15 for more information on scams and frauds.

How to Find Email Discussion Groups

Unlike Web sites or printed publications, email discussion groups are sometimes difficult to find, since the email lists are simply kept in a list management program on a server. There are several directories that attempt to catalog all of the publicly available lists. One is maintained by L-Soft, the company that developed the LISTSERV software (www.lsoft.com/lists/listref.html). It only includes email discussion lists that use LISTSERV, but it is well-maintained and includes over 25,000 lists.

Liszt (www.liszt.com) is another longtime mailing list directory, containing close to 100,000 listings. Not only does Liszt have a searchable database of discussion groups, but it also has a browsable catalog, broken down by categories. See Figure 13.2 for Liszt's search page. To find discussion groups on investing, you can either type the word *invest* in the search box or you can click the [Finance] link (under Business).

And finally, there is PAML, which stands for Publicly Accessible Mailing Lists, at www.neosoft.com/internet/paml. As with Liszt, you can scan the directory by subject or you can search by mailing list name or

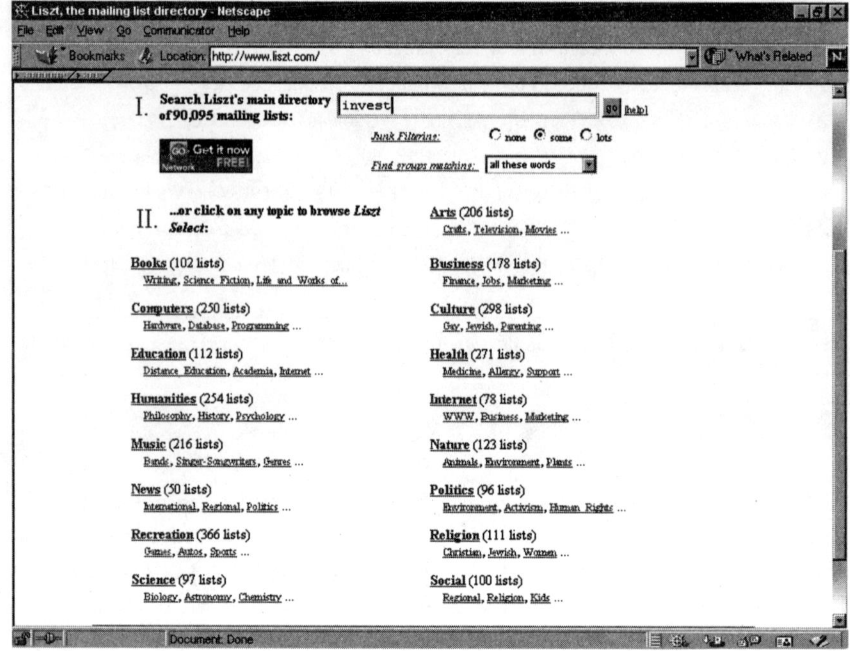

Figure 13.2. Liszt lets you browse through a catalog of mailing lists.

address. Remember that, as PAML's name implies, these directories only include public lists—that is, lists that anyone can subscribe to.

And what if you can't find an existing discussion group that meets your needs? Start one of your own! The challenge, of course, is generating enough interest in it and getting enough subscribers who will participate. There are a number of companies that will host your list for a fee, and some Web-based services that offer free list management in exchange for being allowed to include advertising at the end of each message. A list of Internet service providers who are willing to host mailing lists can be found at www.catalog.com/vivian/mailing-list-providers.html. One example of the free (advertising-supported) list management Web sites is eGroups (www.egroups.com).

Using Usenet

Usenet is one of the early forms of electronic conferencing and is similar in concept to email discussion groups. The principal distinction between the two is that while email groups deliver each participant's message directly to every subscriber's email in-box, Usenet postings are stored and readable on an electronic bulletin board. Individual Usenet conferences or discussion groups are called *newsgroups,* and each newsgroup has a name to indicate its focus.

The naming convention of Usenet newsgroups is similar to that of Web addresses—first an acronym indicating the general area of discussion (e.g., computers, news, recreation), then the general category (e.g., invest, games, taxes), and finally a specific topic (e.g., stocks, mutual funds). Because of how newsgroups evolved, most finance and investment newsgroups are categorized under either *alt* (short for alternative) or *misc* (short for, you guessed it, miscellaneous), two catchall categories. You can browse newsgroups by category or search for newsgroups by name at RemarQ (www.remarq.com). If you find a newsgroup that you want to monitor, click the [Watch this forum] link to create a customized MyRemarQ profile. America Online subscribers can also read newsgroups with the proprietary area of AOL by using the keyword Newsgroups.

One of the biggest drawbacks of Usenet newsgroups is that *anyone* can post a message; there is no need to even go through the simple step of subscribing, as is required with most email discussion groups. As a result, the proportion of irrelevant or argumentative messages is fairly high in newsgroups (sometimes referred to as a *low signal-to-noise ratio* or *a high rate of spam-postings* unrelated to the subject of the newsgroup). See Figure 13.3 for a sample list of subjects appearing in the misc.invest.mutual-funds newsgroup.

Subject:	Number of messages:
Buy & hold or ???	1
Re: managing my elderly mother's finances	2
Charity Football Pool: $17,000 prize money	1
OK, Spammer, what's in it for you????	4
#@#A Fantastic Investment!#@#	1
Oppenheimer Mutual funds!!!	1
The Dow is going to rebound . . .	2

Figure 13.3. Usenet newsgroups tend to have a low signal:noise ratio.

What About Message Boards?

Electronic message boards are similar to Usenet newsgroups in that you *go* somewhere on the Net to read messages. They differ from newsgroups in that they are hosted by individual Web sites, so you just go to a Web address to read and participate. There tends to be less spam and noise on message boards, if for no other reason than it's often too much work for spammers to go from site to site, posting irrelevant advertising. And the managers of many message boards devote a good deal of time to editing irrelevant postings out of the boards. Some of these message boards can be quite useful, particularly if the hosting Web site makes an effort to bring in experts to answer questions and participate in the discussion.

There is no central list of all message boards; the best way to identify them is to watch for them as you visit Web sites. Look for links to [discussion area], [message board], [forum], or [chat room]. Examples of well-designed and active message boards include those on The Motley Fool's site (boards.fool.com), the [Socialize on Morningstar.Net] section of Morningstar's site (www.morningstar.com), and the boards sponsored by Quicken, the financial management software (quicken.excite.com/forums). Note that most boards are organized by *folder* or *conversation*—there will be separate discussion folders on each topic. See Figure 13.4 for a listing of the conversations within the Morningstar site's forum on "Beyond the Basics."

Monitoring Discussion Groups

Clearly, there are plenty of discussions out there on the Web. And you probably don't have time to monitor even a small percentage of them. Fortunately, there are a number of ways for you to set up the equivalent of an electronic clipping service that will watch the publicly accessible discussion groups for any mention of a specific company or topic.

Some Web sites are designed specifically for tracking company news, and will include a feature to monitor electronic discussions. Company Sleuth (company.sleuth.com) is one such site. Once you set up a profile, the site will watch for any mentions of the company or companies you wish to have tracked in public discussion areas, and will notify you when new items appear in one of the public discussion groups that it monitors. See Chapter 12 for more discussion of Company Sleuth.

Another option is Deja.com (www.deja.com), a Web site that began as a way of monitoring discussion groups and has grown to include direct access to Usenet newsgroups, a shopping service, and other features. Of interest in this context, though, is the ability to track any word or phrase

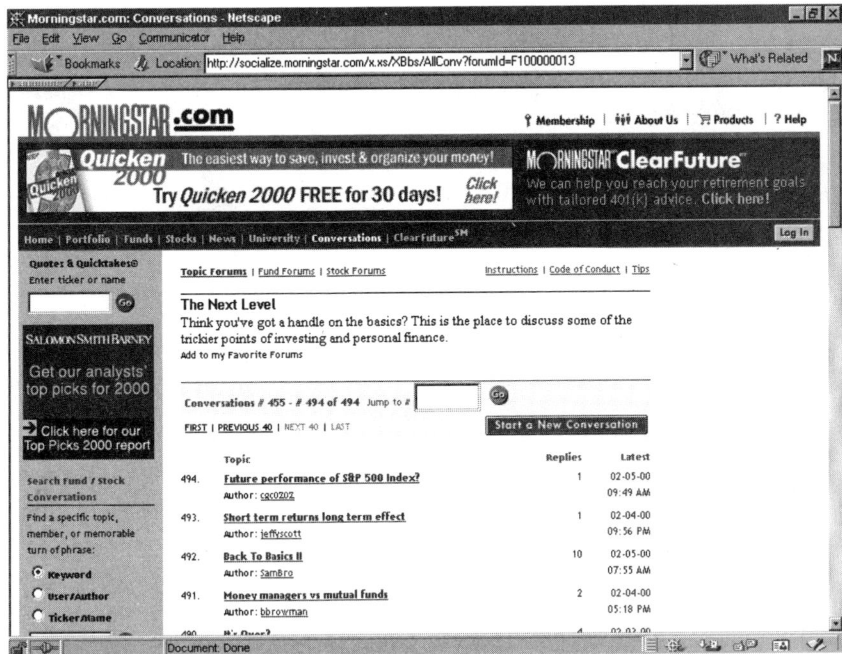

Figure 13.4. Morningstar sponsors a variety of financial forums.

in thousands of Usenet newsgroups and public discussion groups and message boards. Deja.com lets you narrow your search to discussion areas focused on business and finance; unless you want to hear the buzz about a company *anywhere* on the Net, this might be a useful option. If you want to watch for mentions of eToys.com, for example, you may want to limit the search to the two Usenet newsgroup categories *misc.invest* and *alt.invest,* by using the Power Search option. This eliminates mentions such as "I got a good deal on my Beanie Baby through eToys." From the main Deja page, click [Search Discussions], then click [Power Search]. At the Power Search page, type in *etoys* in the Keywords box, pull down the Results Type menu and select Deja Classic, then type **invest** in the Forum search box. See Figure 13.5 for the results of a search for mentions of eToys in the "invest" newsgroups.

If you want to get more comprehensive coverage, eWatch (www.ewatch.com) offers a fee-based service that monitors Usenet groups, electronic discussion groups, forums on America Online, CompuServe, Microsoft Network, and Prodigy, and a number of Web-based message boards. It's not cheap; prices start at $3,600 for 1 to 10 users and go up from there, but this service may well be worth the cost for a company concerned with how

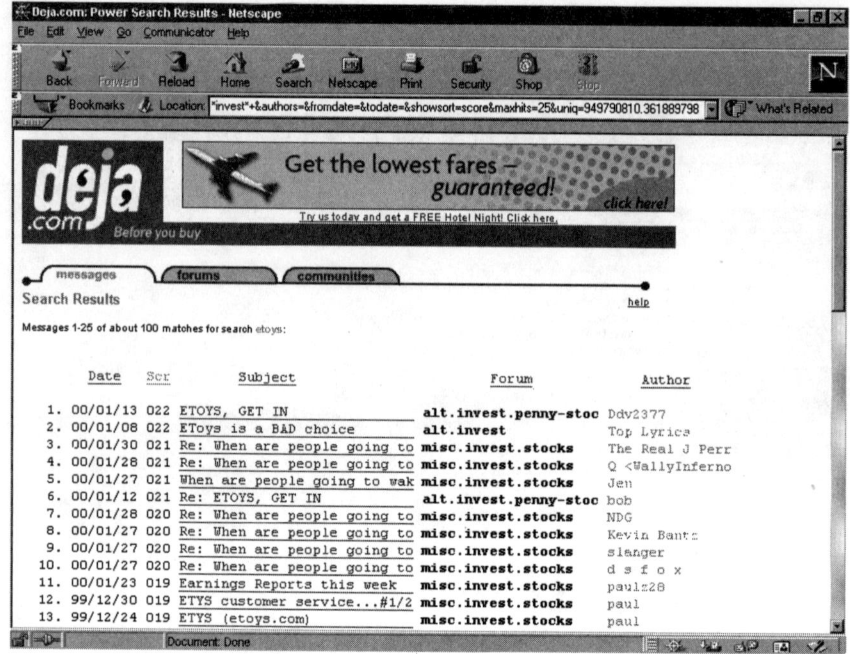

Figure 13.5. Deja.com lets you search for any mention of a company in Usenet newsgroups.

it is being talked about on the Net and wants very specific, fine-tuned monitoring.

Live Chat, or, How Fast Can You Type?

As mentioned previously, some Web sites refer to their message boards as *chat rooms.* This is not to be confused with *live chat* areas, which are sites that allow participants to converse electronically in real time. Live chat participants see what others are typing as they type, and they can respond immediately. Rather than having each message posted (and archived) on an electronic bulletin board, in live chat the participants' comments appear on the screen, then scroll off as later comments replace them. If electronic discussion groups are compared to voice mail, live chat is the equivalent of a live telephone conversation. Unfortunately, many chat areas quickly degenerate into, shall we say, less-than-mature conversations. Participants come and go and, unlike established electronic communities such as long-running email discussion groups, you have no way of getting to know the reputation of the people with whom you are talking. You will probably find that there are more productive ways to use your time than spending it in chat areas. If, however, you want to try out a few, start with the listings in Yahoo!'s Net Events directory (events.yahoo.com). Drill down from the [Business & Economy] category, to [Finance & Investment], and then to [Chat Rooms].

What About AOL and CompuServe?

Strictly speaking, the members-only discussion forums of America Online, CompuServe, Microsoft Network, and Prodigy are not part of the Web, and consequently are beyond the focus of this book. But they deserve mention here simply because one of the selling points of these online services is that not only do they offer access to the Internet but they also provide moderated, value-added message boards for members only. Since these discussion forums are limited to subscribers of the online service, there tends to be far less spam and other irrelevant material on them. This section will look at the discussion areas of America Online and CompuServe—the former because it is by far the largest of the online services, and the latter because it has always focused on attracting and supporting the business and professional community.

America Online

America Online is definitely the 800-pound gorilla when it comes to online services. Its early strategy of mailing CDs of its software to virtually every household in America (or so it seemed) has paid off; it has by far the largest market share of any online service—or of any Internet service provider, for that matter. (To subscribe, go to www.aol.com, click [Download AOL] to get the required proprietary AOL software, and follow the instructions on setting up a subscription.)

Keep in mind that AOL both provides a gateway to the Internet and maintains proprietary content available only to AOL subscribers. It breaks out its content into *channels,* and you will see the main Channels menu when you log on. Click the [Personal Finance] channel, then click [Investing Forums], or use the Keyword: Investing to go straight to the investing discussion groups. See Figure 13.6 for the main Investing Forums screen.

In the left-hand side of the screen, you will see a list of message boards on investing topics. Note that the message boards are listed by general category; when you click on one of the categories, you will see a listing of the subcategories, and you drill down from there. For example, if you click [Stocks A], you will see a list of subcategories of all the discussions of companies whose names start with A—Stocks Aa-Ac, Stocks Ad-Ah, Stocks Aj-Al, and so on. Click on [Stocks Aa-Ac] to get a listing of all the company topics within that category:

AAON Inc. (AAON)

ABC Rail Products Corp. (ABCR)

ACTV, Inc. (IATV)

and so on.

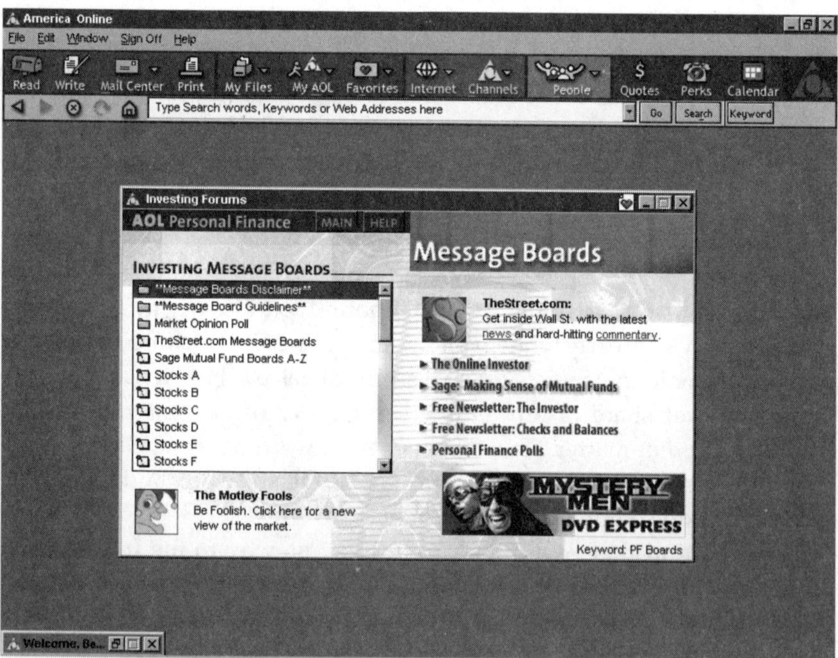

Figure 13.6. America Online breaks out its discussion forums by company.

Within each of these topics are individual postings about the company and its stock. It can be a bit frustrating to have to drill down from category to subcategory to sub-subcategory, and so on, but this structure does ensure that each discussion is focused on a single company.

CompuServe

CompuServe is one of the original online services, dating back to 1979. It became known for its high-quality discussion forums and proactive forum moderators. In an environment of all-you-can-eat pricing by most of its competitors, CompuServe was one of the few services that charged an hourly rate for access to its forums. As a result, it tended to be populated more by professionals who would not balk at paying $50 a month for access to online groups of colleagues and peers. Now, of course, CompuServe offers the same unlimited-use pricing plan as its competitors, but its subscribers still seem to be more focused and business-oriented than those of some of the other online services.

To sign up for CompuServe, go to www.compuserve.com and click the promotional ad to start your subscription. Once you have set up an account, you will have access to all the CompuServe discussion groups. At the main welcome screen, you will see a list of *channels*—CompuServe's name for categories of discussion forums. Click the link for the Personal Finance channel, then click [Forums], or to get there directly, use the GO INVESTORS command. The Personal Finance channel has a number of forums:

- Investor's Forum (which has been in existence since 1982!)
- Personal Finance Forum
- Financial Software Forum
- NAIC Forum (hosted by the National Association of Investors Corporation)
- AARP Forum
- Consumer Savings Forum
- Home Forum (including discussions of financing a home)
- Cars Forum (including discussions of financing an automobile)

Within these forums are lists of *Message Sections*—CompuServe's term for discussion areas—and within each of the message areas are individual folders (just like the message boards on Web sites) and a link to [Chat]. See Figure 13.7 for the front page of the Investors Forum within the Personal Finance channel.

Association Members-Only Discussions

So far, we have looked at email discussion groups, newsgroups, and message boards—all of which at most may require a free registration but do not entail a fee-based subscription—and the online services, which require a monthly fee and offer access to the Internet as well as to a wide variety of proprietary channels of information. A third type of online discussion is that sponsored by investment-related associations and which is often limited to members only. The advantage of such message boards is that the participants are, by virtue of the fact that they're dues-paying association members, perhaps more committed to the exchange

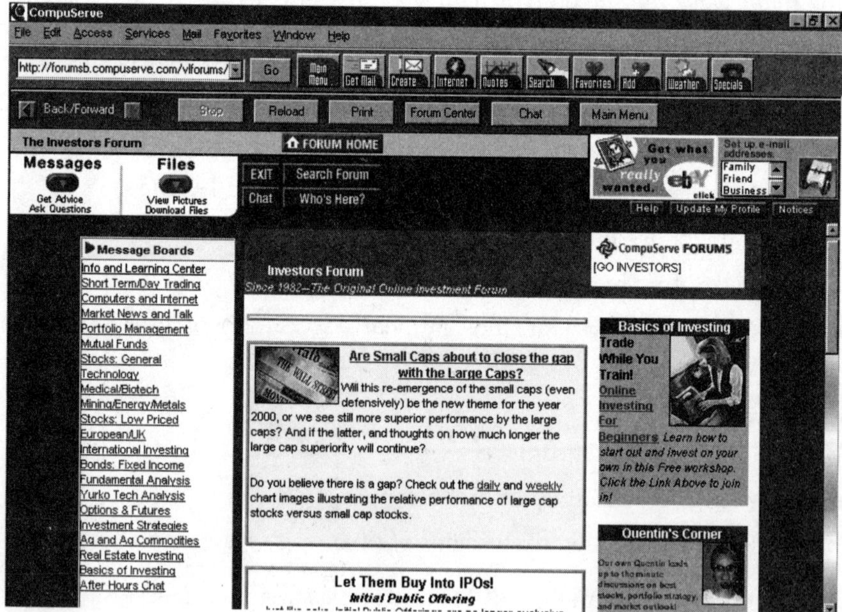

Figure 13.7. CompuServe has a number of well-moderated discussion forums.

of high-quality information. Of course, there are always going to be newcomers who are asking relatively basic questions; they join investors' associations to educate themselves. But there are far fewer spamming messages and irrelevant postings in these members-only discussion groups than there are in the boards accessible by the general public.

American Association of Individual Investors

AAII, the American Association of Individual Investors, has a well-designed message board area on its Web site. Unlike many other subscriber-only sites, it even offers a two-week free trial. Go to www.aaii.com and click [Register] for a trial membership.

The message boards are organized by general area:

- Education
- Investing basics
- Financial planning
- Mutual funds
- Stocks
- Broker issues
- Other investments
- Portfolio management

The structure of each board is simple, and browsing the individual discussion threads is straightforward. See Figure 13.8 for a portion of the Portfolio Management message board.

National Association of Investors Corporation

The National Association of Investors Corporation, or NAIC, promotes education for individual investors. Members receive support in establishing investment clubs, access to seminars and workshops, and subscription to *Better Investing*. NAIC also has several message boards on its site, at www.better-investing.org. Unlike other association message boards, these are not limited to NAIC members, although they do require registration.

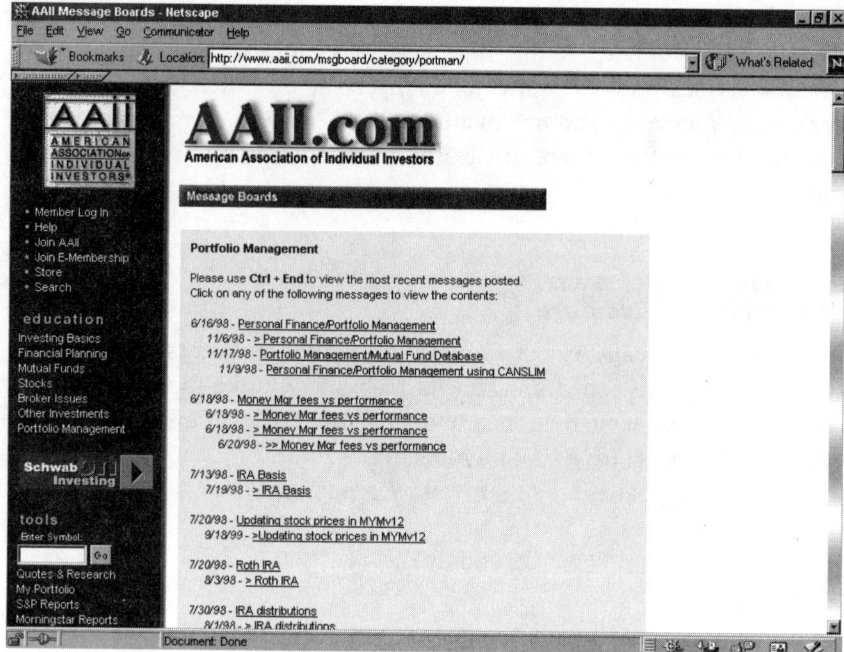

Figure 13.8. The AAII maintains a number of members-only message boards.

They are relatively active; the main I-Club-List board often has over 200 messages posted within just a couple of days. Topics include donor circles; how to provide continuing education within an investment club; evaluating the impact of institutional holdings of a stock; and so on. The postings are usually thoughtful and in-depth.

Investors' Clubs

There are hundreds—maybe thousands—of investors' clubs; small groups of individuals who form a partnership and either make investments collectively or at least collaborate and share research on industries and individual companies. Members contribute to the partnership on a regular basis, and usually each member is responsible for investigating a potential investment periodically. The group shares both the risks and rewards of investing. Investors' clubs often meet on a monthly basis and are usually limited to people in a single geographic area. One useful list of investors' clubs that have a presence on the Net is at www.computerland.net/

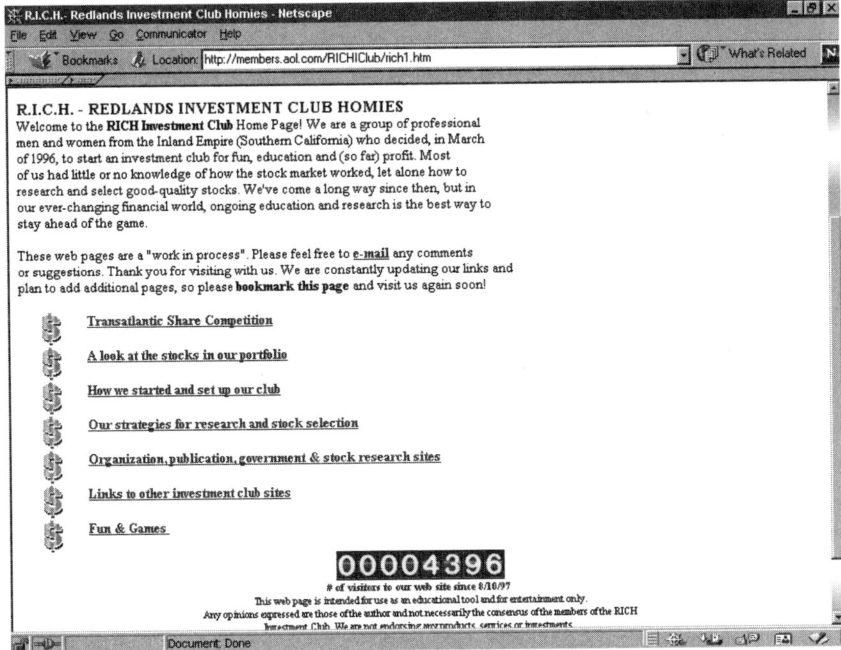

Figure 13.9. Some investment clubs have Web sites that discuss their portfolios and investment strategies.

~missouri/investment_club.htm. While most investors' clubs do not provide online discussion groups (since they often consist of only a dozen or so members), some clubs do maintain Web sites with information on their current portfolios. See Figure 13.9 for an example of an investors' club Web site.

14

Financing College Expenses

Let's face it . . . the two principal reasons why most families invest are for retirement and college expenses. This chapter covers Net resources that help investors find college loans, scholarships, and other financial aid online, and will discuss how to find Internet resources for designing a financial strategy to pay for children's tuition and living expenses. While it won't guarantee your child admission into Harvard, it will at least give you the tools you need to pay for wherever your child decides to go.

Looking for Money in All the Right Places

As more and more Baby Boomer parents face the specter of college tuition for their darlings, there is a corresponding rise in Web sites that provide information on sources for funding. (As one friend whose child just presented him with the bill for the first year's tuition in an Ivy League university said, "I wish I'd made her watch more Saturday morning cartoons. Then maybe she'd just be going to the local community college. . . .") If you start planning early, and look for financial aid from as many sources as possible, you can probably handle the expenses—provided your child doesn't decide to stretch that 4-year undergraduate degree into a 10-year party.

In addition to the resources on the Web, America Online subscribers have access to an area on AOL called Saving For School (yup, that's the Keyword: Saving For School). This area has message boards on various topics pertaining to high school and college (although not much on financing a college education), links to a number of Web resources on planning for your child's college expenses, fact sheets on Education IRAs, and related resources.

When and How to Start Saving

The sites described in Chapter 3 that help you plan for your retirement often also provide guidance on how much you need to save for your child's college education. The Quicken.com site (www.quicken.com), for example, has a section that helps you plan for the financial implications of college, weddings, new children, and so on. Either click on [Retirements] at the initial page and then [Planning], or go directly to www.quicken.com/retirement/planning for a collection of articles and a college planning guide to help you develop your financial strategy.

Likewise, InvestorGuide has a link to a good selection of articles and financial planning calculators and interactive worksheets to assist in planning for your child's college expenses. The simplest way to find all the financial aid information in one place is to go directly to its Classic Web page at www.investorguide.com/FinAid.htm. Figure 14.1 shows a list of some of the resources available at this site.

A number of colleges and universities offer prepaid tuition programs that enable parents to open tuition accounts with a school years before their children are ready for college. The parents lock in tuition costs at current rates and pay into the account on a regular basis; when their children attend college they draw *tuition units* from the account. The National Association of State Treasurers maintains the College Savings Plans Network and a Web site of each state's prepaid college savings program, at www.collegesavings.org. One of the advantages of using a state-sponsored program is that it can often be used for both state-run universities and private colleges and universities. Click [Your State] at the main page, then select your state from the map shown in Figure 14.2 for the College Savings Plans Network Web site for your state.

Finding Scholarship Sources

There are independent programs that fund scholarships for everything from children of Marines, to African-American residents of South Florida enrolled in graduate degree programs in business administration, to gay

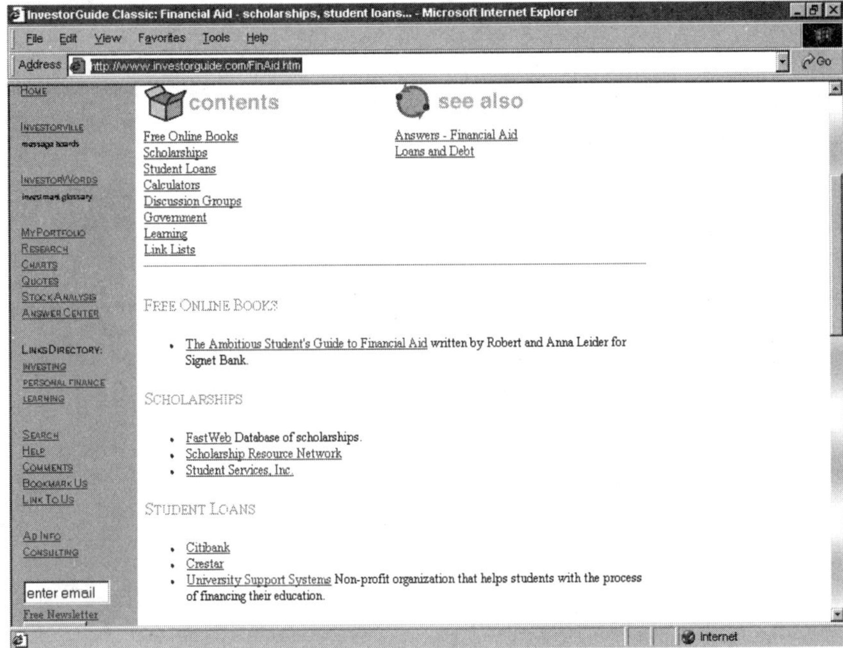

Figure 14.1. The InvestorGuide site includes a good collection of planning guides for college expenses.

students attending a school in Minnesota. How do you find out about these programs? The best way is to ask:

- The guidance counselor at your child's high school
- The financial aid offices of any school your child shows an interest in attending
- Your employer's human resources department—see if they provide financial aid for children of employees, either directly or through a company-sponsored charitable foundation
- The alumni office of the college or university from which you graduated—some schools are known for giving children of alumni preferential treatment
- Professional associations in the subject matter your child is considering—many professional associations offer scholarships to encourage students to consider their field
- Any charitable or nonprofit organizations you or your child belong to—where you worship, service organizations such as Lions, 4-H, or Girl

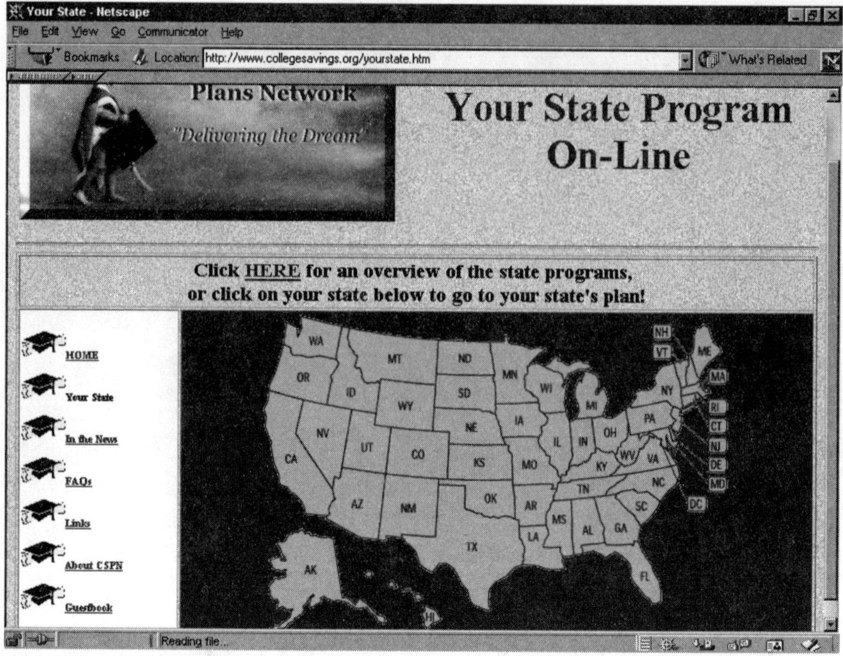

Figure 14.2. The College Savings Plans Network has information on each state's prepaid tuition plan.

Scouts, or groups such as the local chamber of commerce, the American Legion, your union, and your sorority or fraternity

These sources all have the benefit of invoking personal connections between your child and the funding source—something that cannot be replicated by a search on the Web. However, after you have exhausted these sources, it's time to see what you can find online. There are a number of financial aid search services, most of which charge a fee and provide you with a list of 10 or 20 possible scholarship or loan sources. But shop wisely; anyone can set up an electronic store front and offer this service with few credentials or expertise.

One of the best Web sites for general information on advice on student financial aid and sources for identifying loans and scholarships is FinAid (www.finaid.org), maintained by the author of a book on finding financial aid for students. FinAid provides well-designed pages of links to free search services for scholarships and loans. See Figure 14.3 for the page listing scholarship search sites, which is accessible by clicking the [Scholarships] link from the main Web page, then clicking [Other Scholarship Databases].

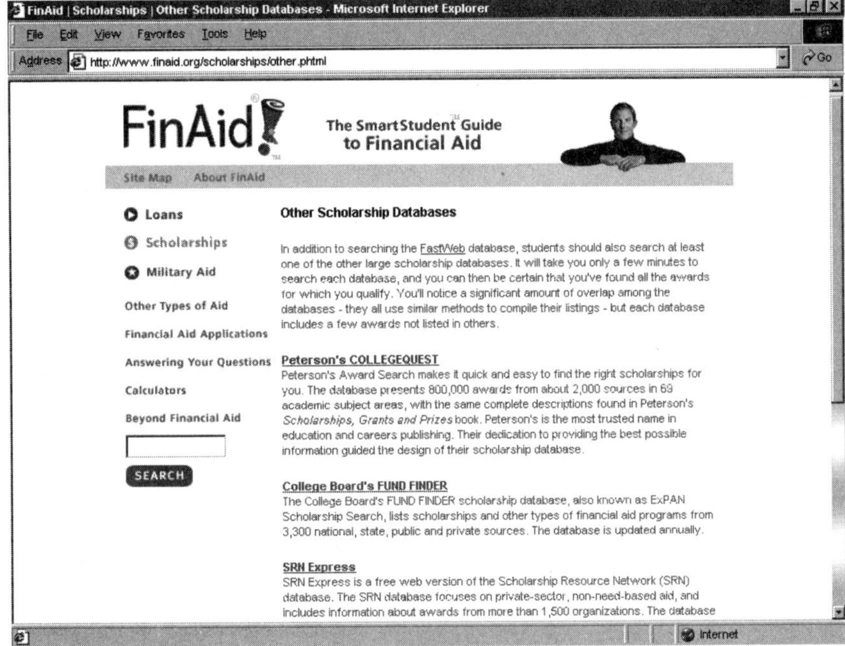

Figure 14.3. FinAid.org provides reviews of the best, free search services for locating financial aid.

Most of the resources listed in the FinAid site will require you to fill out a detailed profile; this may feel intrusive, but the intent is to identify any characteristic that would qualify you for a specialized scholarship. Funding sources often limit their awards to students of a particular ethnic or cultural background or religion, with a specific career objective, or from parents who belong to a particular organization. Search results will usually include a description of the financial aid program and funding organization, along with the necessary contact information. See Figure 14.4 for an example of the information available from the CollegeNET Mach 25 scholarship database.

Sources for Student Loans

While scholarships are more attractive than loans—money that doesn't have to be paid back is preferable to money that does—the available grants, scholarships, and work-study programs often do not provide enough income to cover all tuition, books and other materials, and living expenses. Loans are an alternative, and while the thought of graduating

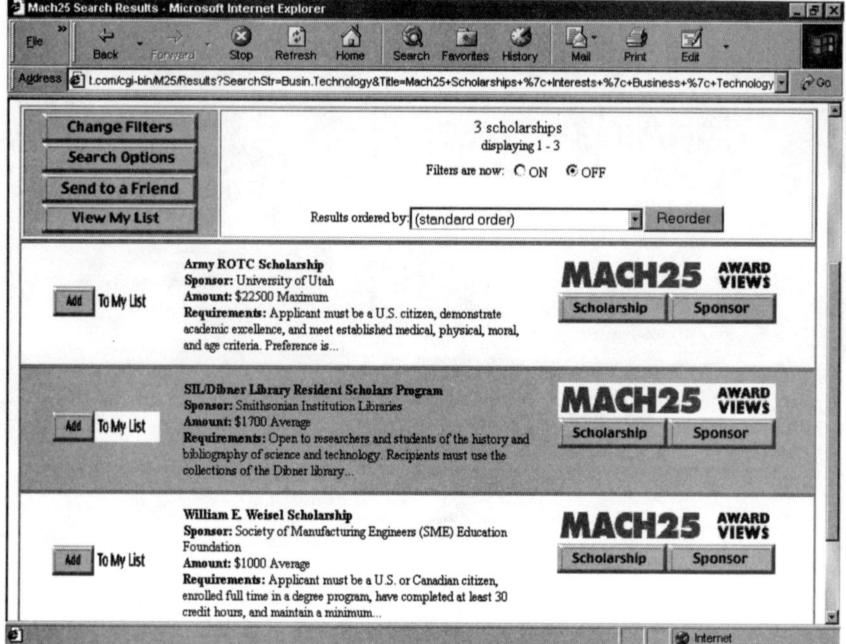

Figure 14.4. The Scholarship Resource Network Express (www.srnexpress.com) provides background information on potential sources of financial aid.

from college saddled with a five-figure debt is daunting to any 18-year-old, at least most student loans are structured to allow for flexible repayment schedules. Federally funded student loans usually offer the lowest interest rate, do not require collateral, offer repayment deferral options, and are sometimes forgiven altogether. (See the next section about loan forgiveness programs.)

And where do you find information on the various student loan options? FinAid, previously described, offers a nice overview of student loan programs at its site, www.finaid.org. (Click on the [Loans] link from the main page.) In addition, look up the Web site for the financial aid office of the school your child is considering attending; many federally funded loans are subsidized by the government but administered by the college or university itself. These days, most schools include their Web addresses on all their correspondence. If your school does not, one way of finding a university's URL is the Web directory maintained by the University of Texas at www.utexas.edu/world/univ. And if you feel adventurous, you can just try guessing the address. As described in Chapter 1, try a few of the obvious forms of the URL, using the following as examples:

- University of California, Berkeley: www.berkeley.edu
- West Virginia University: www.wvu.edu
- Reed College: www.reed.edu

Once you have found your school's site, look for a link to [Financial Aid], [Applying to our school], [Admissions], or [Academic Life]. You will usually see a wide variety of loan programs, along with the necessary application forms and instructions. See Figure 14.5 for an example of West Virginia University's financial aid page describing loan programs.

Nontraditional Sources of College Funding

Scholarships and loans, along with personal savings, are the usual means for financing a college education. However, there are a number of other, nontraditional sources for financial aid. Most of these involve some kind of loan forgiveness program, in which service in a specific program, a

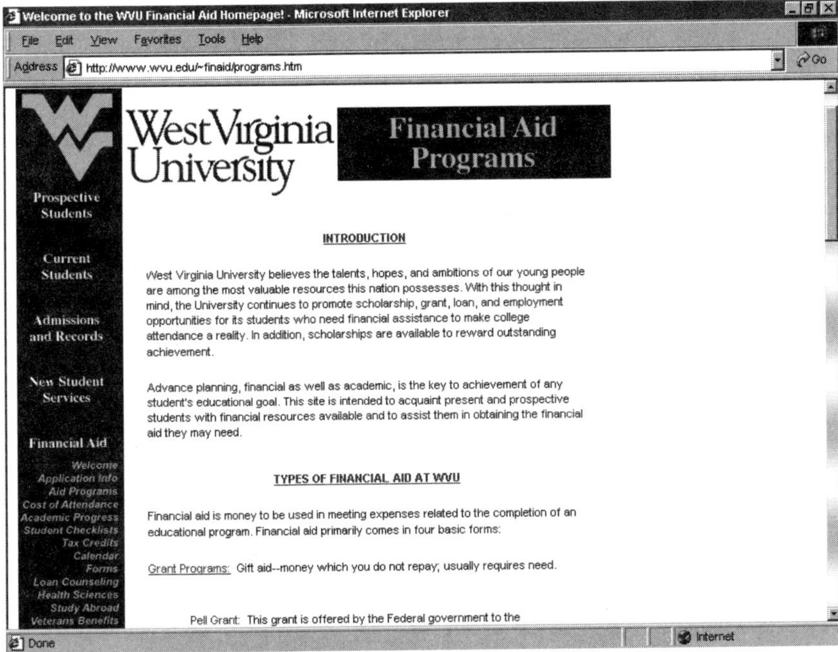

Figure 14.5. West Virginia University's Financial Aid page describes the various kinds of financial aid available.

branch of the military, or profession in an underserved area will result in some or all of your federal student loan being deferred or reimbursed.

Some employers have begun offering to repay student loans in order to attract recent college graduates. While not often publicized, this can be a significant benefit to a new employee faced with having to start repaying those loans. Since repayment of student loans is often used to entice new graduates to geographic areas or professions that are less attractive, students considering loan forgiveness programs would do well to inquire about the availability of such programs as they make decisions about courses of study.

Peace Corps and Related Programs

The Peace Corps (www.peacecorps.gov) is perhaps the best known of the service programs that involve student loan forgiveness. Founded in 1961, the Peace Corps places volunteers in development projects in 80 countries overseas. An assignment lasts for two years; payment of federal student loans is deferred during service; and 30 percent of certain types of loans is cancelled upon completion of the two years of service.

AmeriCorps (www.americorps.org) is collection of several domestic volunteer service programs, including VISTA, the National Civilian Community Corps, and volunteer programs at the state and local level. An education award of $4725 is available upon completion of service, and some student loans can be deferred during service. If the loan qualifies for deferral, AmeriCorps will pay for the accrued interest during the deferral period.

One of the more familiar of the AmeriCorps programs is Volunteers In Service To America. VISTA was founded in 1964 as a kind of domestic Peace Corps, in which volunteers work with community-based nonprofit agencies that address issues relating to poverty, homelessness, illiteracy, and neighborhood revitalization. You can see additional information on VISTA at www.friendsofvista.org.

The National Civilian Community Corps, based on the model of the Depression-era Civilian Conservation Corps, is open to people between the ages of 18 and 24. NCCC volunteers live in one of five campuses that serve the regional needs of the United States and work on environmental projects, disaster relief, education, and public safety. As with the other AmeriCorps programs, education awards and loan forbearance are available to volunteers.

Military Service

The Reserve Officers' Training Corps (ROTC) offers cash incentives and scholarships to college students. Each branch of the military offers its own program:

Army: www-rotc.monroe.army.mil

Air Force: www.afoats.af.mil/rotc.htm

Navy and Marine Corps: www.cnet.navy.mil/nrotc/nrotc.htm

Colleges and universities offer ROTC as elective courses (up to two years), and students are encouraged to join that arm of the military upon graduation. Scholarships of up to $15,000 per year are available; if awarded, the student is required to follow specific academic guidelines and to serve in the National Guard, Reserve, or on active duty upon graduation. Note that not all colleges and universities offer ROTC programs; check the Web site of the ROTC branch being considered for details. See figure 14.6 for the Navy/Marine Corps ROTC site.

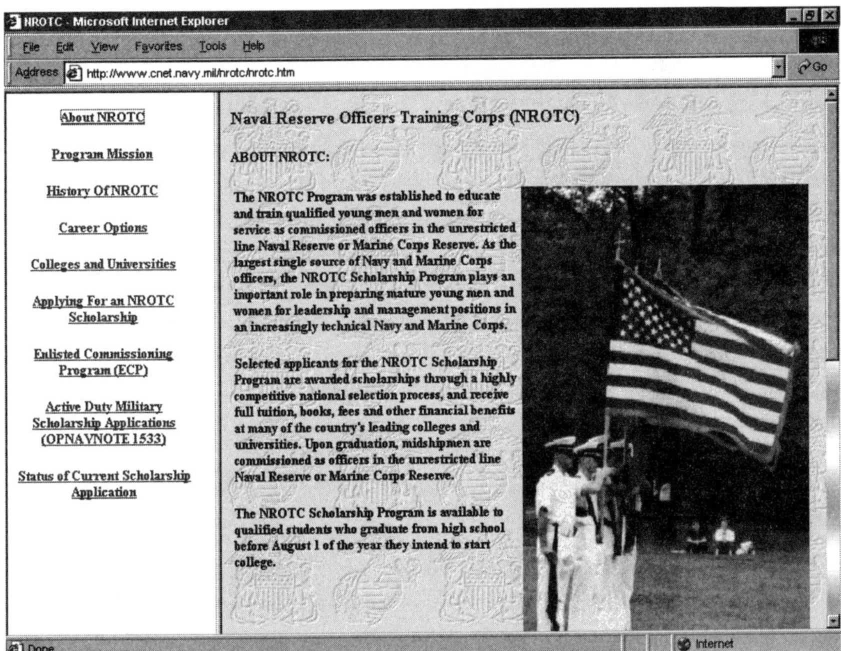

Figure 14.6. ROTC sites include scholarship information and lists of the college that have ROTC programs.

Professional Schools

Many medical and law schools have programs to encourage graduating students to work in underserved areas. The National Health Service Corps (www.bphc.hrsa.gov/nhsc) is a federally funded program that works to increase access to primary medical care to communities traditionally underserved by the profession. Medical or nursing school students can qualify for payment of up to four years of tuition, fees, books, and supplies. In exchange, the students agree to work in a practice site in a federally designated *health professional shortage area* identified as having the greatest need. These are often geographically remote areas or in inner cities. Students pay off their tuition by serving one year in a health professional shortage area for every year of NHSC tuition support, with a two-year minimum.

In a similar program, the National Association for Public Interest Law offers loan repayment assistance programs at a number of law schools. These programs are organized by individual schools and provide relief from student loans for lawyers who pursue public service jobs. See the NAPIL's Web site at www.napil.org for additional information.

We're the Government and We're Here to Help

While we usually think of the government as *taking* our money—in the form of taxes—rather than giving it to us, the federal government can be a real resource when it comes to funding college education. There are a number of federally funded student loan programs that don't require collateral or a prior credit history. Some of these loans can even be forgiven if the recipient serves as a volunteer in the Peace Corps, VISTA, or related programs. And the military has had a long tradition of offering substantial financial aid to students willing to commit to military service after graduation. And, unlikely as it seems, even the Internal Revenue Service can help.

Education IRAs

Chapter 3 looked at Individual Retirement Accounts and related tax-sheltered savings plans. One of the lesser known of these is the Education IRA, which lets you contribute up to $500 a year to an education account for a child under age 18. The contributions to an Education IRA are not deductible, but the amount deposited in the account grows tax-free until withdrawn. For more information about Education IRAs, go to the IRS site at www.irs.ustreas.gov. At the main page, click [Search] and type *Education IRA* in the search box. The site will return a list of IRS forms and publications that describe what is involved in setting up Education IRAs, who qualifies for them, and what restrictions apply. See Figure 14.7 for the results of a search for the phrase *Education IRA.*

U.S. Department of Education

Not surprisingly, the U.S. Department of Education is an excellent source of information on student financial aid. Perhaps most useful is the *Student Guide—Financial Information from the Department of Education,* published each year with updated information on the various grants, student work-study, and student loan programs funded by the federal government. Start at the main Department of Education Web page (www.ed.gov) and click the [Search] button at the top of the page. At the search screen, type

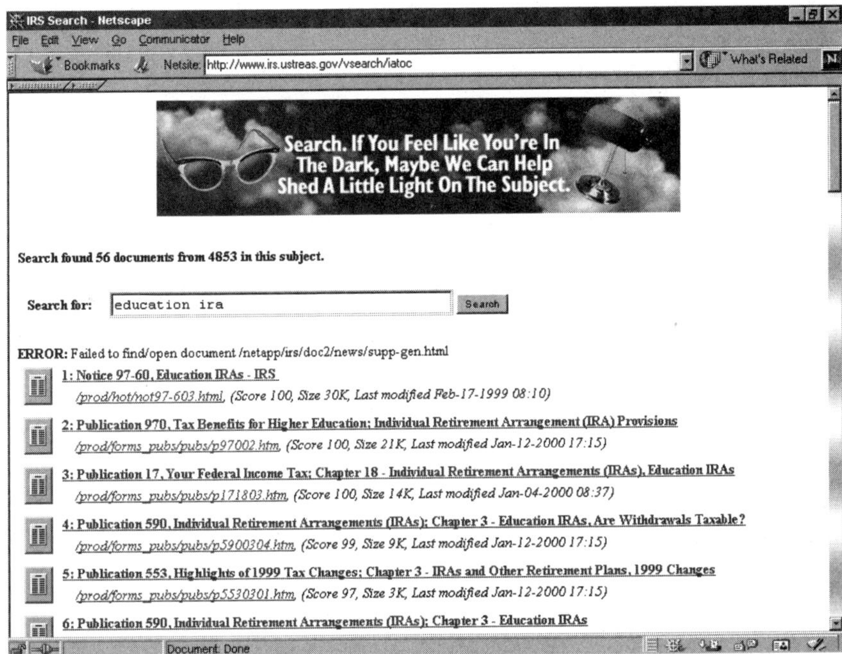

Figure 14.7. Use the [Search] feature on the IRS' Web site to find publications on Education IRAs.

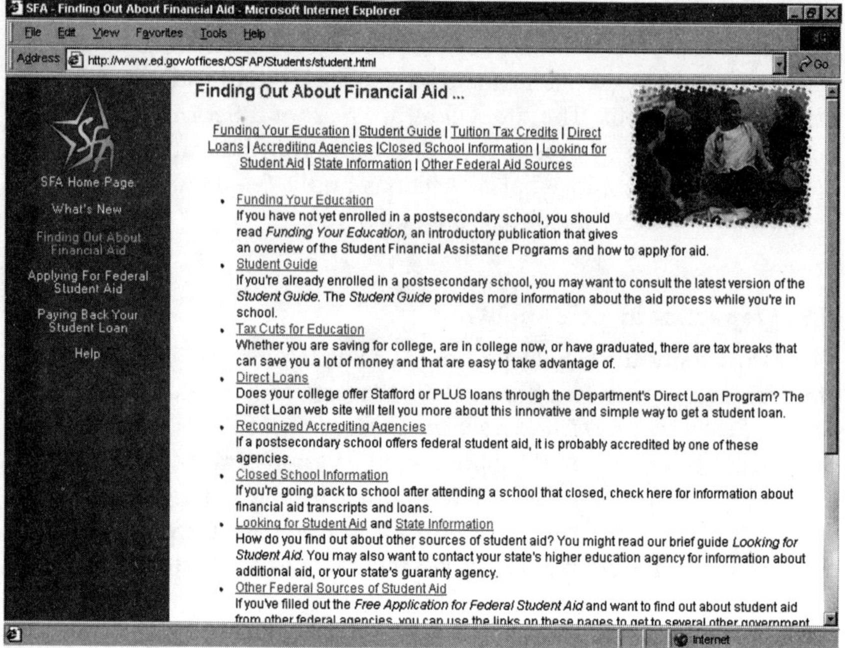

Figure 14.8. The U.S. Department of Education's Web site has a number of publications on student financial aid.

"student guide" (including the quotation marks). The site will return with a list of pages; the link to the *Student Guide* will be near the top of the list. Alternatively, look through the list of [Most Requested Items] at the main Web page; the *Student Guide* is usually among the most popular reports at the Department of Education's site.

At the bottom of the *Student Guide*'s front page, there is also a link, [Finding Out About Financial Aid], that takes you to other sources of information within the Department of Education's site. This page provides information on a variety of student financial aid programs, help for students considering how to pay for college, and related information. See Figure 14.8 for a list of the types of information available through the Department of Education's Office of Student Financial Assistance.

15
Scams and Frauds

As Arthur Levitt, chair of the U.S. Securities and Exchange Commission, has noted, "It is just as easy, if not more, to lose money through the click of a button as it is to make it." It's easy to get swept up in the excitement of the moment, particularly now that electronic brokerages enable investors to execute their own trades. The traditional checks and balances of SEC monitoring and investment house caution do not come into play to protect individual investors, particularly if they rely on information they glean from the Web. As a result, investors have to be more vigilant than ever to detect scams, frauds, and other questionable tactics online. This chapter describes Web-based sources to help you detect and report investment scams. It will also cover the more subtle forms of deception such as insiders promoting their companies' stock and pyramid schemes promoted on the Net.

Running a Reality Check

Yes, if an investment opportunity sounds too good to be true, it probably is. Most people have figured out by now that the sweepstakes letter that promises, "You may already be a winner!" is not necessarily going to be your ticket to early retirement. The smooth-talking telemarketer with the great deal that must be acted upon RIGHT NOW is probably not looking out for your best long-term interest.

Likewise, there are plenty of "opportunities" on the Net that are, shall we say, less than they appear. In fact, the technology of the Web has made it easier than ever for anyone to set up a virtual storefront and appear to be a well-established, reputable business, while actually running the electronic equivalent of a shell game. The Web now lets scam artists reach out and touch millions of people, without having to spend money on postage or long-distance phone calls.

There are plenty of ways to keep your internal scam-meter tuned up. The Federal Trade Commission has a short quiz on its Web site to "Test Your Investment IQ." To find it, go to the FTC's Web site (www.ftc.gov), click the [Consumer Protection] link, then click the [Investments] link. Among the documents listed on this page is the Investment IQ test. Take the test and see how much of a refresher course you'll need in detecting investment fraud. See Figure 15.1 for one of the questions in this test.

Questions to Ask

If someone walked up to you on the street and started telling you about a "once in a lifetime" investment opportunity, you would probably turn and walk the other way. Unfortunately, we sometimes forget that an email about a "great investment" from someone we don't know is equivalent to

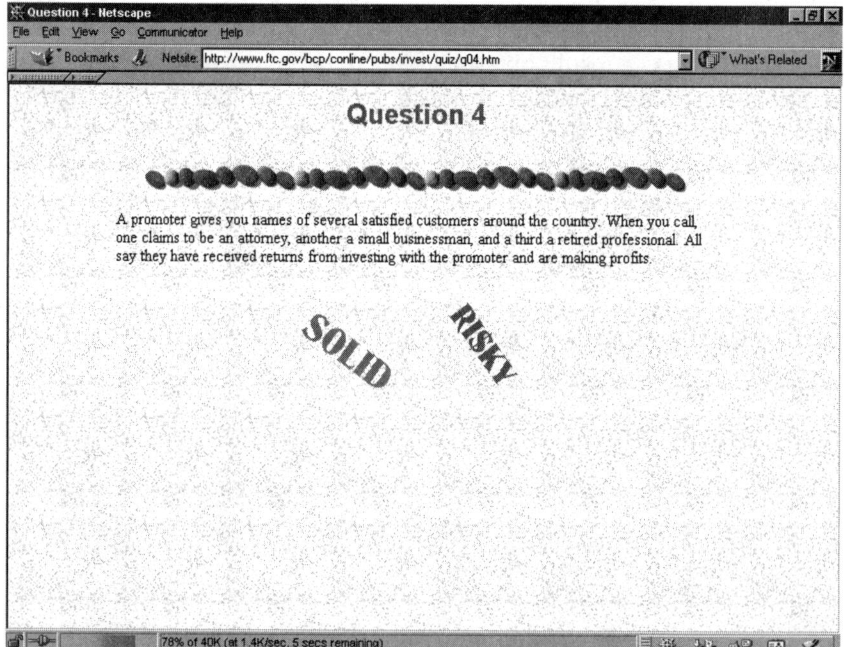

Figure 15.1. The Federal Trade Commission offers a short test to help you evaluate your "investment IQ."

that stranger on the street. The Securities and Exchange Commission hears about many of these too-good-to-be-true offers, and provides a list of 10 questions (www.sec.gov/consumer/10quest.htm) you should ask about any investment opportunity:

1. Is the investment registered with the SEC and the state securities agency in the state where I live, or is it subject to an exemption?
2. Is the person recommending this investment registered with my state securities agency? Is there a record of any complaints about this person?
3. How does this investment match my investment objectives?
4. Where is the company incorporated? Will you send me the latest reports that have been filed on this company?
5. What are the costs to buy, hold, and sell this investment? How easily can I sell?
6. Who is managing the investment? What experience do they have?
7. What is the risk that I could lose the money I invest?
8. What return can I expect on my money? When?
9. How long has the company been in business? Are they making money, and if so, how? What is their product or service? What other companies are in this business?
10. How can I get more information about this investment, such as audited financial statements?

Investigating an Investment

As much as you would like to use the tools on the Web to check out the legitimacy of an investment offer, there are some more traditional steps you should take as well.

Get the solicitation in writing; print a hard copy of any email you receive regarding the investment, or print the pages from the Web site making the offer. Note the full URL and the date that you saw the offer.

If the company is publicly traded, get copies of recent filings from the SEC's EDGAR site at edgar.sec.gov. (See Chapter 9 for more discussion of EDGAR.) If the company is not publicly traded, ask the promoter where the company is incorporated. The state's regulatory body will be able to tell you whether the company is in fact incorporated and if it has an annual financial report on file. But how do you find what number to call?

The Library of Congress has a good directory of state government Web sites, broken out by state. Start at lcweb.loc.gov and click [Using the Library]. At the next screen, click [Explore the Internet], then [State and Local Governments]. This will take you to a set of links for each of the 50 states, which in turn will let you explore a particular state government's Web page. Some states maintain thorough telephone directories; at the least, you should be able to find the office that regulates companies. Look for a Corporations Commission, Department of Commerce, Secretary of State, or Business Services Division (there isn't much consistency in what the regulatory body is called from one state to another).

The information available through states' Web sites varies considerably. To take one example, Maryland allows searches by company name and includes detailed information on companies' filings. While the full text of the filings is not available online, the site provides you with the file number to facilitate ordering a copy of the filing. See Figure 15.2 for the results of a search for companies with the word *History* in their names.

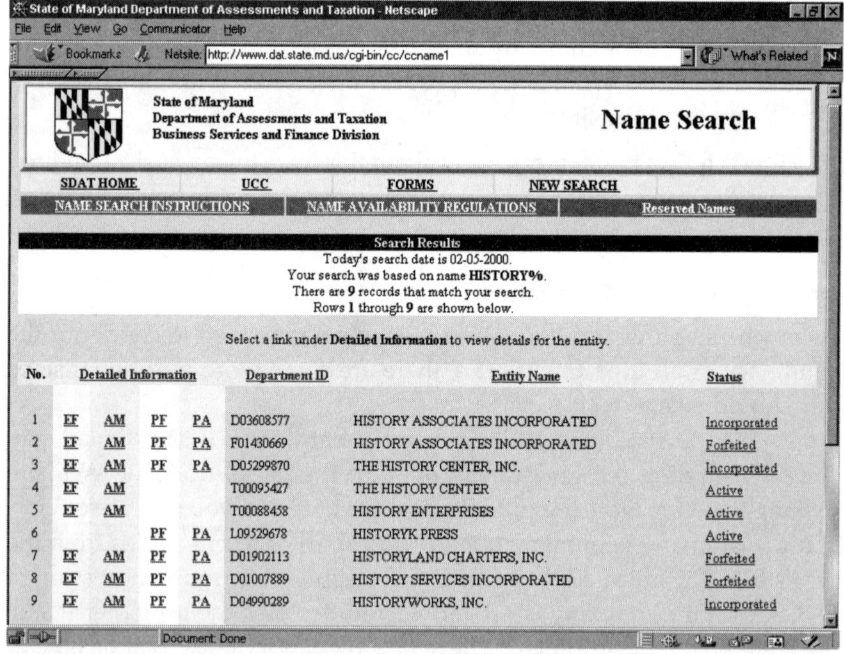

No.	Detailed Information				Department ID	Entity Name	Status
1	EF	AM	PF	PA	D03608577	HISTORY ASSOCIATES INCORPORATED	Incorporated
2	EF	AM	PF	PA	F01430669	HISTORY ASSOCIATES INCORPORATED	Forfeited
3	EF	AM	PF	PA	D05299870	THE HISTORY CENTER, INC.	Incorporated
4	EF	AM			T00095427	THE HISTORY CENTER	Active
5	EF	AM			T00088458	HISTORY ENTERPRISES	Active
6			PF	PA	L09529678	HISTORYK PRESS	Active
7	EF	AM	PF	PA	D01902113	HISTORYLAND CHARTERS, INC.	Forfeited
8	EF	AM	PF	PA	D01007889	HISTORY SERVICES INCORPORATED	Forfeited
9	EF	AM	PF	PA	D04990289	HISTORYWORKS, INC.	Incorporated

Figure 15.2. Maryland lets investors search its corporate records for information on companies incorporated in that state.

Pyramids and MLMs

Just like in what we like to call real life, some "investment opportunities" are actually more accurately called *enrichment schemes for the promoters.* The most common of these are pyramid schemes, many of which have been around in some form or another for decades. Often, you are offered an opportunity to invest in a product or service, with the focus on the commissions you earn by recruiting new investors or distributors. Note that multilevel marketing (MLM) plans also work around the model of distributors and subdistributors. What sets pyramid schemes apart from MLMs is that pyramid schemes focus entirely on gaining commissions by the recruitment of new suckers, er, investors, and the earlier investors make money from the investments of later investors. Eventually, of course, all pyramid schemes collapse, because there are simply not enough people on the planet to support them. A plan that assumes that each new recruit will bring in six more recruits will need 15 *billion* participants by the time the 14th level of marketing is reached. Since there are only 6 billion people alive today, this requires recruiting either unborn generations or extraterrestrials, neither of which are likely candidates for investing in pyramid schemes. See Table 15.1 for the brutal details.

MLMs, on the other hand, focus on the actual product or service being marketed. Investors get a percentage of the commissions earned by the

Table 15.1. How Pyramid Schemes Fall Under Their Own Weight

Level	New Recruits Required to Sustain the Pyramid	Total Number of Participants Required to Sustain the Pyramid
1	1	1
2	6	7
3	36	43
4	216	259
5	1,296	1,555
6	7,776	9,331
7	46,656	55,987
8	279,936	335,923
9	1,679,616	2,015,539
10	10,077,696	12,093,235
11	60,466,176	72,559,411
12	362,797,056	435,356,467
13	2,176,782,336	2,612,138,803
14	13,060,694,016	15,672,832,819

distributors they recruit, but the income is dependent on actual sales, not on the investments of the latest recruits. While MLMs (or *network marketing plans,* as they are sometimes called) sometimes suffer a bad reputation for providing poor-quality merchandise, they can be a legitimate source of income if you are willing to invest the time and energy required to market the product. Established companies such as Amway, Fuller Brush, and Tupperware are forms of MLMs and are reputable and reliable sources of income for people skilled in sales.

The Federal Trade Commission has several one-page reports that describe the warning signs for an illegal pyramid scheme or fraudulent MLM, such as:

- Plans that require new members to spend money on high-priced inventory
- Plans that claim you will make money through continued growth of your distributors' commissions
- High-pressure *opportunity meetings* that encourage you to sign contracts immediately

For a copy of the reports, go to the FTC's site (www.ftc.gov), click the [Consumer Protection] link, then click [Investments]. This will bring you to a list of useful consumer education reports on a number of investment-related issues, including MLMs and pyramid schemes. See Figure 15.3 for a partial list of the available reports.

Traffic Cops on the Information Superhighway

See those flashing red lights in the rearview mirror? That must be the superhighway patrol. Well, perhaps not, but there *are* government agencies and nonprofit groups that serve as watchdogs on the Net. You can report scams to enforcement agencies, look for listings of prior fraudulent activities, and get tips for how to avoid becoming the next victim. Remember, however, that the absence of complaints does not necessarily mean that the company is legitimate; it may just mean that no one has complained yet. Fraudulent companies change names or change officers for the purpose of evading detection, so while the lack of a rap sheet may mean that the company is clean, it might simply mean that it has not been caught yet under its present guise.

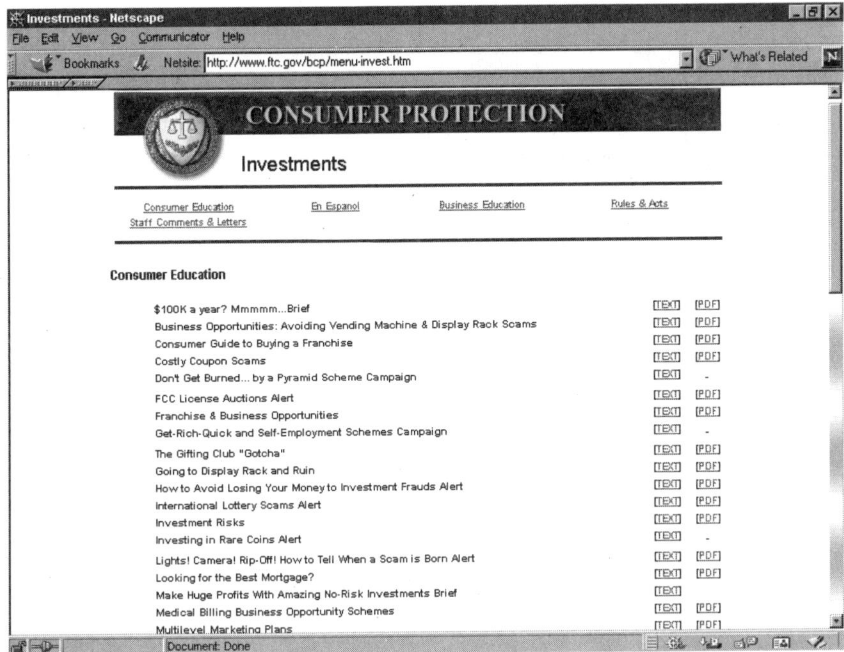

Figure 15.3. The Federal Trade Commission has a number of investment-related reports on its Web site.

The SEC and You

The U.S. Securities and Exchange Commission views itself as "the investor's advocate," and one part of that role is to help investors avoid being fleeced. At the main SEC site (www.sec.gov), click the [Investor Assistance & Complaints] link to get to the material geared to individual investors. At the Office of Investor Assistance and Complaints, click the link to [Protect Your Money] to go to the area that focuses on avoiding fraud. See Figure 15.4 for a listing of information available at this site. You can get a list of recent legal proceedings the SEC is involved in against alleged scam artists; tips on what to watch for in a broker or investment advisor; and help in registering a complaint.

Reading some of the files in the [SEC enforcement actions] area can be a sobering experience. In one case, a company had offered *free* shares of stock for anyone who registered at the Web site or encouraged others to register. The company described itself as the "Internet's Fastest Growing Company." Another section of the Web site said that "we feel that [the company] . . . will grow to become one of the great Internet based busi-

Figure 15.4. The SEC provides information on its Web site to help investors keep from getting defrauded.

nesses of all time." The home page also included a graph that indicated that the company had approximately 10,000 to 12,000 satisfied customers. In fact, the SEC found that the company had only 35 customers and had only received $26 in gross revenues!

The FTC: The Consumer's Watchdog

While the SEC is focused on publicly issued securities, the Federal Trade Commission looks at a wide array of consumer protection issues. As described earlier in this chapter, the FTC has a useful collection of reports and fact-sheets on a variety of investment-related topics. From the main FTC page (www.ftc.gov), click [Consumer Protection]. The FTC has a section specifically focusing on investments, but there are also useful reports under the [Credit], [E-Commerce and the Internet], and [Franchise & Business Opportunities] links. The reports can be displayed on the screen (click the [TEXT] link next to the title) or in Adobe Acrobat format (click the [PDF] link). You will find reports on everything from choosing a credit card to online investment opportunities and investment risks. See Figure 15.5 for the list of consumer protection links at the FTC's site.

Other "Highway Patrol" Organizations

Consumers can turn to a number of government agencies and associations in addition to the SEC and the FTC for help in avoiding and reporting investment fraud. Every state has its own version of the SEC—an agency whose responsibility is to monitor and regulate securities sold in the state. This agency may be called the Securities Commission, Securities Department, or Department of Corporations. Fortunately, there is an association of these state securities regulators, the North American Securities Administrators Association (www.nasaa.org). At the main NASAA site, click [Find Your Securities Regulator], select your state or province (yes, NASAA is more than just U.S. regulators), and you will get a list of the folks to call. See Figure 15.6 for the listing for Indiana.

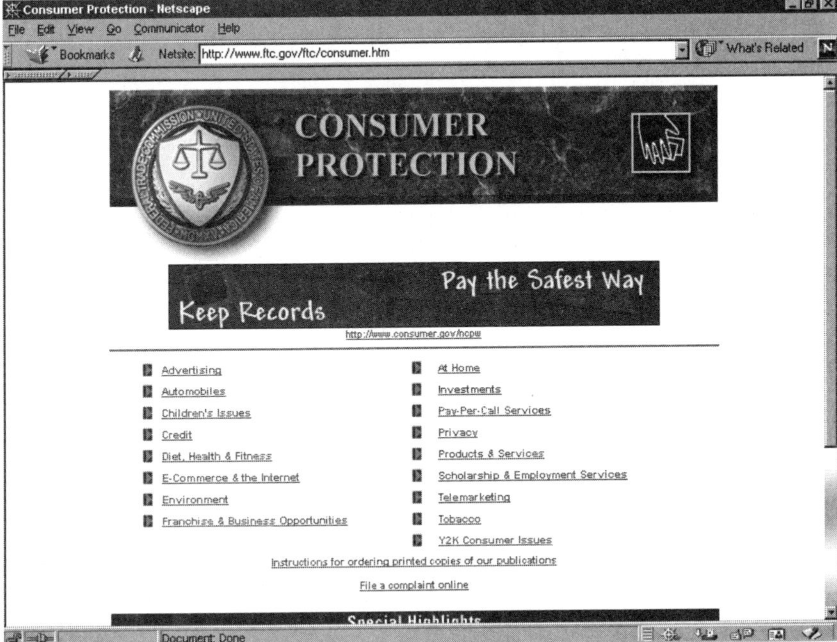

Figure 15.5. The FTC provides consumer alerts on avoiding fraud, managing credit, and other financial topics.

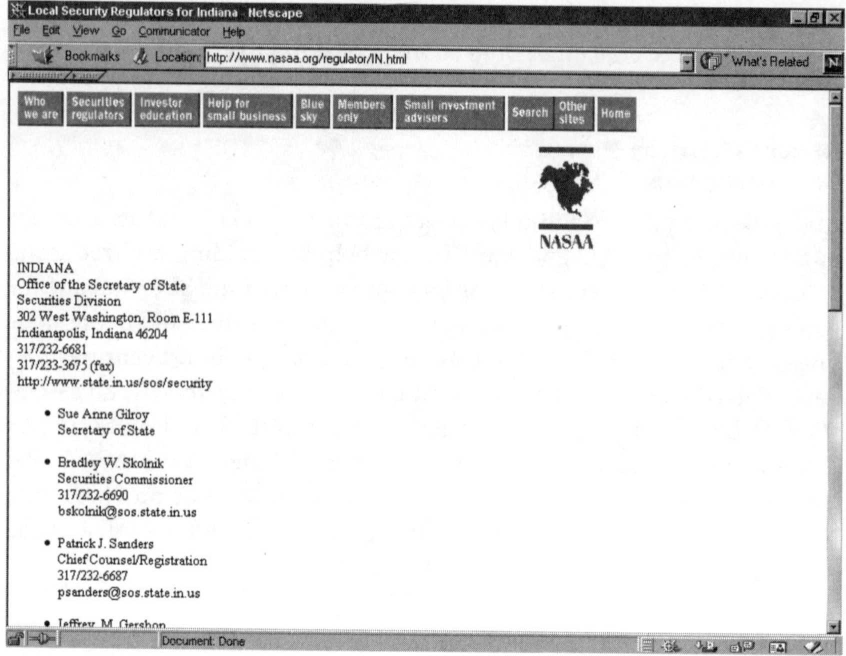

Figure 15.6. The NASAA points you to the securities regulators in each state and Canadian province.

An organization that might not immediately come to mind as a source of help in investment fraud prevention is the U.S. Postal Service. The Postal Inspection Service, which has been around in one form or another since the establishment of the Post Office, was set up to catch everything from stage coach robberies to "mail depredations." Go to the main USPS site (www.usps.gov), click [Inside the Postal Service], then click the link to [Postal Inspection Service]. In addition to Wanted posters for mail fraud criminals, there is a section on consumer fraud, with descriptions of how to recognize various personal-finance-related schemes.

The Better Business Bureau, one of the oldest of the business-supported organizations focusing on ethical business practices, has a useful online library of material on various investment-related issues. Go to the BBB site (www.bbb.org) and click the [Read Our Consumer Tips] link. There is a good selection of reports under the Money & Investments section. Among the titles available are Credit Repair Fraud Proliferates; How the Faithful Can Avoid Investment Scams; Investment Clubs—Are They Right For You?; Protecting Your Financial Privacy in Cyberspace; and Selecting a Financial Planner.

Things Are Not As They Appear

One of the benefits *and* drawbacks of the Net is that it has enabled people to come in contact with others they would never meet otherwise. Electronic mailing lists, chat rooms, and message boards are great ways of exchanging ideas with others interested in investing, to solicit advice, and to hear about new markets and opportunities. Unfortunately, these communications channels are also effective ways for people with less than pure motives to further their agendas. You have no easy way of discerning a person's undisclosed agenda—this helpful participant in a chat room may be an insider hyping a stock, a promoter being paid to inflate the price of a stock, or a short-seller spreading false negative rumors in order to drive down the price of a stock. Several excellent reviews of the various ways that the Net can—and has—been used to defraud consumers by misrepresentation are available on the SEC's Web site. From the main SEC site (www.sec.gov), click [Investor Assistance & Complaints], then [Learn About Investing], then [The Internet and Online Trading]. See Figure 15.7 for a list of the reports available in this area of the SEC's site.

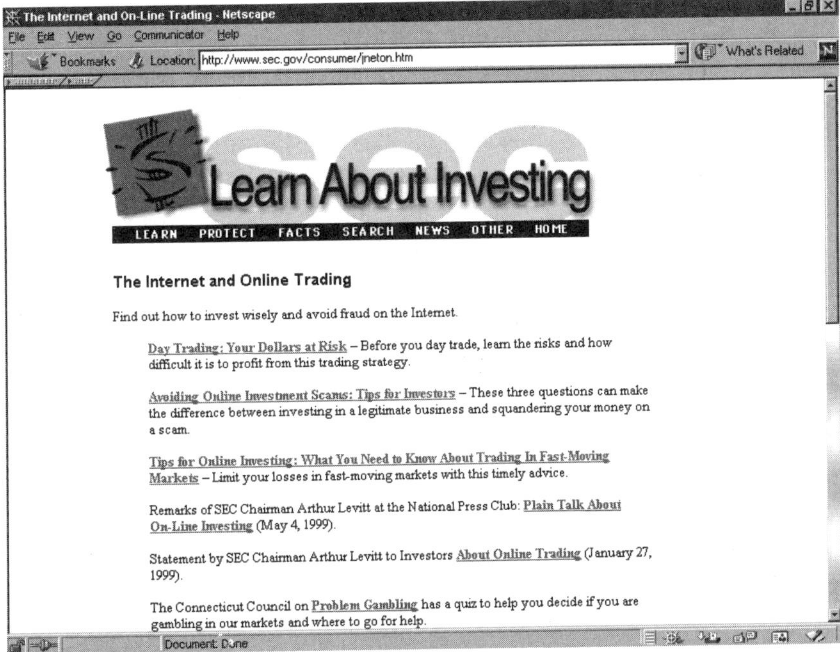

Figure 15.7. The SEC has a number of useful publications on how to spot Internet investment scams.

Another area of possible misrepresentation, whether intentional or not, is what I call the I-Hate-X site. Every large company, particularly those in the consumer market, has a certain number of detractors. Whether it's McDonald's, General Motors, or K-Mart, folks with an ax to grind or a message to tell will set up sites to tell the world what they think about the company. Some sites make it quite clear that they are not the official site. Www.walmart.thecompany.com, for example, is maintained by a current Wal-Mart employee who wants to counterbalance the negative sites about Wal-Mart with his own site telling the world that Wal-Mart is a great place to work, and this site makes it quite clear on the front Web page that it is *not* the official Wal-Mart site (which, by the way, is at www.walmart.com). Other sites, particularly those that do not look favorably on the subject matter of the site, may not be so straightforward.

A related but clearly fraudulent technique has been used to mislead investors. In one such episode in April 1999, an employee of a company posted a message on an investment forum, reporting that the company was about to be bought by another firm. The employee, obviously without the knowledge or consent of his employer, then created a Web site that mimicked that of the Bloomberg financial news service. His message board posting pointed readers to his spoofed site, which appeared to confirm his rumor. The company's stock price rose 32 percent before the fraud was detected. The point of this story is not only to verify any rumor by finding a second news source and checking the company's Web site directly, but also to remember to look at the URL of any Web site you visit. If those defrauded investors had looked at the top of their browser screens, they would have seen an address that did *not* have Bloomberg's name in it—an immediate indicator that the site was not what it appeared to be. If the site had been legitimate, the URL would have contained bloomberg.com. The ease with which people can create free and semi-anonymous Web sites means that the possibility of fraudulent news sites will continue to be an issue for investors.

16
E-Brokerages

Nothing has revolutionized individual investing in the past five years more than access to online trading and electronic brokerages. While there have been discount brokers ever since the U.S. Securities and Exchange Commission deregulated share trade commissions in 1975, the availability of electronic trading to investors at home has created explosive growth in personal investing.

Investors like the immediacy of e-trading—they can check real-time quotes and execute trades immediately, with confirmation of their trade received in seconds. And you can't beat the price—usually $15 to $25 per trade, as opposed to $100 to $300 at full-service brokerages. Of course, most e-brokerages don't offer the same extensive research services and access to a personal broker that you get from the traditional brokerage firms. On the other hand, some e-brokers such as Charles Schwab are recognizing the competitive advantage of offering telephone access to customer service representatives 24 hours a day, 7 days a week. And Merrill Lynch, a traditional full-service broker, now offers online trading, complete with access to personal financial advisors and other perks usually not available to e-broker clients.

This chapter looks at the typical features of electronic brokerages, points you to sites that evaluate the relative merits of the leading e-brokers, and reviews some of the major competitors. Given the stiff competition among brokers today, be sure to check their Web sites for new enhancements and features.

Checklist of E-Brokerage Features

Some electronic trading companies compete mainly on the basis of price, as do most airlines, gas stations, and long-distance phone service companies. And for some investors, particularly those who execute a trade at least once a week, the commission is the primary consideration when selecting an e-broker. For others, access to live financial advisors, availability of proprietary research, or the opportunity to buy shares in initial public offerings is more important. Decide which features you value the most and which ones you won't be using. An experienced trader, for example, may have no need for 24 hours a day, 7 days a week access to account executives. A new investor may find that feature invaluable, but not need electronic notification of stock price changes via email or pager. An investor who tends to buy stock for the long term may not be as concerned about the price of commissions as an investor who trades frequently.

Much has been written about system outages or slow response time suffered by the users of one e-brokerage or another. As a matter of fact, the entire online trading industry has become a victim of its own success. High volume, rapid growth, and high volatility of prices have lead to unexpected demands on e-brokers' online systems. During peak trading times, investors have seen slow response time or have been unable to access their accounts or execute trades. Sometimes these problems have been related to system upgrades or enhancements that were not tested adequately before being introduced. Sometimes they are simply a result of unanticipated volume. While no e-brokerage can promise 100 percent system up-time, you should not encounter access problems frequently. If this is a serious concern for you, consider establishing accounts on more than one e-brokerage. In fact, it might be wise to have accounts with one of the large e-brokerages as well as a smaller firm, on the assumption that a brokerage serving a relatively limited customer base will not be a swamped during a period of high trading volume. Of course, most e-brokerages also let you place orders over the telephone—either with a live operator or through an automated trading system—when their Web sites are down. However, remember that in the case of system problems other traders will be doing the same thing and you may encounter a busy signal.

E-Brokerage Must-Have Features

As discussed earlier, the best choice of e-broker for you will depend on what kind of trader you are. However, some features should be expected of any e-brokerage:

- *Access to current research on stocks and mutual funds.* Most e-brokerages include links to research from third-party sources such as Market Guide, First Call, and Lehman Brothers. Some e-brokerages charge an additional fee for this information.
- *Good system up-time ratios.* Most computer problems—account inaccessibility, slow response time, or a total inability to get to the e-brokerage site—only last an hour or two, but they can sometimes last as long as a day or more. Make sure that the e-brokerage you select will allow you to place your order over the telephone at the lower online trade commission rate if the Web site is down or overly congested.
- *A reasonable per-trade commission.* What is reasonable for you will depend on your trading patterns. Estimate the average frequency and size of your trades and the amount you expect to keep in your account, and calculate the commission you will be charged.
- *Free real-time quotes.* While 15- or 20-minute delayed stock quotes are available on virtually every search engine and portal site on the Web, real-time quotes are usually available only to subscribers. Be sure that your e-brokerage offers account holders access to real-time quotes.
- *Prompt email confirmation of trades.* Be careful, though. Email is vulnerable to the delays and glitches of the Net itself. If you do not receive confirmation of your trade within the amount of time you expect, do not automatically conclude that your trade did not go through. If you reexecute your trade, your e-broker will hold you liable for both the initial and the repeat trade. If in doubt, call the e-broker to confirm receipt and execution of your trade.
- *A Web site that is easy to navigate.* You may have a blazingly fast Net connection at work, but much of your interaction with your e-brokerage will probably be done at home. If you have a 56K modem, remember that a graphics-intense Web site will take much longer to load at home than in the office. If an e-brokerage Web site requires that you go through five or six pages before you can check your account or execute a trade, you may spend more time watching pages load than you do managing your investments.

E-Brokerage Would-Be-Nice Features

Not all e-brokers offer all of the following features and services. In fact, many of them may not be of interest or value to you. And your investment patterns may change over time; be prepared to reevaluate your choice of e-brokers annually to see if you are still getting the best selection of services that meet your needs:

- *Email or pager alerts of stock changes.* Many e-brokerages let you set up a profile with criteria for when you should be notified of market changes—if a security hits a specific high or low, trading volume reaches a certain level, a company makes an announcement, and so on. Notification may be by email, by pager, or as a notice when you log on to your account.
- *Telephone or live-chat access to an account rep who can answer questions.* Yes, most e-brokerages are designed for independent investors who do not need or want to pay for the features offered by full-service brokerages. On the other hand, there may be times when you want to speak to an analyst. If this is important to you, find out whether the e-brokerage you are considering requires that you maintain a higher account balance or has other prerequisites for access to investment professionals.
- *Free check-writing or debit cards associated with your cash management account.*
- *An opportunity to buy shares in initial public offerings.* While IPOs carry an additional risk, there is also the chance to invest in a company whose value will increase exponentially. Who isn't familiar with the astronomical rises in price of Internet-related stock such as Amazon.com (AMZN) or Yahoo! (YHOO)?
- *Detailed monthly statements, including tax-related information on gains and losses.* Note that some e-brokerages provide software that you load on your own PC to track some of this information as well.

Rating the E-Brokerages

In addition to your own evaluation of e-brokers based on the list of features just described, you may wish to consult the investment equivalent of *Consumer Reports* for independent evaluations of the electronic brokerage firms. Use these resources in conjunction with your own assessment of your needs to select the e-brokerage that will best help you achieve your investment goals.

You can also consult investor discussion forums, message boards, and chat rooms to see what individual investors have to say about particular e-brokers. Keep in mind, though, that people are much more likely to post comments about an e-broker they are unhappy with than one with which they are satisfied. That means that the postings may be heavily skewed toward individuals who have had a bad experience, which may or may not be indicative of the e-broker's service in general. See Chapter 13 for more discussion of electronic discussion groups.

Internet Broker Scorecard

Gomez Advisors (www.gomez.com) began publishing its Internet Broker Scorecard in 1997, ranking the quality of a number of online brokers. Since then, this e-commerce consulting firm has expanded its service to include electronic discussion boards in which anyone can discuss any of the rated e-brokers and the ratings assigned to that broker. Gomez has also broadened its scope beyond e-brokers to include rankings of Web-based booksellers, pet stores, grocery services, travel agents, and other e-commerce categories.

The e-brokerage ratings are available by clicking [Brokers] at the main Web page. You can see a ranking of the top 10 e-brokerages by overall score, or see a ranking of all e-brokerages (over 50 at last count). Gomez also provides individual rankings by ease of use, customer confidence, on-site resources such as screening tools or editorial content, relationship services, and cost. Gomez evaluates the e-brokerages for their appropriateness for several categories of investors—the hyperactive trader (that is, someone who values immediate access and fast execution), the serious investor (someone who values high-quality research and investment tools), the life goal planner (the investor focused on long-term growth who values financial planning tools and a stable financial services provider), and the one-stop shopper (the investor who wants a wide variety of financial products easily available from one source). See Figure 16.1 for the initial broker rating page.

Money Magazine

Not unexpectedly, a magazine that focuses on individual investors would be a good source for evaluations of electronic brokerages. *Money* magazine's Web site (www.money.com) provides its ranking of the 15 largest e-brokers, evaluated in ease of use, customer service, system responsiveness, products and tools offered, and cost. At the main page, click the [Investing] link, then click the [Online Brokerage Screener] link to get to the ranking. In addition to a chart showing how each of the e-brokers was

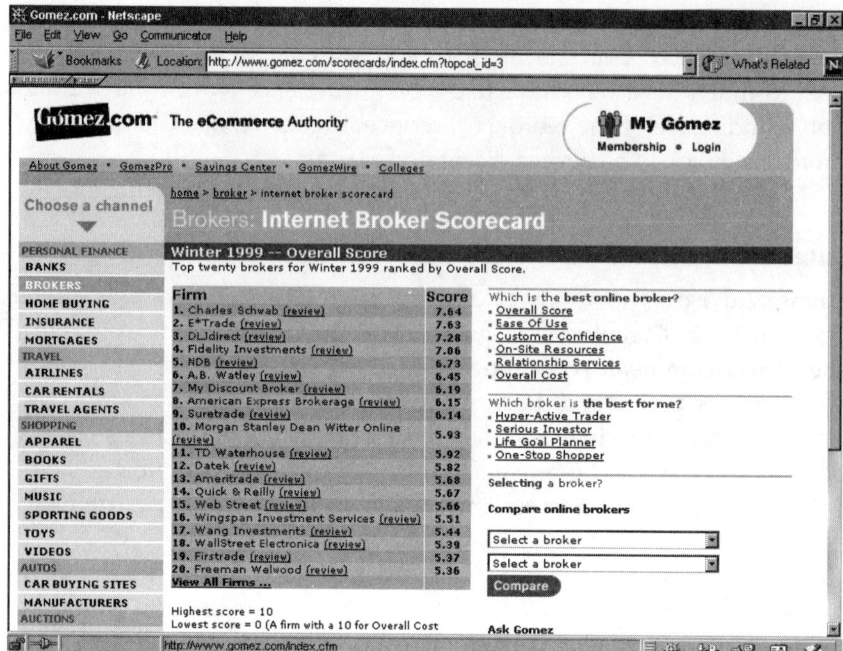

Figure 16.1. Gomez.com provides a well-regarded scorecard of electronic brokerages.

rated on each criterion, the page has links to *Money*'s evaluation of the best e-brokers for four categories of investors—mainstream investors, frequent traders, wealthy investors, and beginning investors. See Figure 16.2 for *Money*'s scorecard of the largest e-brokers.

An additional feature of this site is a customized recommendation of which e-brokers would be best for you, based on your answers to 13 questions. See Figure 16.3 for the initial list of questions to determine your preferences.

SmartMoney

SmartMoney, the magazine published by Dow Jones for individual investors, maintains an e-brokerage scorecard with an attitude—hardly what one would expect from the publisher of the somewhat sedate *Wall Street Journal.* The ranking not only gives scores for the top 21 electronic and discount brokers, but it also includes extensive commentary with an edge. "Low commissions or not, investors expect a certain level of service and reliability from their brokerage firms. That includes . . . having a Web

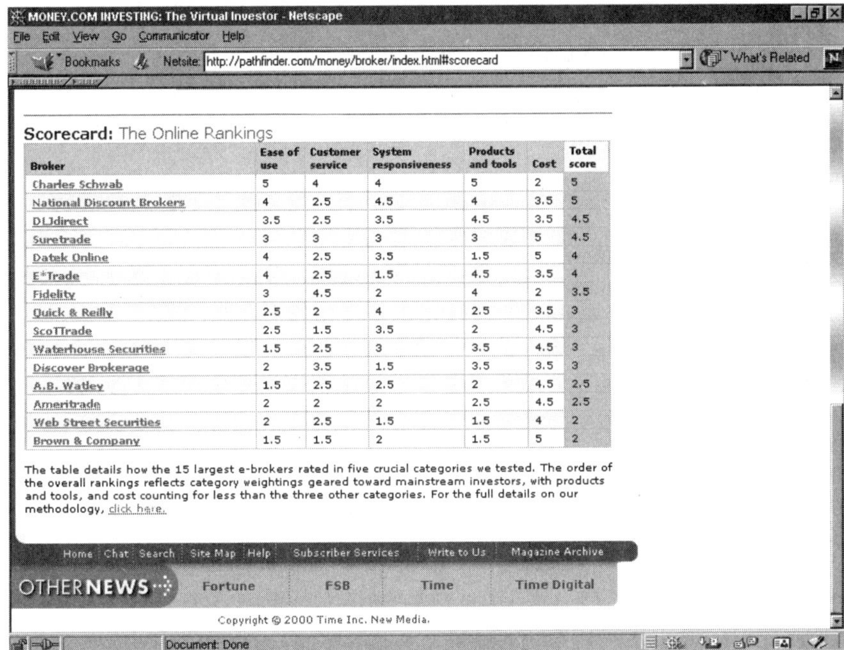

MONEY.COM INVESTING: The Virtual Investor - Netscape

http://pathfinder.com/money/broker/index.html#scorecard

Scorecard: The Online Rankings

Broker	Ease of use	Customer service	System responsiveness	Products and tools	Cost	Total score
Charles Schwab	5	4	4	5	2	5
National Discount Brokers	4	2.5	4.5	4	3.5	5
DLJdirect	3.5	2.5	3.5	4.5	3.5	4.5
Suretrade	3	3	3	3	5	4.5
Datek Online	4	2.5	3.5	1.5	5	4
E*Trade	4	2.5	1.5	4.5	3.5	4
Fidelity	3	4.5	2	4	2	3.5
Quick & Reilly	2.5	2	4	2.5	3.5	3
ScoTTrade	2.5	1.5	3.5	2	4.5	3
Waterhouse Securities	1.5	2.5	3	3.5	4.5	3
Discover Brokerage	2	3.5	1.5	3.5	3.5	3
A.B. Watley	1.5	2.5	2.5	2	4.5	2.5
Ameritrade	2	2	2	2.5	4.5	2.5
Web Street Securities	2	2.5	1.5	1.5	4	2
Brown & Company	1.5	1.5	2	1.5	5	2

The table details how the 15 largest e-brokers rated in five crucial categories we tested. The order of the overall rankings reflects category weightings geared toward mainstream investors, with products and tools, and cost counting for less than the three other categories. For the full details on our methodology, click here.

Home Chat Search Site Map Help Subscriber Services Write to Us Magazine Archive

OTHERNEWS Fortune FSB Time Time Digital

Copyright © 2000 Time Inc. New Media.

Figure 16.2. *Money* magazine evaluates 15 of the largest e-brokerages on five criteria.

site that operates at least as fast as one's toaster oven. Or completing a trade in seconds . . . or minutes . . . not hours. So, you might wonder, is all this too much to ask?"

To get to the broker rankings, go to the *SmartMoney* Web site (www.smartmoney.com), click the [Tools] tab, then the [Broker Meter] link. This will take you to a graphic showing how fast each of the e-brokerage Web sites is. While this may be of passing interest, click the [Broker Ratings] link to get to the heart of the matter. *SmartMoney* grades the e-brokers by cost, breadth of products, mutual fund offerings, extra services, responsiveness, Web reliability, online trading features, and "staying out of trouble," which looks at how well the brokerage meets its legal and regulatory obligations by reviewing data from the National Association of Securities Dealers (see next section for more discussion of this information source).

Unlike other ratings, you can download the full table in an Excel or comma-delimited format and do your own sorting of the information. See Figure 16.4 for the complete table. In addition, you can click the links to each of the rating criteria to see a discussion of the best and the worst of each category.

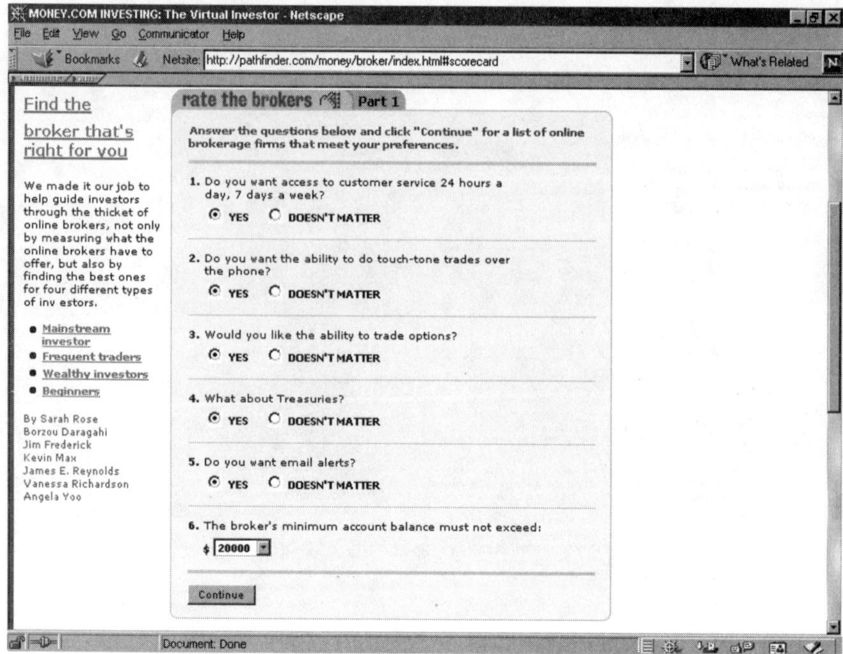

Figure 16.3. The money.com site will select the best e-brokers for you, based on your answers to a series of questions.

NASD Regulation

The National Association of Securities Dealers is the industry organization that regulates its stock broker/dealer members. While it does not provide a scorecard or ranking of brokers, it does maintain a Web page that lets you look up basic information on brokerage firms. From the main NASD page (www.nasd.com), click the [Other NASD Web sites] link, then select [The NASD Regulation Web site] link. At the next page, select [About your broker], then [Perform an On-line Search], and you are finally at the page where you can look up a specific firm or individual broker. The NASD Regulation database will provide you with information on where the firm is located, and in which states it is approved to operate. The NASD also maintains records on complaints filed against the firm, and any criminal convictions, suspensions, or judicial injunctions against the firm. Unfortunately, this information is not available online; you can, however, request that a report on the firm be emailed to you. There is no charge for this report. You should receive the email within 10 business days; if the report is too long for email, it is sent via

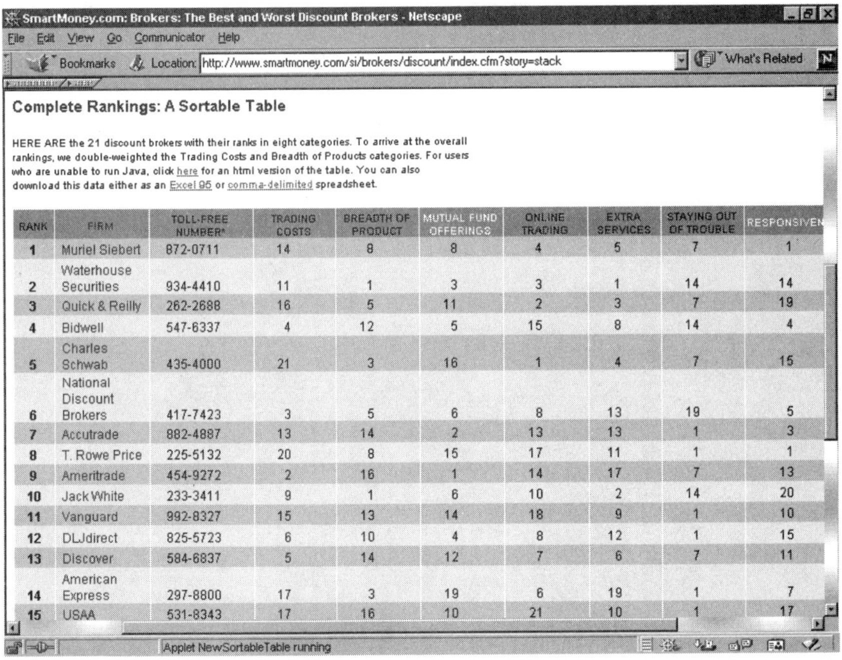

SmartMoney.com: Brokers: The Best and Worst Discount Brokers - Netscape

File Edit View Go Communicator Help

Bookmarks Location: http://www.smartmoney.com/si/brokers/discount/index.cfm?story=stack What's Related

Complete Rankings: A Sortable Table

HERE ARE the 21 discount brokers with their ranks in eight categories. To arrive at the overall rankings, we double-weighted the Trading Costs and Breadth of Products categories. For users who are unable to run Java, click here for an html version of the table. You can also download this data either as an Excel 95 or comma-delimited spreadsheet.

RANK	FIRM	TOLL-FREE NUMBER*	TRADING COSTS	BREADTH OF PRODUCT	MUTUAL FUND OFFERINGS	ONLINE TRADING	EXTRA SERVICES	STAYING OUT OF TROUBLE	RESPONSIVEN
1	Muriel Siebert	872-0711	14	8	8	4	5	7	1
2	Waterhouse Securities	934-4410	11	1	3	3	1	14	14
3	Quick & Reilly	262-2688	16	5	11	2	3	7	19
4	Bidwell	547-6337	4	12	5	15	8	14	4
5	Charles Schwab	435-4000	21	3	16	1	4	7	15
6	National Discount Brokers	417-7423	3	5	6	8	13	19	5
7	Accutrade	882-4887	13	14	2	13	13	1	3
8	T. Rowe Price	225-5132	20	8	15	17	11	1	1
9	Ameritrade	454-9272	2	16	1	14	17	7	13
10	Jack White	233-3411	9	1	6	10	2	14	20
11	Vanguard	992-8327	15	13	14	18	9	1	10
12	DLJdirect	825-5723	6	10	4	8	12	1	15
13	Discover	584-6837	5	14	12	7	6	7	11
14	American Express	297-8800	17	3	19	6	19	1	7
15	USAA	531-8343	17	16	10	21	10	1	17

Applet NewSortableTable running

Figure 16.4. *SmartMoney*'s e-brokerage rating can be downloaded into a spreadsheet for further sorting.

first class mail. See Figure 16.5 for the NASD Regulation registrations list for E*Trade.

Comparison of Selected E-Brokers

Your choice of e-brokerages will depend on a number of factors. Rather than attempt to list them all here, I have described the main features of some of the largest online brokers. Be sure to go through the Web sites of any that you are considering, to see if their current features have changed; then call them to assess their customer service and telephone availability. Table 16.1 provides basic information on six of the major e-brokerages.

Ameritrade

Ameritrade (www.ameritrade.com) has one of the lowest commissions among online brokerages—$8 per trade when placed online, regardless

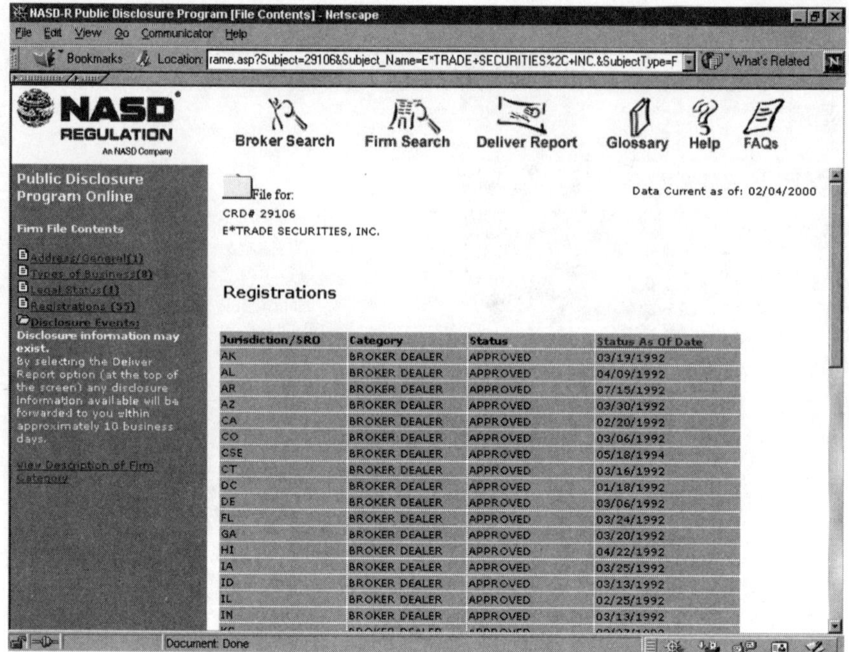

Figure 16.5. The NASD provides information on securities firms and individual brokers.

of the number of shares traded; $12 per trade when done through Ameritrade's automated telephone system; and $18 when done through an Ameritrade broker. The downside of these low commissions is a relative lack of added-value features. The investor information section offers basic company profiles but no access to the in-depth research reports from third-party analysts. Account holders can get 100 real-time quotes for every order placed, and electronic trades are confirmed via email after the market closes for the day. Ameritrade is best suited for high-volume traders who do not need many bells and whistles.

Charles Schwab and Company

Charles Schwab (www.schwab.com) has been one of the leading discount brokerages for years; the fact that it has close to 300 branch offices also means that if its system goes down, you can go into the office for service. Schwab's commissions are relatively high, but you get more features from Schwab than from some other e-brokers. Schwab offers telephone cus-

Table 16.1. Costs and Other Features of Selected E-Brokerages

	URL	AOL Keyword	Minimum Account	Commission for Trade of 1000 Shares
Ameritrade	www.ameritrade.com	ameritrade	$2,000	$8
Charles Schwab	www.schwab.com	N/A	$5,000	$29.95
Donaldson Lufkin Jenrette	www.dljdirect.com	dljdirect	-0-	$20
E*Trade	www.etrade.com	e*trade	$1,000	$14.95
Fidelity	personal400.fidelity. com	N/A	$5,000	$25
National Discount Brokers	www.ndb.com	N/A	-0-	$14.75

tomer service 24 hours a day, 7 days a week; in-depth analysts' reports; industry analyses; financial planning tools; and a full range of investment products and services, including IPOs, annuities, mutual funds, bonds, and money market funds. Schwab is a good choice for the investor who wants added-value research and investment tools and who does not trade so often that the $29.95 commission is an issue.

Schwab's site includes a personalization feature (www.myschwab.com)—you can specify the stocks you want monitored, news you want displayed, and so on. And its main page offers plenty of investment tools for anyone, even if you have not set up an account with Schwab. See Figure 16.6 for the initial Schwab e-brokerage page.

Donaldson Lufkin & Jenrette

DLJ*direct*, Donaldson Lufkin & Jenrette's Web-based brokerage service (www.dljdirect.com), is one of the few e-brokerages that does not require an initial deposit to set up an account. It offers high-quality research and investment information from sources such as Standard & Poor's, Zacks, and its own analysts. While its commissions are about average for e-brokerages, it does not charge a premium for telephone trading, and it

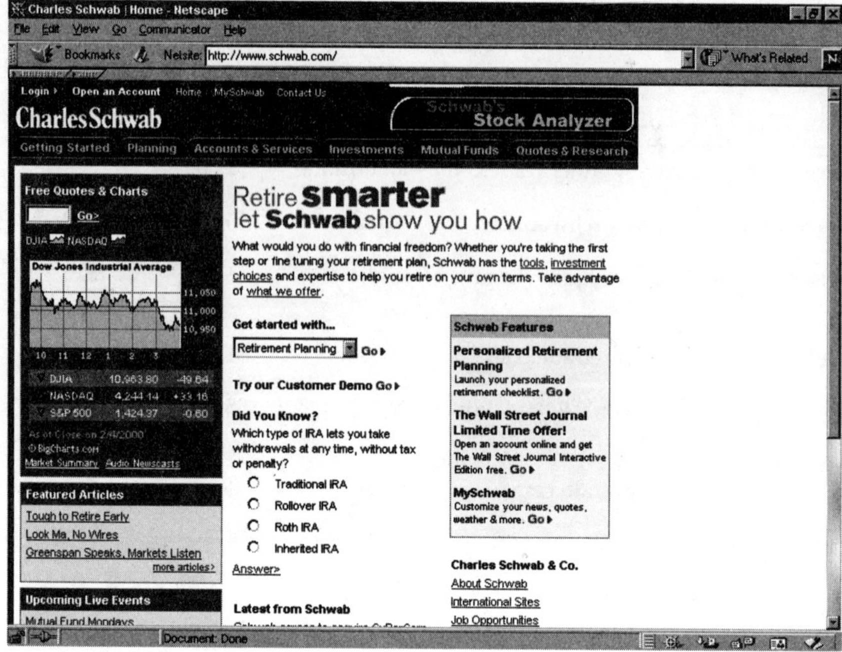

Figure 16.6. Charles Schwab charges higher commissions but offers a wide variety of products and services.

offers customer service 24 hours a day, 7 days a week. DLJ*direct* offers downloadable software, Marketspeed, which streamlines access and navigation and includes proprietary stock management and investment planning tools. DLJ is an e-brokerage for investors who value access to institutional research, financial planning tools, and 24×7 customer service.

DLJ*direct* has a convenient chart spelling out what benefits are available for each level of investor. Click [Account Features] at the main Web page to see a list of what products or services are offered for each type of client. See Figure 16.7 for the main DLJ*direct* Web page.

E*Trade

E*Trade may be the prototype for an e-brokerage. It began offering electronic trading back in 1992 to subscribers of CompuServe and America Online. Once the Web took the world by force, E*Trade launched its Web-based service as well. It offers the usual features of the full-featured e-brokerages—24×7 customer service, investor participation in initial public offerings, notification of changes in a stock price via email, finan-

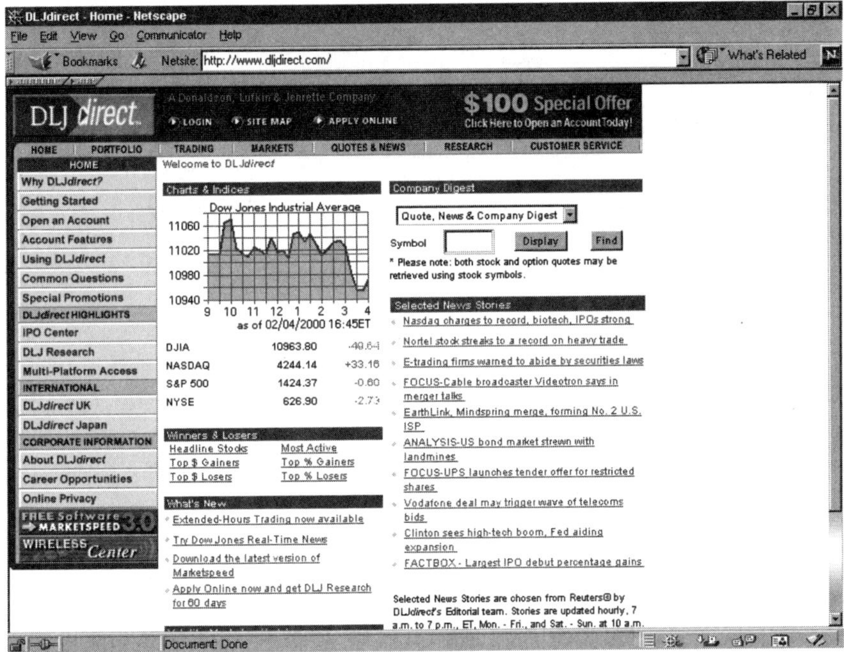

Figure 16.7. DLJ*direct* offers a good selection of value-added research and proprietary software.

cial planning tools, and access to analysts' reports. E*Trade also hosts discussion forums, chat rooms, and live electronic meetings with well-known investment experts. Unlike other e-brokerages, E*Trade offers free access to some of its value-added services to anyone who chooses to become a "member." You can't execute trades as a "member," but you can take advantage of E*Trade's discussion areas and read analysts' research.

E*Trade has suffered more than its share of system crashes and times when investors' accounts were inaccessible. In its 1999 annual report, the company conceded that "we have received, in the past, adverse publicity in the financial press and in online discussion forums primarily relating to systems failures." As the company grows and as its systems staff installs upgrades and enhancements to its online system, some glitches have occurred due to inadequate time to test the changes before implementation. If system reliability is very important to you, E*Trade may not be your best choice. On the other hand, the commissions are reasonable, and E*Trade provides access to a full range of services and features in an easy-to-navigate Web site. See Figure 16.8 for the main E*Trade Web page.

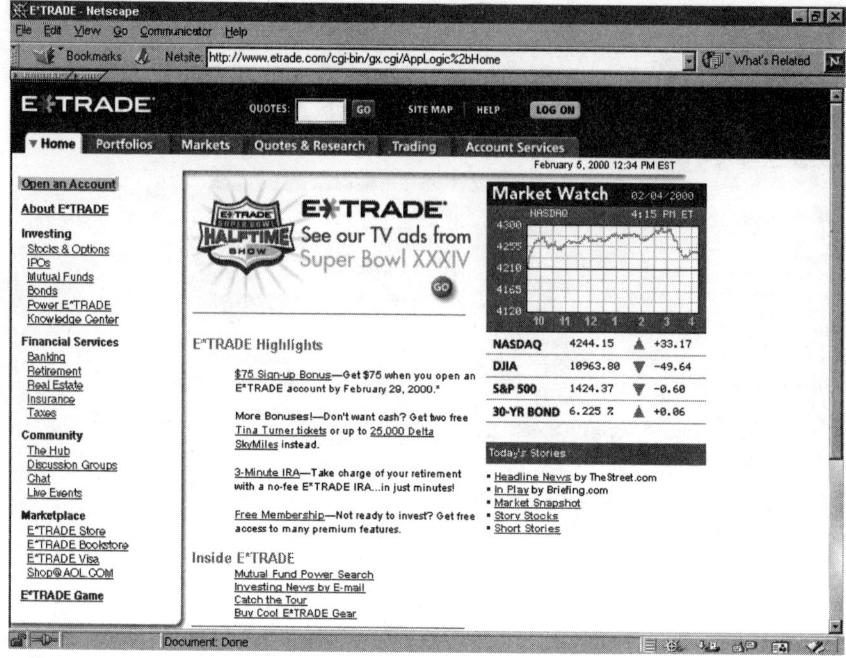

Figure 16.8. E*Trade's Web site is clear and easy to navigate.

Fidelity Investments

Fidelity Investments offers loads of features to personal investors through its Web site at personal300.fidelity.com. Clients can read third-party analysts' reports; use Fidelity's asset allocation tools; get notification of stock price changes via email, pager, or PDA; place orders via two-way pager; contact customer service representatives 24 hours a day, 7 days a week; pay bills electronically from the account; have all or part of a paycheck deposited directly to a Fidelity account; and participate in initial public offerings. While the commission rate is high, telephone orders are the same price as Web trades. Fidelity has a good selection of financial planning tools and would be particularly attractive to investors who hold stocks for the long term (for whom the relatively high commission rate and account minimum are not a concern) and who want a wide range of investment products and information available. Fidelity does not offer the most streamlined of Web sites; the fact that Fidelity provides services for so many types of investors tends to complicate its presentation of products. See Figure 16.9 for the main Web page for the Personal Investing section of Fidelity.com.

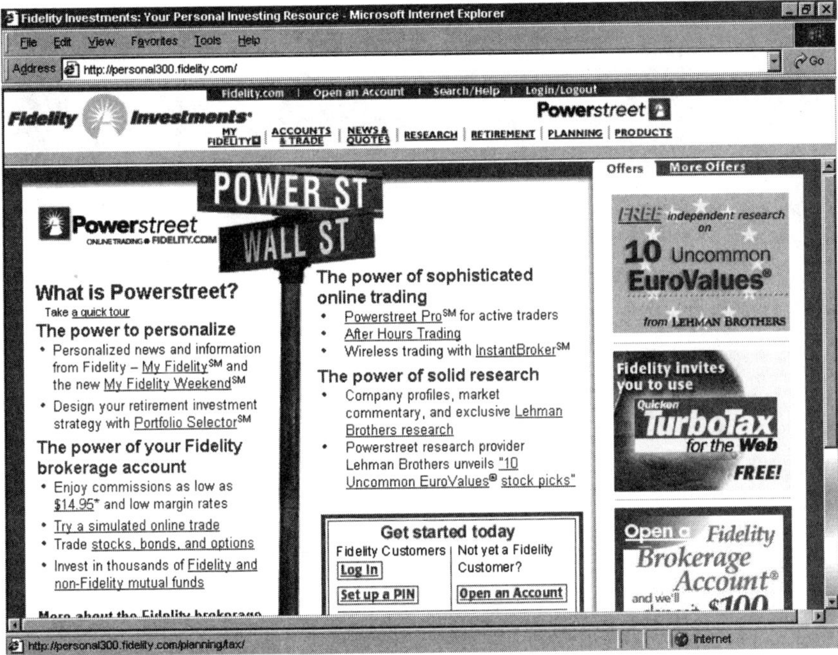

Figure 16.9. Fidelity Investment has a wide array of features for investors.

National Discount Brokers Group

National Discount Brokers (www.ndb.com) is one of the few e-brokerages—along with DLJ*direct*—that do not require a deposit to establish an account, and its commission is also on the low end of the scale. And as a benefit for active traders, NDB charges only a single commission for multiple trades (either all buy or all sell) of the same stock on the same day. It offers electronic notification of your trades via email, pager, fax, or telephone. Cash management accounts come with free check-writing, direct deposit, and automatic bill payment. NDB provides a link to third-party analysts' reports through a partnership with Wall Street On Demand; these reports are also available directly from the vendor's site at www.wallst.com.

NDB also provides a well-designed series of primers on various aspects of investing—futures and options, employee stock options, asset allocation, and so on—in its NDB University page. Just click the [NDB University] link at the main NDB page to see the current lesson and an index of prior lessons. New lessons come out every two weeks or so, and you can request email notification of new lessons as they appear.

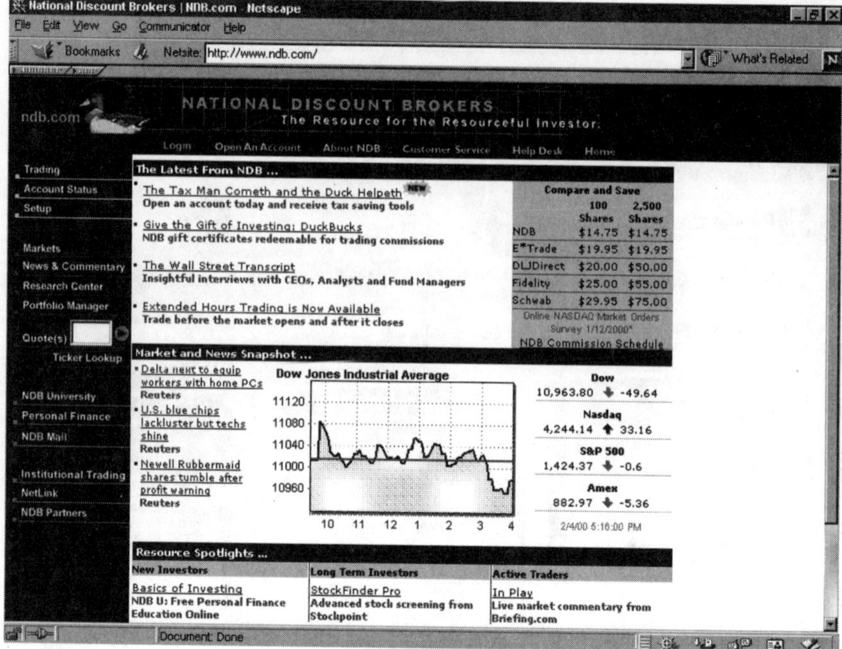

Figure 16.10. National Discount Brokers provides links to a number of investment-related sites.

Surprisingly for such a major player in the e-brokerage field, telephone customer service is only open Monday through Friday. On the other hand, NDB's transaction reports are well-designed and its Web site includes a number of links to personal-finance-related resources. See Figure 16.10 for the NDB main Web page.

Appendix

Referenced Sites and Services

Chapter 1—Internet 101

About.com: www.about.com

Adobe Acrobat: www.adobe.com/prodindex/acrobat/readstep.html

Alta Vista: www.altavista.com

America Online: www.aol.com

AT&T WorldNet: www.att.net

C | Net's ISP Guide: www.cnet.com

CompuServe: www.compuserve.com

EarthLink Network: www.earthlink.net

Google: www.google.com

GTE Internet: www.gte.net

HotBot: www.hotbot.com

Lycos: www.lycos.com

Northern Light: www.northernlight.com

Search Engine Watch: www.searchenginewatch.com

WorldCom: www.wcom.com

WWW Virtual Library: vlib.org/Overview.html

Yahoo!: www.yahoo.com

Chapter 2—Financial Basics Online

About.com: www.about.com

AltaVista: www.altavista.com

American Association of Individual Investors: www.aaii.com

American Association of Retired Persons: www.aarp.org

American Savings Education Council: www.asec.org

Disclosure, Inc.: www.disclosure.com

EduStock: library.thinkquest.org/3088/

Federal Deposit Insurance Corporation: www.fdic.gov

Fidelity Investments: personal300.fidelity.com

HotBot: www.hotbot.com

Internet Public Library: www.ipl.org

Michigan State Government; Corporation, Securities and Land Development Bureau: www.commerce.state.mi.us/corp/invested.htm

NASDAQ: www.nasdaq.com

National Association of Securities Dealers: www.nasd.com

New York Stock Exchange: www.nyse.com

Personal Wealth: www.personalwealth.com

Securities Industry Association: www.sia.com

Standard & Poor's: www.standardandpoors.com

U.S. Federal Trade Commission: www.ftc.gov

U.S. Securities and Exchange Commission: www.sec.gov

U.S. Social Security Administration: www.ssa.gov

ValueLine Inc.: www.valueline.com

Virtual Stock Exchange: www.virtualstockexchange.com

WWW Virtual Finance Library: www.cob.ohio-state.edu/dept/fin/overview.htm

WWW Virtual Library: vlib.org/Overview.html

Yahoo!: www.yahoo.com

Yahoo!'s Investment Challenge: quote.yahoo.com/t1 (that's the letter T and the number 1)

Chapter 3—Financial Planning Online

Call For Action affiliates: www.experian.com/customer/action.html

Debt Counselors of America: www.dca.org

Equifax: www.equifax.com

Experian: www.experian.com

401Kafé: www.401kafe.com

InvestorGuide: www.investorguide/Retirement.htm

National Foundation for Consumer Credit: www.nfcc.org

Quicken's Retirement Planner: www.quicken.com/retirement/planner

TransUnion: www.transunion.com

U.S. Internal Revenue Service: www.irs.ustreas.gov

Vanguard Group: www.vanguard.com

Yahoo!: www.yahoo.com

Chapter 4—Wall Street Hits the Web

Alta Vista: www.altavista.com

Armchair Millionaire: www.armchairmillionaire.com

EDGAR Online: www.edgar-online.com

FirstCall Corp.: www.firstcall.com

Market Guide Inc.: www.marketguide.com

Motley Fool: www.fool.com

Multex: multex.multexinvestor.com

Quicken: www.quicken.com

TheStreet.com: www.thestreet.com

Wall Street on Demand: www.wallst.com

Wall Street Journal Interactive Edition: www.wsj.com

Wall Street Research Net: www.wsrn.com

Yahoo!: www.yahoo.com

Zacks Investment Research: www.zacks.com

Chapter 5—Stock Screening on the Web

About.com: www.about.com

CyberInvest.com: www.cyberinvest.com

Hoover's Online: www.hoovers.com

Hoover's StockScreener: www.stockscreener.com

Intellifact.com: www.intellifact.com

InvestorGuide: www.investorguide.com

Money: www.money.com

Quicken: www.quicken.com

SmartMoney: www.smartmoney.com

Wall Street City: www.wallstreetcity.com

Chapter 6—Bonds on the Net

About.com's bonds guide: bonds.about.com

Bond Market Association: www.investinginbonds.com

Bondtrac: www.bondtrac.com

FinanCenter: www.financenter.com

Library of Congress' catalog of government agencies: lcweb.loc.gov/global/executive/fed.html

Money: www.money.com

MSN MoneyCentral: moneycentral.msn.com/investor

SmartMoney: www.smartmoney.com

Standard & Poor's: www.standardandpoors.com/ratings/index.html

U.S. Bureau of the Public Debt, Department of Treasury: www.publicdebt.treas.gov

Women's Wire: www.womenswire.com

Chapter 7—Finding and Evaluating Mutual Funds Online

About.com's mutual fund guide: mutualfunds.about.com

Barron's: www.barrons.com

Business Week: www.businessweek.com

CyberInvestor: www.cyberinvest.com

Dow Jones: dowjones.wsj.com

E*Trade: www.etrade.com

Individual Investor: www.individualinvestor.com

misc.invest.mutual-funds FAQs: www.moneypages.com/syndicate/faq/toc.htm

Money: www.money.com

Morningstar: www.morningstar.com

Motley Fool: www.fool.com

Mutual Fund Café: www.mfcafe.com

Mutual Fund Education Alliance: www.mfea.com

Quicken: www.quicken.com

RemarQ: www.remarq.com

U.S. SEC's EDGAR filings: edgar.sec.gov/edaux/formlynx.htm

USA Today: www.usatoday.com

Vanguard University: www.vanguard.com

Wall Street Journal: www.wsj.com

Washington Post: www.washingtonpost.com

Worth: www.worth.com

Chapter 8—Advanced Investing

About.com's day trading guide: daytrading.about.com

DayTraders: www.daytraders.org

EDGAR Online: www.edgar-online.com

FinancialWeb: www.financialweb.com

IPO Central: ipocentral.hoovers.com

IPO-Home: www.ipo-fund.com

IPO Resources: www.iporesources.org

MarketWatch: cbs.marketwatch.com

National Association of Real Estate Investment Trusts: www.nareit.com

North American Securities Administrators Association: www.nasaa.org

REITNet Online: www.reitnet.com

U.S. Securities and Exchange Commission: www.sec.gov

Chapter 9—Uncle Sam and Financial Information

Congressional Budget Office: www.cbo.gov

EDGAR Access: edgar.disclosure.com/ea

EDGAR Online: www.edgar-online.com

FedStats: www.fedstats.gov

FedWorld: www.fedworld.gov

Library of Congress: lcweb.loc.gov

LIVEDGAR: www.livedgar.com

Stat-USA: www.stat-usa.gov

U.S. Bureau of the Census: www.census.gov

U.S. Bureau of Economic Analysis: www.bea.doc.gov

U.S. Bureau of Labor Statistics—Links to Worldwide Statistics Sites: stats.bls.gov/oreother.htm

U.S. Internal Revenue Service: www.irs.ustreas.gov

U.S. Securities and Exchange Commission's EDGAR filings: edgar.sec.gov

U.S. Social Security Administration: www.ssa.gov

Chapter 10—Covering the News

ABC News: www.abcnews.com

AJR Newslink: ajr.newslink.org

Business Week: www.businessweek.com

CBS News: www.cbsnews.com

Excite: www.excite.com

Forbes: www.forbes.com/forbes/current

Fortune: www.fortune.com

GO Network: mypage.go.com

HotBot: www.hotbot.com

NBC News: www.nbc.com

Newsletter Access: www.newsletteraccess.com

Reuters: www.reuters.com/news

Standard & Poor's: www.personalwealth.com

Wall Street Journal Interactive Edition: www.wsj.com

Yahoo!: www.yahoo.com

Chapter 11—High-Powered Online Services

DialogSelect: www.dialogselect.com

DialogWeb: www.dialogweb.com

Dow Jones Interactive: djinteractive.com

InSite 2: www.insite2.gale.com

Lexis-Nexis: www.lexis-nexis.com

Lexis-Nexis Universe: web.lexis-nexis.com/ln.universe

Northern Light: www.northernlight.com

ProQuest: www.umi.com/proquest

Chapter 12—Scoping Out a Company on the Net

AltaVista: www.altavista.com

Anonymizer: www.anonymizer.com

AskJeeves: www.aj.com

Career Mosaic: www.careermosaic.com

Company Sleuth: company.sleuth.com

CorporateInformation: www.corporateinformation.com

Dow Jones: www.dowjones.com

Dow Jones Interactive: djinteractive.com

Excite: www.excite.com

GO Network: infoseek.go.com

Hoover's Online: www.hoovers.com

HotBot: www.hotbot.com

Monster Board: www.monsterboard.com

Society of Competitive Intelligence Professionals: www.scip.org

U.S. Securities and Exchange Commission's EDGAR filings: edgar.sec.gov

Wall Street Research Network: www.wsrn.com

Yahoo!: www.yahoo.com

Chapter 13—Let's Talk About It

America Online: www.aol.com

American Association of Individual Investors: www.aaii.com

Company Sleuth: company.sleuth.com

CompuServe: www.compuserve.com

Deja.com: www.deja.com

eGroups: www.egroups.com

eWatch: www.ewatch.com

Internet Mailing List Providers: www.catalog.com/vivian/mailing-list-providers.html

Investment Clubs on the Net: www.computerland.net/~missouri/investment_club.htm

Liszt: www.liszt.com

L-Soft's email discussion lists: www.lsoft.com/lists/listref.html

Morningstar: www.morningstar.com

Motley Fool's message board: boards.fool.com

National Association of Investors Corp.: www.better-investing.org

PAML (Publicly-Accessible Mailing Lists): www.neosoft.com/internet/paml

Quicken's message boards: quicken.excite.com/forums

RemarQ: www.remarq.com

Chapter 14—Investing for College Expenses

AmeriCorps: www.americorps.org

College Savings Plans Network: www.collegesavings.org

FinAid: www.finaid.org

InvestorGuide: www.investorguide.com/FinAid.htm

Marine Corps ROTC: www.cnet.navy.mil/nrotc/nrotc.html

National Association for Public Interest Law: www.napil.org

National Health Service Corps: www.bphc.hrsa.gov/nhsc

Navy ROTC: www.cnet.navy.mil/nrotc/nrotc.htm

Peace Corps: www.peacecorps.gov

Quicken.com's "Planning" section: www.quicken.com/retirement/planning

Scholarship Resource Network Express: www.srnexpress.com

University of Texas Web Directory: www.utexas.edu/world/univ

U.S. Air Force ROTC: www.afoats.af.mil/rotc.htm

U.S. Army ROTC: www-rotc.monroe.army.mil

U.S. Department of Education Web page: www.ed.gov

U.S. Internal Revenue Service: www.irs.ustreas.gov

Volunteers In Service To America (VISTA): www.friendsofvista.org

Chapter 15—Scams and Frauds

Better Business Bureau: www.bbb.org

Library of Congress: lcweb.loc.gov

North American Securities Administrators Association: www.nasaa.org

U.S. Federal Trade Commission: www.ftc.gov

U.S. Postal Service: www.usps.gov

U.S. Securities and Exchange Commission: www.sec.gov

U.S. Securities and Exchange Commission "Ten Questions to Ask About Any Investment Opportunity": www.sec.gov/consumer/10quest.htm

U.S. Securities and Exchange Commission's EDGAR filings: edgar.sec.gov

Chapter 16—E-Brokerages

Ameritrade: www.ameritrade.com

Charles Schwab: www.schwab.com; www.myschwab.com

DLJ*direct*—Donaldson Lufkin Jenrette: www.dljdirect.com

E*Trade: www.etrade.com

Fidelity Investments: personal300.fidelity.com

Gomez Advisors: www.gomez.com

Money: www.money.com

National Association of Securities Dealers: www.nasd.com

National Discount Brokers: www.ndb.com

Smart Money: www.smartmoney.com

Wall Street On Demand: www.wallst.com

Index

About the Author

Mary Ellen Bates is the owner of Bates Information Services, a research firm specializing in providing business research to business professionals. She has been online since the late 1970s and worked in libraries and information centers for 15 years before starting her own business in 1993. She is the author of *The Online Deskbook* (Information Today, 1996); *Super Searchers Do Business: The Online Secrets of Top Business Researchers* (Information Today, 1999); and the coauthor, with Reva Basch, of the 2nd edition of *Researching Online For Dummies* (IDG Books, 2000). She has edited or contributed to several other books about the Internet and information retrieval, including *Secrets of the Super Net Searchers* and *Internet Tools of the Profession.* She is a contributing editor of *Information Advisor* and *EContent,* and writes frequently about the online industry. She is an often-requested speaker at information industry conferences and has made presentations at international conferences in Mexico, Germany, Denmark, the United Kingdom, Sweden, and the United States.

Mary Ellen has a bachelor's degree in Philosophy from the University of California, Santa Barbara, and a master's degree in Library and Information Studies from the University of California, Berkeley. She now lives online and in Washington, D.C., with her companion and her dog. She is a back-of-the-pack marathon runner and still listens to the Grateful Dead.